DANDELION
& QUINCE

DANDELION & QUINCE

EXPLORING THE WIDE WORLD
OF UNUSUAL VEGETABLES,
FRUITS, AND HERBS

MICHELLE MCKENZIE

PHOTOGRAPHS BY RICK POON

ROOST BOOKS
BOULDER
2016

CONTENTS

INTRODUCTION

———

Not long ago, I was perusing shelves in a beautiful old bookstore in the Marais district of Paris where I stumbled upon a series of notebooks entitled *Les Éditions de l'Épure*. Each short volume was dedicated to a single fruit or vegetable—the subject generously illustrated, discussed, and given its due as the focus of a number of recipes. Most of the featured ingredients were common and had been discussed ad infinitum before and since: apricots, beets, peas, potatoes, and so on. But quite a few of the petit volumes were devoted to "outliers"—fig leaves, cardoons, chrysanthemum, rhubarb, quince, spirulina, licorice root—the sorts of plant matter that sound lovely in high literature or stories by A. S. Byatt but that most of us cannot imagine cooking up in our own kitchens.

I soon relocated to San Francisco, where the markets explode with all things strange, lovely, and hyperseasonal. There was so much on offer, and shoppers seemed to be consistently curious but also completely apprehensive about new foods. I might hear someone say, "These pea shoots are sweet and beautiful, but what do I do with a pound of them?" Unable to just listen, I found myself stepping in to assist the shoppers around me. I began doling out recipes, techniques, and menu suggestions like the mushroom monger at the market on the Avenue de Saxe. Unbeknownst to me, I'd begun reciting the contents of *Dandelion and Quince*.

The less familiar and more unique your produce, the more exciting the dish and, often, the deeper the flavor. In Italian, this idea is called *brutta ma buona*, meaning "ugly but good." *Dandelion and Quince* is a celebration of that absolutely perfect notion.

Every day, I test out this idea at 18 Reasons, a community cooking school in San Francisco's Mission District. As program director, my days are long and demanding, yet they give way to such a satisfying exhaustion. I teach the elemental, and its returns are ample.

On a recent Monday, I was in the midst of an already nine-hour day, aproning up to teach the first of three, three-hour classes in a series on the egg. I was lost in a moment of dread. Having had no time to eat or wash my face, I felt a tinge of resentment rising from the bottom of my otherwise empty stomach. Then Guenter walked through the door. Dependably early, his arrival swiftly pulled me back together.

I had met Guenter only a few months earlier, when he arrived forty-five minutes before the start of a one-hour lunchtime class. He was slightly hunched, with his pants hiked high, somewhat frail, and looking a bit confused. He handed me a homemade gift certificate that read, "Happy Father's Day! Redeemable for one cooking class at 18 Reasons." Above the text was a stock photo of a pan. He must be older than eighty, and I admit to having doubts about him. *He isn't here because he wants to be*, I thought. I expected him to flounder or fuss; he did neither. He sat on a stool and smiled at me through the entire class. Then he and I and the remaining twelve guests sat at the long, wooden table and passed around platters of the day's menu. While many of the others, mostly women, chatted effortlessly about banalities, Guenter asked poignant questions. He cleaned his plate. He never stopped smiling. There was a moment of silence as several students gathered to leave. Wanting to keep that sweet grin for just a bit longer, I asked Guenter why he had come. "My wife just died," he said. "And I am learning to cook for the first time in my life." I cried.

The lesson that day had been based on a composed salad of toasted rye berries, shaved kohlrabi, Reed avocado, and flowering cilantro. I had dreamed of this salad while perusing the Castro farmers' market the afternoon before. Now it felt showy and shallow. I was teaching a man to survive with this? I kicked myself for days, wishing I had simply fried an egg.

But on that exhausting Monday, months later, I would have a chance to redeem myself and Guenter, who'd signed up for nine hours of egg instruction! I would get to teach him the tricks for a perfect poach and how to achieve a speedy but silky carbonara—simple, hearty food for the man! (Writing this now, I feel those exclamation points in the tips of my typing fingers.)

This is where my certainty and satisfaction lie, in the faces and stories of the people I teach. I receive immense pleasure connecting with people and watching them learn about food. For some, it is about hedonism; for others, survival; and for many, the arousal of interest is merely an escape from the tedium of their daily routine. I see people eat in hope of forming a community, for distraction, or to satisfy a displaced hunger. At times, sensing the disparate needs of those around me can be daunting, as I try to define my offering in a way to meet them all. So I have begun to think my service is simply to add a dose of texture to their lives, to engage them in a new way. I find peace here.

HOW TO USE THIS BOOK (AND HOW TO STOP)

There is so much at the farmers' market and local grocery yet to be discovered by the everyday shopper: wild mustard flowers, kumquats, spigarello, nettles, fava leaves, and sunchokes. Professional chefs have already embraced these blossoms, berries, leaves, and roots, and we—their approving patrons with our increasingly curious palates—are ready to prepare them in our own homes. Where arugula and kale once seemed exotic, now they're as everyday as peas and potatoes. The same can be true for the ingredients in this book. They belong in our home kitchens. These are simple foods that satisfy important nutritional and spiritual needs: to eat a diversity of plant life, grown with care, and prepared by our hands for our community. I hope this book will both inspire you and ease your way.

As a teacher, I strive to write recipes that are practical, though sometimes edging on aspirational—I want home cooks to stretch. A very good meal is to be found in a pot of lentils and a soft-boiled egg. Yet I believe that stepping into unknown territory nourishes vitality, and with food as my work, I contribute directions there in the form of recipes.

With time, I encourage you to step away from my recipes and find your own compass in the kitchen. Learn from steps one and steps two and from tasting constantly and making mistakes. Then when you hear the quiet, playful voice of ambition, close this book and approach an unknown ingredient with your now skilled hands, knowing palate, and innate curiosity. Please take as much pleasure in cooking as you do in eating. Feed yourself in creative ways. Then feed another.

REGARDING MY WAY WITH RECIPES

My recipes are the product of accumulation, alchemy, and a lot of practice. I learned much from college, culinary school, and restaurants. I am a voracious reader and consume cookbooks from cover to cover. Stacks of books on food anthropology, history, cooking chemistry, and related memoirs line the walls of my living room. And some of the most engrossing and useful knowledge has come from the farmers, grocers, Chinese doctors, and home cooks who surround me. I have created community through food; I've learned from, shared with, and forged connections to people with whom I was already interconnected.

There are more ideas and adventure maps floating around inside my head than I can possibly include in one book. As such, I often share a few extra ideas at the start of each section. When these suggestions aren't self-explanatory, I propose them knowing that the idea has already been elucidated in some great book or on some wonderful website; I hope you'll use these tips to search them out and extend your education.

You may have developed preferences for peeling, washing, salting, and storing your produce. But I want to share my own preferences because they may be new ideas and because it will save repeating them in each recipe.

The success of these recipes depends largely on the thoughtful purchase, storage, and preparation of fruits and vegetables. Buy produce from sources you trust; you want unsprayed, freshly harvested specimens. If you do this, your food is likely to be both safe and delicious, and you will be less prone to washing items that shouldn't be washed, such as mint, squash blossoms, fennel fronds, and huckleberries. Excessive water is the enemy of most edible plants (it speeds up spoilage and can damage delicate leaves), so when it is required, wash just before cooking.

All vegetables should be trimmed of their roots and stems unless otherwise noted. Discard the papery covering of onions, garlic, and shallots or save it for stock. I use both the white and green parts of green onions. I rarely peel thin-skinned fruits or vegetables such as carrots, parsnips, potatoes, radishes, persimmons, baby turnips, or burdock, but I will scrub them under water with a bristle brush, as needed.

Dried legumes should be sorted before soaking; they often contain stones or debris.

Chiles (fresh or dried) are always stemmed. They are sometimes seeded if I want to reduce their heat further. Heat is always optional—feel free to ignore instructions for added chiles or freshly ground black pepper.

All greens are washed and thoroughly dried (salad spinner or, if delicate, spread on a clean kitchen towel) unless otherwise noted. I only wash the leaves of herbs if they are incredibly sandy. I never wash their blossoms, but

I do rinse their stems (which can be tied with twine and simmered with beans, in soups, and under grains).

All fruits are best purchased in small quantities, stored at room temperature, and eaten within a few days of ripening. Refrigerated fruit suffers a loss of flavor that cannot be regained. That said, I am almost as practical as I am romantic, and I understand the need to refrigerate some foods, especially highly perishable berries.

Although many hearty vegetables can be stored at room temperature for multiple days (for example, cabbage, cauliflower, and potatoes), many will wilt and wither. The best bet is to refrigerate your vegetables in an airtight container lined with a few sheets of paper towel; when the paper becomes saturated with water, replace and reseal. The exceptions to this rule include vegetables with a protective outer layer (usually a woody or papery skin), such as winter squash, onions, shallots, and garlic; I keep these in a woven basket in a cool, shady spot.

I commonly use whole spices and toast them in a dry skillet over moderate heat until their fragrance is apparent and they've turned a shade darker. Once cooled to room temperature, I grind them myself or add them whole to a dish. Other times, I'll sauté them in hot fat; this is another way of coaxing out their aromatic compounds. Black peppercorns are an exception to the toasting rule: I use a standard pepper grinder, and I use it sparingly.

With the exception of tiny sesame seeds, I toast all seeds and nuts in a 375°F to 400°F oven; toasting in a skillet on the stove too often leads to shallow and uneven browning and doesn't provide enough depth of flavor. Walnuts, pecans, hazelnuts, almonds, and peanuts take approximately 10 to 12 minutes; pine nuts and most seeds take 5 to 7 minutes.

Use a scale when precision is necessary (such as in baking and preserving) and easy eyeing when an approximation is all you need. I find measuring in cups and teaspoons a tedious task. So while I've done the work and provided measurements, I recommend you see them as a training tool. Once you can recall what 6 ounces of fava leaves looks like and how they cook down to a quarter of their volume, you can begin to shop and cook freestyle; you will imagine, purchase, and employ the right mound of mint, handful of peas, or pinch of Marash chile. Eventually, gathering and preparing food will become even more efficient and enjoyable. Recipes will become mere templates, ideas, and ratios that you alter to fit your needs and wants. And cooking in this way is exceptionally rewarding.

I've rarely provided measurements for salt since salts vary greatly in both density and salinity and because, as just mentioned, I find teaspoons tiresome. If you constantly taste as you cook, you'll learn what each kind of pinch tastes like, and soon enough you will season food effortlessly. In my kitchen, "fine sea salt" is a blue cylinder of La Baliene, and "coarse sea salt" is Maldon, Jacobsen, or fleur de sel. Kosher salt (such as Diamond Crystal) is a wonderful

alternative to fine sea salt and more affordable. Gray salt is great for cooking and is high in minerals, but I have yet to spend the energy to climb the learning curve. Find a few salts you love, use them often, and know them well. When I do say "a pinch of salt," I am referring to roughly ¼ teaspoon.

Serving sizes are merely suggestions, but I consider the nature of the dish when writing recipes and offering estimates. For instance, the Winter Root and Quince Tagine will likely be served as a main dish and makes wonderful leftovers; I assumed full-belly portions and that you'd want to make a bit more than you need for a single meal. In contrast, Eggs Baked with Dandelion and Cream won't hold or reheat well, so I offered measurements suitable for three to four people, knowing you could easily halve the ingredients if you're feeding one or two.

I've added tips and tricks throughout the book, and I hope you'll see the broader applications of such instructions. These small pieces of advice can make your cooking more effortless, efficient, and exploratory.

If you can't find a particular ingredient, in most cases, you can use a substitute. Consider the flavor, texture, and nature of what you need, then seek out something similar. For instance, spinach leaves can step in for nettles, blackberries easily replace huckleberries, green onions make sense in ramp recipes, and turnips can be used instead of kohlrabi.

You should always taste a dish throughout the cooking process and again right before serving.

ON BALANCING A DISH

Seasoning is about tasting and tweaking, fine-tuning to bring out the best in the food. There are two main considerations for balancing a dish: flavor and texture. And there are two main times to think about both while cooking: the beginning and the end.

When planning a dish or a meal, think in terms of complementary elements. Your finished dish should be more than the sum of its parts. Consider why a plate of mozzarella, tomato, basil, olive oil, red pepper flakes, balsamic vinegar, and salt is so popular. Each ingredient complements the others. Eat each alone and they're good; eat them together, and the dish is dynamic. Tomatoes at their peak offer sweetness and acidity. Mozzarella offers a richness that makes food especially satisfying, both physically and chemically (the fat in the cheese intensifies flavors). Basil gives herbaceousness, freshness, and sweetness. Balsamic vinegar's acidity brightens. Olive oil balances the acid of both the tomato and the vinegar. Red pepper keeps it interesting by hitting the mouth with pops of heat. And finally, salt provides the salinity necessary for enlivening all the ingredients. What's missing? Textural contrast. So swap a fine variety of salt for one with large, crunchy flakes. Alternatively, serve the salad on grilled bread. Either way, you have a perfectly balanced, almost addictive dish.

The following lists provide a rough guide to help you choose ingredients with complementary elements of flavor and texture. It is not extensive, and many foods fall into multiple categories. However, these are the most relevant for home kitchens.

ELEMENTS OF FLAVOR

SALTY—sea salt; kosher salt; cheese; cured meats; capers; olives; anchovies; fish sauce; soy sauce; shio koji; miso; Worcestershire sauce; some vegetables (such as celery)

SOUR—vinegars; sour cream; crème fraîche; tomatoes; tomato paste; citrus and other fresh fruits (such as grapefruit and pineapple); dried fruits; pickles

SWEET—tomatoes; tomato paste; fresh and dried fruits; vegetables (such as roasted beets, sweet potatoes, squash, red bell peppers, sugar snap peas, and carrots); beans; nuts; honey; sugar; agave; pomegranate molasses; molasses; maple syrup; fruit juices

RICH—oils (such as olive, nut, coconut, argan, and grapeseed); all dairy products; avocado; nuts and nut butters; tahini (sesame seed paste); animal fats; offal

HOT— fresh and dried chile peppers; black peppercorns; ginger; garlic; hot sauces; horseradish; wasabi; spicy greens and vegetables (such as watercress, arugula, and radishes)

BITTER—broccoli rabe; radicchio; grapefruit; dandelion; endive; eggplant; citrus rind; walnuts

PUNGENT/FUNKY—garlic; onions; shallots; some cheeses; fermented foods (such as preserved lemons, fish sauce, and miso)

UMAMI (implies a savory or meaty flavor and usually involves salt, proteins, fermentation, or a combination of these)—seaweed; meats (such as ham, chicken, turkey, and steak); cured meats (such as salami, pancetta, bacon, and speck); fish; cured fish (such as sardines and anchovies); smoked foods (such as cheese, tofu, fish, meat, paprika, and salt); pickled products; cheese; fermented foods (such as black beans); mushrooms; miso, broths, and stocks; Worcestershire sauce; fish sauce; tahini; sauerkraut

ELEMENTS OF TEXTURE

CRUNCHY—coarse sea salt; nuts; crispy pork (such as bacon, pancetta, and roasted speck); toasted bread, breadcrumbs, and breaded foods; fried onions and shallots

CRISP—pickles; raw apples; shaved raw vegetables (especially radishes, fennel, and turnips); some lettuces (such as little gem, romaine, and iceberg)

CREAMY—avocado; puréed vegetables (such as potatoes and cauliflower); soft cheese (such as ricotta, fromage blanc, and fresh goat cheese); crème fraîche; custards; foams; raw fish

SOFT—most cooked vegetables; cooked fish; custards; beans; most gelatin treatments; animal proteins cooked over slow, low heat (such as short ribs and lamb shank)

CHEWY—rice; grains; mushrooms; hard cheese; animal proteins cooked over fast, high heat (such as chicken breast and steak)

Before you start cooking, taste what you can. How sour is your red wine vinegar? How sweet and floral is your honey? How grassy is your olive oil? Is the fresh arugula mild or intensely peppery? Taste, taste, taste! Consider the end use and then remain attentive.

CHOOSE AN ACID WITH AN APPROPRIATE FLAVOR PROFILE. Most sources of acid have a very unique flavor. Think of the notable difference between limes and lemons or between a delicate sherry vinegar and a concentrated balsamic. Pick the one that will work with your dish, not over, behind, or against it.

CHOOSE A SUGAR WITH AN APPROPRIATE FLAVOR PROFILE. Options for sweetening a dish include honey, palm sugar, muscovado, date sugar, whole cane sugar, granulated sugar, maple syrup, date syrup, agave nectar, and molasses. Here again, you need to think of the dish as a whole. Maple syrup can add a lovely caramelized flavor that heightens the natural flavor of a roasting kabocha squash but clashes with the delicate freshness of cucumbers.

GET CREATIVE WITH YOUR SOURCES. While it can be easy to reach for a squeeze of lemon or a spoonful of vinegar, it can be more fun (and delicious) to add an ingredient that lends a relatively gentle effect. For example, the zest of a lemon might add just enough acid to a dish in which the juice would be a distraction; imagine a raw scallop in the shell or a sauté of baby pea shoots in butter. The subtle sourness of pomegranate juice or labne enlivens a bowl of braised lamb with pumpkin, whereas lemon juice would be comparatively brash.

START WITH LESS, AND AGAIN, REMAIN ATTENTIVE. If you overdo any element, you can sometimes use the complement to adjust and fix. So if there's too much acid, a little fat can help and vice versa. But this is far from ideal. Better to season carefully and avoid the need for corrective measures.

After cooking and just before you serve, have a little taste of your dish and ask yourself these two questions:

Is there a dullness I want to enliven? If so, which flavor element is missing? (More often than not, the answer is salt or acid or both.)

Are the textures satisfying, or is more contrast needed?

If you're a little unsure, there is a safe way to tinker and tweak: you can take out a small sample, put it in a bowl, and add what you think it needs. Taste and compare to the original. If it tastes better, adjust the entire dish. If not, then you're ready to serve. (This is a good time to get kids involved in the kitchen—they love this part! And if they help make decisions about it, they are more likely to eat it.)

Last, beware of palate saturation. Remember that when your taste buds have been exposed to something a few times, they become less sensitive to those particular flavors. If you've been grabbing bites for a while, it's good to have a break and a glass of water. Or get a second opinion.

In the end, it's all about trusting your judgment. Relax and take note of what you've learned in the process. Then serve your dish with aplomb.

ON PREPARING FOR FUN AND SUCCESS IN THE KITCHEN

My primary recommendation for food prep is to sharpen your knife. Having a good, sharp knife and a big, heavy cutting board will truly transform your cooking experience. Imagine attempting to work at a tiny, cramped desk with pens low on ink and a superslow computer. Wouldn't you find the work—regardless of its actual nature—frustrating and difficult? Preparing food on small or shoddy cutting boards with dull knives is the equivalent kitchen experience. Invest and reinvest in these two tools.

I use a maple chopping block that is 2 feet wide by 2 feet deep. I sharpen my carbon steel knives using a Japanese whetstone and have them professionally cared for once every few months.

I don't promote the use of highly specialized or expensive equipment. Most of the recipes in this book can be made with the following common tools:

- A heavy cutting board, preferably of maple wood
- A sharp (6- to 10-inch) chef's knife
- A wooden spoon
- A fish spatula, spider strainer, and slotted spoon
- A Microplane and a box grater
- A Japanese mandoline (optional but very useful)
- One small (1- or 2-quart) and one medium (4-quart) saucepan (Heavy-bottom pans are ideal.)
- One small (9- or 10-inch) and one medium (12- or 14-inch) sauté pan or skillet (Sauté pans have slightly higher sides than skillets, which slows the rate of evaporation.)
- One large (approximately 7-quart) pot or Dutch oven
- A 7-quart pressure cooker (Although not essential, this facilitates the efficient cooking of beans, grains, stocks, and soups.)
- A blender and/or food mill
- A 7- or 14-cup food processor and/or a large, heavy mortar and pestle
- A spice grinder and/or a small mortar and pestle
- A medium fine-mesh strainer
- One round 9-inch springform cake pan
- Two 9 × 2-inch loaf pans

- One tart pan (10-inch round and/or 13 × 4-inch rectangular)
- A digital scale
- Dry and liquid measuring cups
- A pastry brush
- Glass jars (pint- to quart-size) with tightly fitting lids
- An offset spatula and a bench scraper (These two inexpensive tools can ease many tasks.)

Mise en place is a French phrase meaning "everything is in place." It implies that your cooking station is set up and that all ingredients are prepped and ready before you to begin cooking. This may seem less efficient than sautéing your onions as you start to chop your garlic, but in practice, it facilitates a skillful and graceful experience. Getting everything in its place first will ultimately save you time and make the time spent more peaceful and pleasant.

Preheat your cooking element beforehand, so it is at the desired temperature when you are ready to use it. Ovens and grills need more time than you think, and having an oven thermometer is useful. Pans on a stovetop should be hot before you add your fat, and the fat should be hot (but not smoking) before adding your ingredients.

When baking, it is essential that you use exactly the amounts listed in the recipe—any more or any less and the recipe might not work. To achieve accuracy, weighing all ingredients with a digital scale is ideal. However, if you are going to use measuring cups, remember the following guidelines.

Dry and wet ingredients both are measured in cups and spoons, but there is a notable difference. Measuring cups for dry ingredients are made of metal or plastic and usually come in sets of ¼, ⅓, ½, and 1 cup. Measuring cups for liquid ingredients are made from clear glass or plastic with a pour spout, with the measurements marked on the sides. Measuring spoons typically come in sets of ¼ teaspoon, ½ teaspoon, 1 teaspoon, and 1 tablespoon. The same spoons are used for both wet and dry ingredients, but it is important to use the correct type of cup for either liquids or dry ingredients.

To measure a dry ingredient such as flour or salt, spoon it into the required dry measuring cup or spoon until it is higher than the rim. Do not pack it down (unless it is brown sugar, which is measured firmly packed). Using the flat side of a table knife or offset spatula (a baker's most useful tool!), sweep off the excess even with the rim. Loose dry ingredients, such as raisins, can be scooped into dry measuring cups; fill the cup but do not pack it tightly unless the recipe says to do so.

To measure a wet ingredient such as stock or olive oil, set a clear liquid measuring cup on a flat surface. Pour the liquid into the cup, then scoot down so your face is level with the meniscus (the base of the center of the curve), which should meet the desired measurement line. To measure a small amount of liquid like vanilla extract, carefully pour the ingredient into a measuring spoon until it reaches the rim.

Last, enjoy the process.

ON LETTING GO

Recipes are wonderful—they help people make dishes they have never seen or tasted before. But when it comes to teaching you how to cook, recipes fall short. They're often seen as formulas to be executed mathematically. And following rules won't lead to ecstatic fun. Moreover, most recipes fail to teach us the reasons for the steps they require. You can make a recipe over and over with the same ingredients, and the results will always vary; heat, humidity, pan composition, and the age of ingredients are all factors that affect the final dish. If you learn why things are happening and how you can change them, you are more likely to avoid mishaps and disappointments because you'll proceed from intuition rather than from blind obedience. Recipes should be references. With knowledge and practice, your intuition will arise naturally; with intuition will come greater ease; and with greater ease, you are more likely to tap into the personal creativity that makes a moment really rich.

ON ATTUNING TO THE BODY

I value my vitality. And a sense of physical well-being is integral to my feeling alive.

It is becoming common knowledge that favoring whole, intact foods supports optimum health; and when organically grown, they offer exceptional flavor and greater nutritional value. Yet even within the whole foods doctrine, few are discussing the overall effect certain ingredients have on our individual systems. In many of my cooking classes, I loosely reference the dietary tenets of Chinese medicine, which classifies foods according to their energetic properties rather than their component parts. I studied these ideas years ago, and after years of practice, I now feel them in my bones. Students' faces light up with curiosity, and they ask for more; the information naturally resonates. We know that we are impacted physically, emotionally, and mentally by the fruits, grains, seeds, eggs, meats, and dairy products we eat. Discerning these effects in your body is challenging at first, but just like learning a new language, you will eventually decipher physical clues effortlessly.

I am not a trained Chinese medical practitioner, but I have tried to weave my experience with the discipline into my recipes. Integrating Eastern and Western philosophies can help evolve our thinking and heal our bodies. It is beyond the scope of this book to develop this topic fully, yet I hope my few personal examples help illustrate the approach.

In the spring, as tender greens emerge from the ground, I begin to grow bored with cozy hibernation; I am ready for a brisker pace of life, greater creative output, and more time playing outdoors. I am drawn to foods like ripe stone fruit, raw shoots and leaves, and quickly blanched vegetables. I tend to forgo substantial, complex carbohydrates, and my meat consumption drops a bit.

In contrast, as the days shorten and the air turns colder, the produce is slower to grow, becomes denser and heavier, and a lot of it heads underground. Simultaneously, I want to rest, to think more and do less, and to spend more time inside and around my stove. I seek warming foods: roasted root vegetables, caramelized pumpkins, braised joints of meat, and hearty grains. During both times of transition, there is a broad synchronicity between the season's change, my personal energy, and the produce and meat available around me. Even within each season (and microseason), cooking requirements are more finely drawn; for example, whether I need to roast a plum to warm and contract its energy or whether I should steam a pumpkin to lighten and cool it depends on many factors—sleep, exercise, and stress, to name but three.

Every food has many energetic properties, and each of us—with our particular constitutions—has unique vulnerabilities and concerns. Garnering a glimpse of this understanding will greatly enhance your well-being. For example, raw dates are sweet, warming, strengthening, expansive, and dampening. When they arrive at the market each September, it is the time of year when folks around me are getting sick. I've noticed that if I am at all compromised—with even the slightest hint of a stuffy or runny nose—the dampening energy of fresh dates exacerbates my symptoms, and I'm likely to get quite sick if I eat more than two. So I listen and respond: I forgo the pleasure of the sweet, sticky, earthy fruit for the preferred, albeit more subtle, pleasure of a clear nasal passage and an optimally functioning mind.

Although the chapters of this book present foods in alphabetical order, I urge you to eat with the seasons. Purchasing the foods of your region will make it relatively easy to stay in balance with your specific environmental and other needs. Even then, pay close attention to how certain foods and cooking methods affect your unique being. *Aliveness* is the goal.

DANDELION & QUINCE

ASIAN PEARS

Asian pears aren't unsightly or rare or difficult to use. Their name isn't difficult to pronounce, and they don't require special handling. They sell for about three dollars a pound, and the late harvest varieties emerge as we tire of apples and await citrus. Why then do so few people use this fruit?

The name *pear* might be a disservice, confusing patrons whose minds associate that term with something quite different. While Asian pears do share similar flavor characteristics with the other members of the *Pyrus* genus (floral honey, nuts, butter, vanilla, citrus), they look completely different. Asian pears are fairly round and lack the neck seen on European varieties. They range in size, like apples do. Depending on the variety, the skin may be ivory, mustard yellow, brown/russet, monochromatic, or flecked. They look demure when compared to a curvy, blushing Bartlett pear with its spicy-sweet aroma. Yet Asian pears are brighter and more refreshing. Moreover, they have many qualities that make them suitable for preparations in which the more typical Bosc and d'Anjou won't suffice. They remain relatively firm even when ripe; they offer a crisp, barely juicy bite; and their flesh only marginally discolors when exposed to the air.

There are at least a dozen varieties of Asian pears at my local farmers' market. The varieties I've tasted range in flavor and brightness, from highly aromatic and bubblegum-like to mellow with thin threads of caramel and green walnut. They also have slightly different textures, from gritty to buttery. Many markets offer samples so you can taste before purchasing, and if they don't, ask. Seek pears that are firm but not hard and have smooth, unpunctured skin. Russet varieties should be deep golden brown, and yellow varieties should be a bright yellow. Store them at room temperature for up to two weeks.

Asian pears can be slipped right into several recipes in this book besides the ones in this chapter:
- Julienne an Asian pear and add it to the Daikon Slaw with Shio koji (see page 56).
- Poach it as you would the quince (for Poached Quince see page 194), shortening the cooking time slightly.
- Use an Asian pear instead of the persimmon in the Kohlrabi Salad with Persimmons and Sheep's Milk Cheese (see page 167).
- In the fall, when figs aren't in season but dandelion is, use Asian pears alongside pancetta in Baby Dandelion Salad with Fresh Figs and Pancetta (see page 64).

PICKLED PEARS

These pickled pears are the perfect accompaniment to cured meats and sharp cheeses. They are also my chosen late-night snack. I like to eat them standing up in the kitchen, my right foot perched on my inner left thigh, with a pickled pear in one hand and leftover cold steak in the other.

3 small Asian pears (1 pound; such as Hosui or Shinko), cut in quarters

2 cups white vinegar

¼ cup granulated sugar

1 cup water

1 tablespoon black peppercorns

1 teaspoon fine sea salt

Pour boiling water into two pint-size jars with tight-fitting lids; drain and set aside to air-dry.

Place all the ingredients in a large saucepan; bring to a boil over high heat. Reduce the heat until the mixture is at a low simmer (too many big, rapid bubbles can really damage the flesh of the pear). Cook the pears for 8 to 10 minutes, or until the flesh is easily pierced with a paring knife. Remove the pan from the heat and allow the mixture to cool to room temperature. Transfer the pears to the sterilized jars, pour the remaining brine on top, and secure the lids. Store in the refrigerator for up to one month.

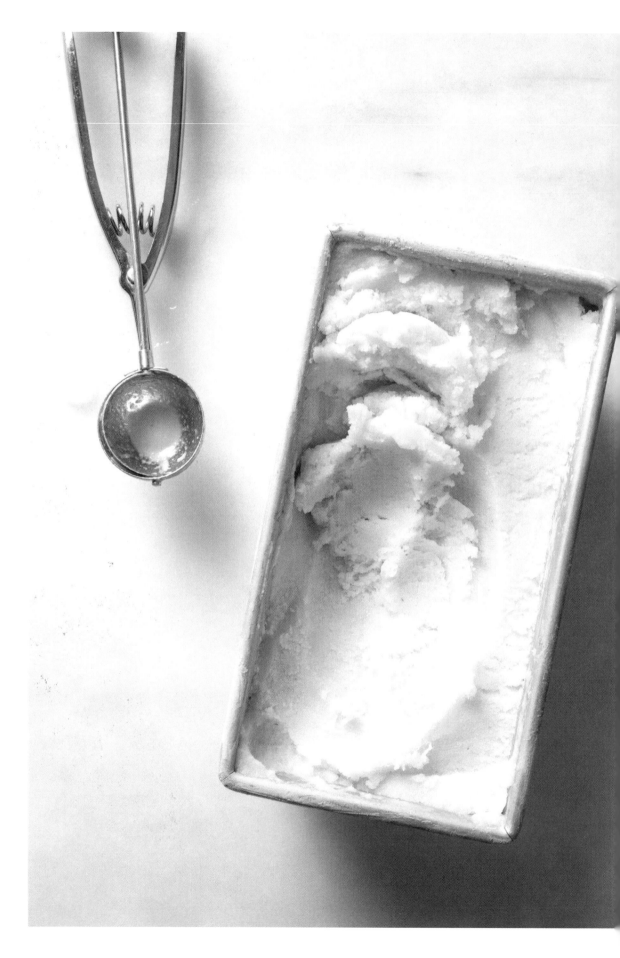

SHINKO PEAR AND BUTTERMILK SORBET

===== Makes 3 cups =====

To me, most ice cream tastes mostly of sugar, which is an aggressive and one-dimensional flavor on its own. But my opinion has more than a few exceptions. I have fond memories of my aunt's freshly churned peaches and cream ice cream, and I've enjoyed many a sorbet (especially chocolate). Recently I tasted a delicious sweet potato ice cream–like concoction on top of a sweet potato cake that had me entranced. I also enjoy this buttermilk sorbet; it is mildly sweet, bright and floral, easy to make, and beautiful to serve.

2 Asian pears (1 pound), peeled and cored (I prefer the Shinko variety for this.)

¾ cup brown rice syrup

½ cup granulated sugar

1 cup water

2 cups buttermilk

2 egg whites

Pinch of fine sea salt

Chop the pears into a ½-inch dice. Combine with the brown rice syrup, granulated sugar, and water in a medium saucepan; bring to a boil. Reduce the heat until the mixture is at a simmer, and cook, stirring occasionally, until the sugar dissolves and the pear has softened, about 15 minutes.

In a blender, combine the pear mixture with the buttermilk, egg whites, and sea salt. Blend on high until thoroughly puréed. Cool in the refrigerator for 1 hour, or up to overnight.

Transfer the mixture to an ice cream maker, and follow the manufacturer's instructions. When churning is complete, transfer the sorbet to an airtight container and place in the freezer for at least 1 hour. The sorbet will keep, frozen, for up to three weeks.

RYE BERRIES, CHICORY, PEAR, AND WALNUTS

Makes 4 to 6 servings

Rye is thought to have originated in mountainous Asia Minor, where its undemanding nature granted it rein over the more finicky crops like wheat and barley. Rye's nutritional profile is similar to that of other cereal grains—it is high in vitamins B and E, iron, fiber, protein, and trace minerals. It contains phytic acid and should therefore be soaked overnight before cooking. Store rye berries in a sealed container in a cool, dark, dry cupboard.

This grain dish is hearty and delicious. The rye berries are chewy and deeply nutty, the pear sweet, and the mustard perfectly pungent.

¾ cup rye berries, soaked overnight and drained

5 cups water

Fine sea salt

1 teaspoon raw honey

1 teaspoon Dijon mustard

1 teaspoon sherry vinegar

1 tablespoon + 1 teaspoon walnut oil

1 cup walnuts

1 Asian pear (about 8 ounces)

2 shallots

2 small heads radicchio

2 tablespoons chopped thyme

Freshly ground black pepper, to taste

Heat a large Dutch oven or stockpot over moderately high heat. Add the rye berries and toast for approximately 5 minutes, stirring occasionally. When the berries have darkened considerably and give off a nutty aroma, pour them into a strainer and rinse well with cold water to stop the cooking. Return the rye berries to the pot and add 2½ cups of the water; cover and leave overnight.

Preheat the oven to 375°F. Strain the rye berries and cover with 2½ cups fresh water and 2 pinches of salt; bring to a boil over high heat. Reduce the heat and simmer for approximately 45 to 60 minutes, or until the berries are tender and the liquid is absorbed. Add the honey, mustard, vinegar, and 1 tablespoon walnut oil.

Meanwhile, spread the walnuts on a sheet pan lined with parchment paper, and toast in the oven for approximately 8 to 10 minutes. While still hot, toss with 1 teaspoon walnut oil and a pinch of salt. Cool, roughly chop, and set aside. Slice the pear in half lengthwise and remove the core. Thinly slice each half into half-moons, about ⅛ inch thick. Thinly slice the shallots. Tear the radicchio leaves into 2-inch pieces.

To the rye berries, add the shallots, walnuts, and thyme; stir to combine. Add the pears, radicchio, a pinch of salt, and a few grinds of black pepper; toss gently.

A STEAMED PEAR TO SOOTHE A COUGH

All members of the pear family clear heat, energize the lungs, and nourish the body with fiber and potassium. I once suffered a persistent dry, hot cough, and this simple home remedy put all syrups, drops, and pills to shame. The combination of pears and a mild sweetener soothed my irritated throat and cooled my system. You can use Chinese rock sugar in place of the brown rice syrup.

1 Asian pear, peeled
   (approximately ½ pound)
1 tablespoon brown rice syrup
½ cup water

Cut the pear in half lengthwise; remove the core and seeds. Place the fruit, cut side up, in a small saucepan. Spoon ½ tablespoon of the brown rice syrup into the center of each half. Pour the water into the pan and bring to a simmer over moderately high heat; cover the pan. Cook the pear for 15 to 20 minutes, or until it is soft and slightly transparent. Serve the pear warm, in a bowl, and top with the warm syrup. Consume one a day, as long as symptoms persist.

BOLTING HERBS

Herbs may be my signature ingredient. I buy gobs and all sorts of them. I treat them as the precious items I believe them to be, picking each leaf from the stems. I use the stems too: tied with twine in a pot of beans or braising pan, pickled, or sliced and sautéed. I rarely consider herbs a garnish; they are integral, not decorative. Herbs boast more complicated flavors than most edible plants and are versatile, medicinal, and beautiful.

All plants bolt, or go to flower and eventually to seed. This is a part of their natural life cycle. Because many plants are only vaguely recognizable at this stage, farmers have a hard time selling them, and they end up in the chicken coop or compost bin. This is unfortunate.

Bolting herbs can easily be used as in their nonflowering phase in almost any recipe; the flavor is more floral and relatively subdued—in some cases, slightly more bitter, which is not a bad thing—and the plating prettier. Purchase bolting herbs that have no yellowing or wilting (or clip the affected branches); store them in a vase of water; and change the water every day or so. Trim what you need as you need it. If you have more than you can use immediately, you can dry the branches and harvest the pollen, or you can make flower vinegar.

Harvesting pollen from your herb bouquet is a simple preservation technique that leaves you with a unique powder. This powder can be used like a dry spice and works particularly well with flowering fennel, dill, and parsley. Place a bunch of flowering herbs bud-side down in a brown paper bag. Use twine to tie the bag around the branches; wrap the twine up the branches a bit, so you are able to hang them upside down with the bag affixed. As the herbs hang and dry, the bag will catch any pollen that falls.

Pollen can be sprinkled on eggs, soups, roasts, and just-grilled vegetables. Its uses are really endless. The dried leaves that remain on the stem can be crumbled and used to flavor soups, stews, and sauces.

Preserving in vinegar is also a practical solution to the question of too many herbs (flowers or no flowers). Simply put good-quality white wine vinegar in a sterilized jar, stuff it full of herbs, cover, and leave it in a sunny spot for one to two weeks. The longer the infusion, the stronger the infusion; when it reaches your desired intensity, strain and bottle it. Use your flower vinegar to make vinaigrettes. Or make a mignonette sauce: Combine about ¼ cup vinegar with 2 tablespoons finely chopped shallots, a pinch of salt, and a few grinds of black pepper. Chill the sauce until cold and spoon over oysters or other shellfish.

PEAS AND THEIR SHOOTS, LETTUCE, TICKLEMORE, AND CHIVE BLOSSOMS

Makes 4 to 6 servings

This dish can serve as a salad, side dish, or entrée. It is bright, substantial, and—once those peas are shelled—quick to please. If you can't find chive blossoms, a handful of finely chopped chives will do the trick.

3 tablespoons unsalted butter

4 cups shelled English peas

Fine sea salt

¼ cup water

Zest of 1 lemon

Freshly ground black pepper

2 teaspoons fresh lemon juice

3 tablespoons extra virgin
   olive oil

4 heads little gem lettuce
   (romaine or Bibb make good
   alternatives), washed and
   cut in quarters

1 pint pea shoots

6 ounces Ticklemore cheese
   (or ricotta salata), cut into
   roughly ⅛-inch slices

1 cup baby mint leaves (or
   large leaves, torn or roughly
   chopped right before use)

1 cup chive blossoms or
   rosemary flowers, torn

Coarse sea salt

Melt the butter in a large frying pan over low heat. Add the peas, a pinch of fine sea salt, and the water. Raise the heat and bring to a boil. Cook for 2 to 3 minutes, or until the peas are tender and bright green. Remove from the heat and stir in the lemon zest and a few grinds of black pepper. Taste, and add more salt if needed.

Meanwhile, in a medium bowl, whisk together the lemon juice with a pinch of fine sea salt; add the olive oil and whisk to combine.

Place the peas on a serving platter, reserving a few for garnish. Toss the lettuce with the lemon vinaigrette. Layer half the dressed lettuce with half the pea shoots, cheese, mint leaves, chive blossoms, a pinch of coarse sea salt, and two hits of freshly ground black pepper. Add the second layer of each ingredient, then scatter the few reserved peas over the top.

> Ticklemore is a kick-ass British cheese with a supercute name. If you know a shop nearby that sells Neal's Yard Dairy products, ask if they'll order some. Cheesemongers really like people who really like cheese, so there is a good chance they'll accommodate your wish (or find you a delicious substitute) and become your friends to boot.

CARAMELIZED CARROTS WITH LENTILS, LABNE, AND FLOWERING CILANTRO

Makes 4 servings

If you believe you abhor cilantro, I urge you to try it in its flowering stage. Once bolted, the leaves and flowers taste more like the plant's seed, coriander: assertive but slightly sweet, with notes of lemon rind and pine. As a garnish, the white buds and feathery leaves echo and integrate the characteristics of caramelized carrots, earthy spinach, bright labne, and hearty lentils.

Lentils are cheap, fast food. They are filling, nutritious, and teem with a minerality that complements so many foods. While half a cup of lentils is all you need for this particular recipe, I recommend making twice or thrice that. You'll find yourself inspired to make more meals or snacks out of small and simple things like fried eggs, leftover grains, or roasted carrots.

½ cup dry black (Beluga) or
   brown (Spanish) lentils

Fine sea salt

Red wine vinegar

Extra virgin olive oil

20 baby carrots, scrubbed

1 tablespoon honey

½ lemon

⅛ teaspoon orange flower water

2 cups labne

2 cups baby spinach leaves

Coarse sea salt

1 cup flowering cilantro

Preheat the oven to 450°F. Pick through the lentils and remove any stones; place them in a small saucepan with a pinch of fine sea salt and enough water to cover by approximately 1 inch. Bring to a boil over high heat, then lower the heat and simmer for about 20 minutes, or until the lentils are just tender. Check on them a few times; they should retain a slight bite. Lentils can quickly turn to mush. Drain off any remaining water and season the lentils with a splash (about 1 teaspoon) of red wine vinegar, a good drizzle (about 1 tablespoon) of olive oil, and salt to taste.

Line two sheet pans with parchment paper. Pat the carrots dry, if wet, and divide between the pans. Toss each lot with another 2 pinches of salt, ½ tablespoon honey, and enough olive oil to coat every carrot. I toss everything right in the pan, using my hands to distribute the wet ingredients evenly. Spread the carrots in an even layer, making sure there is space for water to evaporate quickly (½ inch or so between each carrot). Roast for approximately 25 minutes, or until sticky and caramelized. Season each batch with a squeeze of lemon and a few drops of orange flower water. Cool slightly.

Spoon labne onto a platter (or divide it among serving plates); use the back of the spoon to sweep the creamy mixture across into a thin, asymmetrical base. Top the labne with a loose pile of lentils. Finish with a few alternating layers of carrots, spinach, coarse sea salt, and cilantro flowers.

SMOKED TROUT AND POTATO HASH
WITH DILL BLOSSOMS

Makes 2 servings

Flowering dill is lanky and delicate, vivid and fragrant. It is somewhat sour; certainly floral; and reminiscent of caraway, celery, and anise. This herb pairs especially well with tomatoes, asparagus, fava beans, all root vegetables, basmati rice, fresh cheese, pork, and fish—especially when smoked.

This smoked trout hash can handle a substantial quantity of even the strongest dill blossoms. While hash is deeply spontaneous and malleable, I formulated this recipe as an easy reference; please get playful and consider using golden beets, that half-yellow onion wrapped in plastic wrap on the fridge shelf, or bits of pork pulled from last night's roast. With hash, you get to serve thrift and receive fun; pig and fish are interchangeable.

---

2 tablespoons extra virgin olive oil

2 tablespoons unsalted butter

4 Yukon gold (or other waxy variety) potatoes, cut into ½-inch dice

Fine sea salt

1 red onion, finely diced

1 smoked trout filet (approximately 4 ounces), deboned and pulled into 1-inch pieces

Zest of ½ lemon

Freshly ground black pepper

½ cup dill fronds and dill blossoms, roughly chopped

2 eggs

Coarse sea salt

Place a large skillet over moderately high heat; add the oil and 1 tablespoon of the butter. Cook the potatoes with 2 pinches of fine sea salt, stirring occasionally (too much, and you'll mash the potatoes), until golden, about 10 to 12 minutes. Add the red onion and cook, stirring occasionally, until it is translucent, 5 to 7 minutes more. Remove from the heat and gently stir in the trout and lemon zest. Season to taste with more salt and freshly ground black pepper. Stir in half of the dill fronds and blossoms.

Melt the remaining tablespoon of butter in a medium skillet over moderate heat; when the butter's foam subsides, fry the eggs until they are cooked to your liking. Serve the eggs over the warm hash, topped with coarse sea salt, black pepper, and the remaining dill blossoms.

BUDDHA'S HAND

SIX CITRUS RICE SALAD · *18*

CARROT AND CITRON SOUP · *20*

CHEESE PUMPKIN AND CITRON HUMMUS · *21*

WALNUT AND CITRON CIGARS · *22*

FERMENTED CITRON AND HONEY TEA · *24*

Don't ignore that crazy looking, lumpy, thick-skinned citrus in the form of clustered fingers. It is intensely flavorful and more versatile than you may think. Buddha's hand is one of several varieties of citron, an aromatic citrus fruit that contains little flesh. Other citrons include the etrog and diamante (yuzu is actually a bitter orange), but Buddha's hand is the one most readily available stateside. This Chinese symbol of happiness is harvested in the winter, when we all can use its bright color and sweet, floral fragrance.

Select firm fruits that are heavy for their size; the smoother the skin, the better. Avoid any with bruised or soft spots, as this spoilage quickly spreads. Store Buddha's hands at room temperature, on a plate in a single layer, as piling them in a bowl can lead several of them to spoil quickly. They keep this way for three to four days.

Citrus fruits are alkaline to the blood and exceptional sources of vitamin C. Citrus peel is relatively warming (versus citrus flesh, which is cooling), and the oils in the rind are particularly healing for ailing lungs, compromised mucosa, slow digestion, and chronic stress.

The Buddha's hand is all peel and pith, but unlike the rind of the common Eureka lemon, it is barely bitter. You often see it candied and folded into fruitcakes and occasionally shaved into a salad dressing, but I like to use the whole fruit, stem to fingertip, in a variety of ways. I've included my favorites in the following pages, but a few more preparations (including the common) warrant mention:

- Thinly slice any chicory (such as Treviso or Belgian endive), and toss it with a vinaigrette of red wine vinegar, shaved citron peel, pecorino sardo, and sliced toasted pecans.
- Marinate olives by tossing them with warm olive oil, cracked fennel seed, shaved citron, and chile de arbol.
- Candy the rind in sugar syrup, then dip in tempered dark chocolate, or chop and make panforte. Both are wonderful holiday gifts that keep for a few months.
- Fold undipped, roughly chopped candied rind into a quick bread batter (fruitcake is a classic, but I'm partial to chocolate-rye) or a yeasted dough (such as Italian panettone).

SIX CITRUS RICE SALAD

Makes 4 to 6 servings

Late one winter night I was at home testing recipes and got swept up in a creative current. By my sink sat a strainer of soaked rice. My chopping block was strewn with remnants from more than a few dishes: quince cores, crispy shallots, pints of picked herbs. The room was filled with the strong fragrance of ripening citrus on my dining room table. The evening before I had talked Thailand with a well-traveled friend. This salad emerged from all that inspiration.

Using a mandoline makes shaving the citrus an easy job; you are after a $\frac{1}{16}$-inch slice, as anything thicker is too bold and bitter. When just cooking for myself, I double this salad's punch by using twice the quantities of lime juice, fish sauce, and chile de arbol.

---

4 cups Perfect Steamed Rice, at room temperature (see page 286)

1 teaspoon fresh lemon juice

1 teaspoon fresh lime juice

1 teaspoon white shoyu or soy sauce

1 teaspoon fish sauce

Pinch of palm sugar

2 garlic cloves, minced with a pinch of salt

1 or 2 chiles de arbol, very thinly sliced (seeds included)

¼ cup Shallot Oil (see page 225)

Fine sea salt

3 green onions, thinly sliced

½ cup shaved Buddha's hand

½ cup shaved mandarinquats

1 cup pomelo segments, torn or cut into 1-inch pieces

1 cup Crispy Shallots (see page 225)

1 cup roasted salted peanuts, roughly chopped

1 cup cilantro leaves, roughly chopped

1 cup mint leaves, roughly chopped

Place the rice in a large mixing bowl and use a fork to fluff it well. In a small bowl whisk together the citrus juices, shoyu, fish sauce, palm sugar, garlic, chile de arbol, Shallot Oil, and a pinch of sea salt. Dress the rice and use the fork to toss thoroughly. Add the remaining ingredients and toss gently with clean hands. Taste, and adjust the seasoning, adding more fish sauce, chile, citrus juice, oil, or salt to suit your palate.

CARROT AND CITRON SOUP

Makes 4 to 6 servings

This is a simple soup that is as delicious cold as it is piping hot. Make a double batch, but reserve some for freezing before you stir in the crème fraîche; it keeps and reheats exceptionally well.

1½ pounds carrots, scrubbed

2 tablespoons extra virgin olive oil

2 tablespoons unsalted butter

3 shallots, thinly sliced

½ cup shaved Buddha's hand

2 black cardamom pods

Fine sea salt

4 cups water

½ cup Homemade Crème Fraîche (see page 284), plus more for serving

Cut the carrots in half lengthwise, then slice them, flat-side down, into ½-inch-thick half-moons. Melt the olive oil and butter in a large saucepan over moderately high heat. Add the shallots, Buddha's hand, black cardamom pods, and a pinch of sea salt; sauté for 4 to 6 minutes, or until the shallots and Buddha's hand begin to brown. Add the carrots, 3 pinches of salt, and enough water to cover by approximately 1 inch; bring to a boil. Reduce the heat and simmer until the carrots are very tender, about 30 minutes.

Remove the soup from the heat; discard the black carda-mom pods. Purée in batches in a blender until smooth, adding salt to taste and thinning with a bit of water, as needed, until you reach your desired consistency. Return the soup to the pot and whisk in the crème fraîche. Taste, and adjust the seasoning. If you like, top with an additional spoonful of crème fraîche to serve.

CHEESE PUMPKIN AND CITRON HUMMUS

Makes approximately 6 cups

This purée can be eaten on its own or scooped up with pita, lavash, or raw/quickly blanched vegetables. It can also serve as a condiment to plainly seasoned meats, hard-boiled eggs, or steamed grains. Sweep a spoonful across a plate and top it with a cup of cooked chickpeas, a few wedges of caramelized cheese pumpkin, braised lamb belly, lamb's quarter, thinly sliced red onion, and a sharp lemon vinaigrette, and you have an elegant meal. When I make hummus, I make a big batch, knowing how quickly it disappears. If you desire a smaller yield, this recipe is easily halved.

2½ pounds cheese pumpkin (or other winter squash)

Extra virgin olive oil

2 chiles de arbol, cut in half

Fine sea salt

¼ Buddha's hand (3 to 4 ounces), cut into 2-inch dice

1 garlic head, cloves separated and peeled

1 cup cooked chickpeas (I used sprouted chickpeas; see page 238 to make your own.)

¼ cup tahini

2 teaspoons fresh lemon juice

Preheat the oven to 425°F. Line two sheet pans with parchment paper.

Peel the pumpkin, cut it in half lengthwise, and remove the seeds. Cut the pumpkin into a 2-inch dice; divide the pieces between the two pans. Toss each batch with 2 tablespoons olive oil, half the Buddha's hand, half the head of garlic, 1 chile de arbol, and 2 pinches of sea salt. Spread the ingredients into an even layer across each pan. Roast for approximately 35 to 45 minutes, or until tender and caramelized.

Discard the chiles, and place all the ingredients (including the garlic cloves) in a food processor with a pinch of salt. Purée until smooth, adding 1 to 1½ cups olive oil while the machine is running. Taste, and adjust the seasoning, adding more olive oil, lemon juice, and/or salt as needed.

WALNUT AND CITRON CIGARS

Makes 20 cigars

There is a tiny shop on the edge of San Francisco's Mission District that is full of some of my most-loved ingredients: bulk bins of watermelon seeds, five varieties of tahini, plastic buckets of perfect olives, both Jordanian and Lebanese couscous, and flaky lavash. Each time we nod good-bye, Sami, the owner and cashier, reaches around the register and hands me a treat. Once he gifted me with a white root for brushing my teeth. There was also a small paper bag of roasted chickpeas. But most of the time, he slips me a cookie—date filled, pistachio laden, or phyllo with walnut. Recently, while staring at half a citron, Sami's phyllo sweet came to mind, and this delicious treat came to life.

FILLING

¼ medium Buddha's hand (about 3 ounces)

½ cup (3½ ounces) granulated sugar

1½ cups (5 ounces) raw walnuts

CIGARS

Ten 10 × 10-inch sheets phyllo pastry (9 ounces)

½ cup unsalted butter, melted

Preheat the oven to 375°F. Line a baking sheet with parchment paper.

In the bowl of a food processor, pulse the Buddha's hand and sugar until you have wet crumbs. Add the walnuts and pulse until finely ground (don't go too far, or you'll have nut butter).

Cut the sheets of phyllo in half, and work with one rectangular half-sheet at a time, keeping the rest covered with a slightly damp towel as you go. Brush a half-sheet with melted butter and place a tablespoon of filling just above the edge of the short end closest to you. Fold the left and right sides inward so they overlap the filling slightly. Bring the short edge over the filling, and roll into a cigar shape (this is the same method used for rolling Spring Rolls with Daikon, Yuba, and Sprouts on page 58). Repeat until all the pastry and filling has been used.

Lightly brush the tops of the cigars with the remaining butter and bake for approximately 20 to 25 minutes, or until a deep golden brown. Remove from the oven and cool on a wire rack. Stored in an airtight container at room temperature, these little pastries will keep for four days.

FERMENTED CITRON AND HONEY TEA

Makes approximately 16 servings

This is one of my favorite home remedies. A cup of this tea soothes a dry cough and aching throat, and it is quite delicious.

---

1 cup raw honey

¼ teaspoon fine sea salt

½ cup filtered water, warmed

1 Buddha's hand (12 to 14 ounces)

Stir the honey and sea salt into the warm water until dissolved; set aside. Think of this as a sort of honey brine, which is necessary for the fermentation and preservation process.

Scrub the Buddha's hand lightly; pat dry. Thinly slice the citron into ⅛-inch slices (I use a mandoline for this, but a sharp knife will do fine). Pack the slices into a clean, dry 12-ounce jar, spooning the honey brine between each layer. When the final layer of citron has been added, pour the remaining brine on top; there should be at least ¼ inch of liquid rising above the fruit.

Place a double layer of cheesecloth on top of the jar; secure this permeable lid with a rubber band. Keep the jar at room temperature for five days. Remove the cheesecloth, cap the jar tightly, and store in the refrigerator for up to a year.

To prepare the citron tea, dissolve a spoonful of the fermented citron honey in 1 cup filtered water.

BURDOCK

My encounter with burdock is one of my most potent memories of my chef's training program at the Natural Gourmet Institute (NGI) in New York City. The NGI specializes in concurrently teaching culinary techniques and the ancient arts of healing the body through food. Our instructors told us burdock was primarily a Japanese vegetable, referred to as *gobo*, and we prepared a common recipe: sautéed burdock with carrot, wakame, and shoyu (known as *kinpira*). I was taken by the root's firm texture; sweet smell of fresh earth; and nutty, herbaceous flavor. I was disappointed we didn't explore it further. I wanted to take it off the macrobiotic plate. I wanted to braise it in butter, pickle it with sugar, or toss it with pasta (farro penne, lacinato kale, green olive, lemon, and chile). Fast-forward a decade, and I am still excited by this fibrous root. I continue to find new ways to enjoy its utterly unique character.

Burdock must be cooked to be enjoyed. Much of its flavor lies in its skin. So although it looks dark and gruesome, please don't peel it; simply trim the ends and scrub along all sides with a stiff brush. Once cut, the white flesh will begin to turn brown; many folks may want to combat this reaction with acidulated (lemon) water, but I don't bother.

While burdock grows wild all over the place, it is not always easy to find. Look for it in the fall and winter at farmers' markets, Japanese grocers, and "specialty" supermarket chains. If demand increases, more farmers and foragers will do the hard work of harvesting and bringing roots to market.

Purchase or forage roots that are firm, avoiding any that appear limp or shriveled (a sign of moisture loss). To store burdock, wrap it in paper towels and place it in an airtight container; refrigerated this way, it will maintain its integrity for up to a week.

I truly hope you'll seek out this precious wild weed. Besides boasting exceptional flavor, burdock is also high in soluble fiber and antioxidants. Brewed as a tea or broth, it acts as an herbal medicine, detoxifying the kidneys, liver, and blood. (The same is true for Red Clover Blossom Tea; see page 81).

POACHED CHICKEN AND BURDOCK BROTH

Makes 6 to 8 servings

When the flu season hits, I build my immunity with mushroom teas and powders (available in pill form), umeboshi plums (one plum a few times a week), and this fortifying broth. If you'd like to make this a more substantial dish, you can add ½ cup rice or barley after you skim the water.

1 whole chicken (3½ pounds), giblets removed and reserved for another use

12 cups filtered water, cold

Fine sea salt

2 leeks, sliced ¼ inch thick

8 spring onions, trimmed and thinly sliced

5 burdocks, sliced ¼ inch thick

4 carrots, scrubbed and sliced ½ inch thick (alternatively, use baby carrots left whole)

4 garlic cloves, thinly sliced

One 2-inch piece of ginger, thinly sliced

1 chile de arbol

One 4-inch piece of kombu

Sesame oil

Place the chicken in a pot just large enough to hold it and the vegetables. Cover with the water and bring to a boil over high heat. Lower the heat until the broth is at a slow simmer. Skim any foam that rises to the top and discard. Add 3 pinches of salt and simmer for 20 minutes.

Add the vegetables, garlic, ginger, chile de arbol, and kombu. Once the broth returns to a simmer, cook for 25 minutes more. The chicken should be cooked (you can pierce the thigh joint to peek at the flesh to see if the juice runs clear), and the vegetables should be tender. (The burdock is cut in slices half the size of the carrot slices so they cook at the same rate.) Turn off the heat and allow the soup to rest for 15 minutes.

Remove the chicken from the broth and let the meat rest for 10 minutes more. Meanwhile, discard the kombu and chile; taste, and adjust the seasoning.

Carve the bird into eight pieces, or shred the meat into bite-size pieces. Serve the chicken in soup bowls with the vegetables and broth poured over it. Finish each bowl with a drizzle of sesame oil.

BRAISED BURDOCK

I've kept this braising recipe simple so you can easily use the braised burdock in other dishes. You can toss it with farro penne, braised lacinato kale, Anchovy Butter (see page 253), and chopped parsley. You can spoon a quarter cup onto a bowl of brown rice laden with wakame salad, soft-boiled eggs, pea shoots, and sliced chiles. You can also serve it on its own, as a side for any roasted joint.

Braising in a mixture of olive oil and water can be used for a variety of vegetables; try it with carrots, fennel bulbs cut in half, and baby turnips. The cooking time will vary widely among vegetables, and the only way to determine the right length is to taste for texture as you cook.

4 burdocks (approximately 10 to 12 ounces)
½ cup extra virgin olive oil
Fine sea salt
1 cup water

Cut the burdocks into 2-inch pieces. I like to make little owl-eye shapes by cutting on the diagonal, giving the root a quarter turn, then cutting on the diagonal again.

Heat the oil in a large sauté pan over moderately high heat; add the burdock and fry until lightly brown. Turn the burdock gently with tongs, making sure the pieces caramelize evenly; this takes 5 to 7 minutes total.

Lower the heat and season with 2 pinches of sea salt. Add the water (it should come halfway up the sides of the burdock) and cover the pan; cook for 5 to 7 minutes. Uncover and cook for 8 to 10 minutes more, or until the burdock is tender. If the water evaporates before the roots are tender all the way through, add a few tablespoons incrementally and as needed.

BURDOCK FRITTERS

I created these fritters when I needed a new way to consume large amounts of sprouted fenugreek. I had a full quart with a maximum one-day shelf life. Made with burdock and onions, these little root pancakes would beg for a fresh garnish. Moreover, their flat shape would facilitate a massive mound of the curly, white-and-lime-green shoots. Even if you can't find or don't like such strongly flavored sprouts, the fritters themselves are worth the work of grating burdock.

Fritters are the meal I have when I don't really want a meal. They're easy to throw together, require one bowl and one skillet, and fulfill that vague need that only small bits of fried food can.

3 burdocks (about 8 ounces), grated

1 onion, sliced ¹⁄₁₆ inch thick

2 to 3 serrano chiles, minced

½ cup chopped cilantro

½ teaspoon fresh lime juice

¾ teaspoon fine sea salt

½ cup chickpea flour

2 eggs, beaten

Coconut or grapeseed oil, for frying

1 quart fenugreek, clover, or onion sprouts (see page 238 to make your own)

Lime wedges

Coarse sea salt

In a large mixing bowl, combine the burdock, onion, minced chiles, cilantro, lime juice, and fine sea salt; rub the chickpea flour into the mixture using your fingers. Add the beaten eggs and mix thoroughly. Line a plate or pan with paper towels.

Set a large skillet over moderately high heat; add about ¼ cup coconut oil. When the oil is hot, drop in walnut-size balls of the burdock batter, making sure you do not over-crowd the pan (keep about ½ inch of space between the fritters); immediately use the back of a spoon to give each a little press, flattening it slightly.

Fry until the exterior of each fritter is golden brown and crispy, about 2 to 3 minutes per side, using a spoon or spatula to turn them only once (too much moving and flipping, and they'll fall apart). Add more oil between batches, as needed. Remove the fritters from the oil and drain on the lined plate. Top with sprouts to cover; season with a squeeze of lime and a hit of coarse sea salt.

BURDOCK AND MUSHROOMS ON DANISH RYE

Makes 2 to 4 servings

The summer I spent in Copenhagen I enjoyed doing as the Danes do: spending spare minutes outdoors; eating poppy seed pastries as a first meal every day; drinking beer and eating tiny sausages (*snackpølser*); admiring great art (Odilon Redon's *Buddha in His Youth* still lingers in my mind); and eating a lunch of *smørrebrød*, or tiny open-faced sandwiches. Oh, the *smørrebrød*! I consumed myriad toppings on those little squares of sprouted black bread: beef with horseradish and fried onions, creamed herring with beets and dill, cultured butter with local cheese and pickles, and egg salad with anchovy and chervil.

Today I still eat open-faced sandwiches on Danish rye, and this particular spread—hearty and earthy—keeps for up to five days without any noticeable loss of flavor (see also Open-Faced Sandwich of Danish Rye, Beet Relish, and Horseradish Crème Fraîche, page 124).

MUSHROOM SPREAD

2 tablespoons extra virgin olive oil

4 tablespoons unsalted butter

2 burdock roots (about 10 ounces), cut into ¼-inch dice

2 shallots, finely diced

2 spring onions, thinly sliced

Fine sea salt

2½ pounds assorted mushrooms (such as shiitake, cremini, oyster), roughly chopped

Freshly ground black pepper

⅓ cup verjus (or white wine)

1 cup water (or Kombu Stock; see page 281)

SMØRREBRØD

4 pieces Danish rye bread (see headnote), sliced ¼ inch thick

Softened butter

1 cup Mushroom Spread

2 green onions, thinly sliced

Handful of Quick Pickled Shallots (see page 222)

Watercress leaves

Dill, roughly chopped

Chive blossoms (optional)

Place a large sauté pan over moderate heat; add the olive oil and butter. When the butter's foam starts to subside, add the burdock, shallots, spring onions, and 2 pinches of sea salt. Sauté for 10 minutes, stirring occasionally, until the burdock begins to brown. Add the mushrooms, another pinch of salt, and 2 grinds of black pepper. Cook, stirring occasionally, until the liquid the mushrooms released evaporates and the pan is nearly dry.

Add the verjus, and once again, cook until the pan is nearly dry, about 4 to 5 minutes. Add the water, and reduce the heat to a simmer. Cook for approximately 20 minutes, or until all of the liquid has evaporated and the burdock is completely tender (add more water if your roots need more time). Taste and adjust the seasoning. Remove the pan from the heat and let cool slightly.

Put the mushroom and burdock mixture in a food processor, and pulse until it forms a loose paste; taste and add more salt, if needed. Spread the bread with softened butter and cover each slice with a few tablespoons of the spread. Garnish with green onions, pickled shallots, watercress leaves, dill, and chive blossoms, or as you like.

CARDOONS

Its prehistoric appearance, prickly exterior, and bitter bite don't help my case for the cardoon. Moreover, like fava beans and artichokes, it takes several whole plants to yield a small dish for two. Yet what they lack in comeliness and ease, they more than make up for in interesting texture; a wild, herbaceous flavor; and a biochemical nature that eases the body's digestion of many favorite, fatty foods (such as cheese, cured pork, cream, and deep-fried batter).

Cardoons are in the edible thistle family (with artichoke, milk thistle, and sunflowers) and contain phytochemicals that are associated with an improvement in liver and gallbladder function and the lowering of cholesterol. So it's interesting that this plant comes to us in the spring, a classic time for tonifying the system.

With a fairly long growing season, especially in California, cardoons are typically available from early November through late June. Very young stalks are tender enough to be eaten raw. When they are older, the stalks can become bitter and stringy, so cooking is required. Seek firm plants with grayish green leaves that show no sign of wilt or rot.

For most recipes, I start by parboiling cardoons: run a paring knife down the sides to remove the leaves; strip off any tough or stringy layers; cut into 3- or 4-inch pieces and simmer in salted water for 25 to 35 minutes, or until tender. At that point, they can be stored in the cooking liquid for up to four days; drain them right before you use them.

While I've included only three recipes here, there are many ways to enjoy this ancient and distinctive plant:

· Young, tender, and raw; shave and toss with lemon, olive oil, pecorino, and
  black pepper
· Stewed with white beans and showered with bottarga; include good country
  bread for sopping
· Cooked with pork shoulder, rosemary, and chile de arbol then folded into
  al dente pasta
· Braised with beef, preserved lemon, olives, and spices to make a classic North
  African tagine
· Poached with swordfish, capers, and olive oil; finished with lemon and parsley
· Baked into a gratin

OLIVE OIL–BRAISED CARDOONS, FRIED EGGS, AND ALMOND PICADA

Makes 3 to 6 servings

The bulk of the work for this dish can be done up to two days in advance. Make the picada ahead and store it in an airtight container at room temperature; refrigerate the cardoons submerged in the olive oil. Prepping ahead makes this a great brunch dish or a just-walked-in-the-door-from-work-and-starving dinner.

Extra virgin olive oil

Fine sea salt

1 pound cardoons, trimmed, peeled, and cut into 3-inch pieces

Coarse sea salt

Juice from ½ lemon

6 eggs

1 cup coarsely ground Almond Picada (recipe follows)

½ cup parsley leaves

Place a large sauté pan or shallow Dutch oven over moderate heat; add enough olive oil to reach a depth of 1 inch. Heat until slight bubbles begin to form. Add 2 pinches of fine sea salt. Place the cardoons in the oil in one even layer. Braise for 55 to 65 minutes, or until the thistles are very tender.

Preheat the oven to 250°F. Remove the cardoons with a slotted spoon and divide them between serving dishes (three plates if you'd like 2 eggs per person; six plates for 1 egg per person); season with coarse sea salt and a few drops of fresh lemon juice. Keep the plates warm in a low oven.

Raise the heat under the sauté pan slightly (you want the olive oil hot but not smoking). Crack three eggs into small bowls or ramekins. Tip the eggs into the olive oil and fry until the white is just set and brown and crispy around the edges, about 2 minutes; season each egg with a pinch of coarse salt. Using a slotted spoon, transfer the fried eggs to the plated cardoons. Repeat with the remaining three eggs, keeping the other dishes warm in the oven until you are ready to serve.

Garnish each plate with about 2 tablespoons picada and a scattering of parsley leaves.

ALMOND PICADA

Puréed to a paste, picada can be used to thicken soups and stews. Chopped coarsely, it makes a great garnish for any dish that can shine through the bold flavor of the roasted nuts and garlic and that benefits from substantial crunch, such as fried eggs, raw or grilled chicories, and braised meats. These are a few examples of my favorite complements to picada; there are many.

Makes approximately 1 cup

Two ½-inch slices country
   sourdough bread, cut into
   ½-inch dice
1 cup blanched almonds
3 garlic cloves, peeled
3 tablespoons extra virgin olive oil
Fine sea salt

Preheat the oven to 375°F. On a baking sheet, toss the bread, almonds, and garlic with the olive oil and a pinch of sea salt. Roast for approximately 10 minutes, or until golden brown. Cool to room temperature.

Transfer the ingredients to a food processor and process to coarse crumbs or a paste (depending on its use).

CARDOON AND PARSNIP SOUP

Makes 4 servings

This is a soup to bridge the seasons, made with the last of winter's parsnips and the first of spring's cardoons. I garnish my bowl with Katz Meyer lemon olive oil; its sweet citrus notes brighten the bowl.

2 tablespoons extra virgin
   olive oil
2 leeks, sliced ½ inch thick
Fine sea salt
3 parboiled cardoons, sliced
   ½ inch thick
3 parsnips, sliced ½ inch thick
Lemon olive oil or extra virgin
   olive oil, for serving
Freshly ground black pepper

In a large pot, heat the oil over moderately high heat; add the leeks and 2 pinches of sea salt. Soften the leeks for 2 to 3 minutes, then add the cardoons, parsnips, and enough water to just cover. Simmer for 35 to 40 minutes, or until the parsnips are very soft. Purée everything in a blender with another pinch of salt, thinning with water and adjusting the salt until you achieve your preferred thickness. Rewarm over low heat. Serve with a drizzle of lemon olive oil and a few grinds of black pepper.

BUTTERMILK-FRIED CARDOONS

Makes 4 servings

The moment the first cardoons hit the hot oil, I break open a beer. My friends keep me company by the stove, and we eat each batch as soon as it emerges, dousing it with chiles and Italian fish sauce.

CARDOONS

3 parboiled cardoons

1 cup buttermilk

Fine sea salt

BUTTERMILK BATTER

1 cup all-purpose flour

⅛ teaspoon fine sea salt

½ cup buttermilk

¼ cup beer (or sparkling water)

FOR FRYING

1 quart grapeseed, rice bran, or olive oil

1 cup all-purpose flour

Chile flakes

Colatura, or other good fish sauce (optional)

4 lemon wedges, plus extra for serving

Coarse sea salt

Preheat the oven to 250°F. Pat the cardoons dry and place them in a large bowl. Add the buttermilk and a good pinch of fine sea salt; mix to combine. Let the mixture stand for 30 minutes at room temperature.

Meanwhile, prepare the buttermilk batter. Mix the flour and sea salt in a medium mixing bowl; make a well in the center. Slowly add the buttermilk and beer to the well, whisking constantly until just smooth and combined—do not overmix or the gluten in the flour will develop. Let this mixture stand for 15 minutes.

Line a large plate with paper towels and a sheet pan with parchment paper. In a deep-fryer or large saucepan, heat the oil to 355°F. Drain the prepared cardoons (discard the buttermilk used for soaking), dust with the flour, then dip each piece in the buttermilk batter, shaking off the excess in between. Deep-fry in batches, turning occasionally, until crisp and golden (2 to 3 minutes; be careful as the hot oil may spit). Drain on the paper towels and then transfer to the sheet pan; keep warm in the oven until ready to use. Garnish with chile flakes, a light sprinkling of Colatura, a squeeze of lemon, and a pinch of coarse sea salt before serving. Serve extra lemon wedges on the side.

CELERIAC

Possibly the most unsung of all vegetables, celeriac's gnarly, dirty facade tends to turn people off. This is a shame, considering everything underneath that brown, creviced skin is dense with satisfying texture and flavor. Celeriac—also called celery root—is a kind of celery (there are many wonderful varieties of this common biennial) prized for its enlarged root versus its stalks or leaves.

Although this root is firm, it can be sliced or shredded thin and eaten raw, preferably well dressed in a strong vinaigrette. It also yields a phenomenally silky soup and an addictive mash (add horseradish, please). However, in my mind, celeriac is its sweetest, most earthy self when caramelized in a pan or hot oven.

When cooked, celery root grounds our energy and warms our systems. Like celery, it supports the nervous system, stimulates the appetite, and aids in digestion.

You will spot celeriac intermittently throughout the fall and winter. Purchase small, heavy roots; the larger, lighter ones can be pithy inside. Store celeriac with the skin on, in the refrigerator, for up to one week after purchase. Peel and discard the skin (and any nooks holding dirt) before using it. If you find celeriac with the leaves still attached, use the slightly bitter greens in soups, stews, or stock.

There are several classic recipes for this root that are wonderful and warrant mention here:
· Celeriac remoulade—raw matchsticks of celeriac tossed with mayonnaise, Dijon mustard, and black pepper
· Celeriac mash/purée—especially alongside short ribs and crunchy bitter greens
· Potato and celeriac gratin
· Celeriac soup—finished with crème fraîche, black pepper, and chervil or chives

CELERIAC GALETTE

Makes 4 servings

This basic savory galette can be adapted for a variety of roots and tubers; simply adjust the quantity of liquid and cooking time based on how fibrous the vegetable is.

1 large celeriac (1 pound)

¼ cup extra virgin olive oil

4 tablespoons unsalted butter

Fine sea salt

Freshly ground black pepper

3 tablespoons roughly chopped thyme (or oregano), plus more leaves for serving

½ cup water

Coarse sea salt

Preheat the oven to 400°F. Using a mandoline, slice the celeriac crosswise into $\frac{1}{16}$-inch rounds; place in a medium mixing bowl and set aside.

Heat a 9-inch ovenproof frying pan (I use cast iron) over moderately high heat; add the olive oil and butter, and swirl both around the bottom and sides of the pan.

Pour the warm fat over the sliced celeriac; add a pinch of fine sea salt and a few grinds of black pepper; toss with about 2 tablespoons of the chopped thyme. Place the celeriac in the oiled pan, overlapping the slices to create a tight circular pattern; you will have 2 to 3 layers. Drizzle any remaining fat and herbs on top and add the ½ cup water. Bake until the celeriac can be pierced easily with the tip of a knife, about 45 minutes.

Remove the pan from the oven and transfer to the stove. Sauté over high heat (leaving the celeriac slices undisturbed) until the bottom and edges are golden and crispy, about 8 minutes. Cool for 15 minutes before unmolding.

Use an offset spatula or paring knife to loosen the edges of the galette. Flip the pan onto a serving platter, board, or plate; tap the bottom. Lift the pan; rearrange any celeriac slices that may have fallen out. Sprinkle the galette with coarse sea salt and a bit more black pepper; top with a few leaves of fresh thyme, oregano, or marjoram.

CELERIAC BAKED WITH CHESTNUTS AND SOURDOUGH

Makes 8 to 10 servings

The most coveted dish of the American holiday meal is usually the bready one: stuffing. I crave my Aunt Sherry's casserole brimming with her secret bacon, biscuit, and cornbread mix. It is dense and moist, smoky and rich. I also really like this combination; earthy celeriac contrasts with the sweet chestnuts, and the sourdough holds its shape amid a relatively light base.

1 loaf country sourdough bread (approximately 1½ pounds), cut into 1-inch cubes

4 tablespoons unsalted butter, melted

4 ounces pancetta (or bacon), cut into ¼-inch dice

¾ cup unsalted butter, plus 1 tablespoon for baking dish

2 medium yellow onions, finely diced

1 medium leek, thinly sliced

Freshly ground black pepper

Fine sea salt

2 celery roots (about 3 pounds), cut into ½-inch dice

6 cups turkey or chicken stock

3 tablespoons finely chopped fresh oregano

¾ cup chopped fresh parsley

½ pound peeled chestnuts (see page 176), cut roughly into ½-inch dice

1 egg, lightly beaten

Arrange the bread in a single layer on a baking sheet, and let stand, uncovered, at room temperature overnight (or up to two nights). Alternatively, bake the bread in a 300°F oven until dry but not browned, about 15 minutes.

The day you wish to serve the dish, preheat the oven to 400°F. Brush a 13 × 9-inch casserole with 1 tablespoon of the melted butter and set aside. Place the bread cubes in a large bowl and set aside. Heat a medium skillet over low heat and add the diced pancetta. Cook for 4 minutes, or until it starts to release its fat. Turn the heat up to moderately high and allow the pancetta to continue cooking until crisp, approximately 6 minutes more. Remove the pancetta with a slotted spoon (leaving the fat in the pan), and drain on a plate lined with paper towels.

Return the pan to moderate heat. Add the onions, leek, a few grinds of black pepper, and 2 pinches of sea salt. Sweat the onions and leeks until they are soft and translucent, about 8 to 10 minutes. Add the celery root and cook until just tender, approximately 15 minutes.

Add the remaining melted butter, stock, and a pinch of salt. Bring the mixture to a boil, then immediately remove from the heat. Add the oregano, parsley, and chestnuts. Pour the stock mixture over the reserved bread cubes; add the pancetta and beaten egg, and stir to combine.

Allow the mixture to sit for approximately 10 minutes, so the flavors begin to meld and saturate the bread. Spread in the buttered pan. Bake for approximately 40 to 45 minutes, or until the liquid is absorbed and the top has turned a deep golden brown. Remove from the oven; rest 20 minutes before serving.

CARAMELIZED CELERIAC, HONEY, AND JUNIPER SALT

Makes 4 to 6 servings

Celeriac's punchy flavor can hold its own next to other, similarly strong ingredients. Juniper—with its sharp, piney flavor that is most often associated with gin—makes a fun pairing.

JUNIPER SALT

2 tablespoons juniper berries

2 tablespoons coarse sea salt

CARAMELIZED CELERIAC

4 pounds celeriac

½ cup extra virgin olive oil

1 tablespoon honey

In a spice grinder, pulse the juniper berries until finely ground. Transfer the ground juniper to a small bowl and toss with the sea salt.

Preheat the oven to 450°F. Cut the celeriac into planks, 1½ inches thick; cut each plank into thick matchsticks, 1½ inches thick. Finally, cut your matchsticks into 1½-inch-thick cubes. This precision will ensure that every piece of celeriac caramelizes at the same rate—you don't want your honey to burn, as it quickly turns bitter.

In a large roasting pan, toss the diced celeriac with the olive oil, honey, and juniper salt. Spread it out across the pan, making sure there is space between the pieces so that water can evaporate and hot air can circulate easily. Roast in the middle of the oven for 30 to 40 minutes, gently tossing once to ensure even caramelization.

> Juniper is most often associated with gin, but the dark purple berries can be used to season strongly flavored foods such as pâté, pickles, fatty cuts of pork, sauerkraut, and earthy roots. Steep juniper berries in vinegar or oil, stir them into marinades and brines, or crush them with salt, as I do in this recipe.

CELERY LEAVES

Even the most conscientious of farmers' markets cut edible trimmings of plants before arranging displays. Cauliflower cores, radish tops, beet greens, and celery leaves are too often missing from the plants offered for sale. So I poke around the stands looking for these trimmings and will brazenly ask for them. I'm often met with stares and a series of questions (especially "Do you have chickens?" assuming I could not possibly be feeding myself with this compost material). After I explain my delight in cooking and eating their bird food, most sellers bag it up for free.

Embrace this quirkiness and ask your farmer for the cut leaves, especially those of celery. And you can stop composting the tops from your store-bought celery immediately. These salty, herbaceous greens are available year-round but seem best in the late spring and early fall. Seek stalks and leaves that are a dark, vivid green. Refrigerate the leaves in an airtight container, layered with paper towels, as you do all herbs. If needed, wash the leaves gently right before using them.

Celery leaves make a good substitute for parsley (and vice versa) in many common applications:
· Chopped into Dandelion Gremolata (see page 66)
· Baked in a quiche
· Pounded into pesto
· Added to a marinade
· Mixed into a stuffing (for fowl or fish)
· Tossed in salad classics such as chicken with walnuts, tabbouleh, or Waldorf

CELERY LEAF SALAD WITH DUCK EGGS AND BASIL OIL

Makes 6 servings

The monochromatic palate of this salad is particularly pleasing to me, as is its preponderance of little crunchy things. The unique combination of bitterness and salinity makes celery leaves a perfect partner for the perfumed basil, crisp peppers, and rich eggs; if you can't find celery leaves, you can use parsley or watercress instead.

   If you overcook a boiled egg, you'll end up with a rubbery white and a chalky yolk with an unsightly gray ring. Preferable is a just-set white and a wonderfully creamy, bright yellow yolk. Try the method described here (and as pictured on page 46).

6   duck eggs
    Coarse sea salt
    Freshly ground black pepper
3   tablespoons salt-packed capers, soaked in water
    Extra virgin olive oil
1   tablespoon red wine vinegar
    Fine sea salt
3   tablespoons Basil Oil (recipe follows)
3   cups celery leaves
½   cup baby basil leaves (or large leaves, torn or roughly chopped right before use)
2   long Italian roasting peppers (or other Cubanelle variety), thinly sliced
2   cups pitted green olives (such as Castelvetrano), cut in half
2   medium shallots, thinly sliced

Place the duck eggs in a medium saucepan; add cold water to cover. Bring to a boil over high heat. Once rapid bubbles rise, immediately remove from the heat. Cover the pan and let it stand for 11 minutes, then transfer the eggs to a bowl of ice water. Once cool, gently crack the eggs and peel under the water. Pat the eggs dry, then cut into quarters, lengthwise; season each piece with coarse sea salt and freshly ground black pepper.

   Drain the capers with a fine-mesh strainer, leaving behind the salt that has settled at the bottom of the bowl, and rinse. Pat the capers very dry with paper towels—too much moisture makes the next step tricky. Set a small frying pan over moderately high heat; add a thin layer of olive oil (about 1 tablespoon). Fry the capers in one even layer for 2 to 4 minutes, or until they are brown and crispy (but not black). Use a slotted spoon to remove them from the pan, and set them aside until they have cooled to room temperature.

   In a small bowl, whisk together the vinegar, a pinch of fine sea salt, and the basil oil. Scatter a handful of the celery leaves across a serving platter; top with a few basil leaves, peppers, olives, shallots, and capers; drizzle a spoonful of vinaigrette over everything. Add a layer of eggs. Top the eggs with the remaining celery leaves and ingredients, as before. Finish the salad with a pinch of coarse sea salt.

BASIL OIL

Makes approximately ¾ cup

Fine sea salt

2 cups basil leaves

¾ cup extra virgin olive oil

Bring a medium saucepan full of water to a rolling boil; add 2 pinches of sea salt. Get a small bowl of ice water ready, and set it aside.

Blanch the basil leaves in the boiling water for 20 seconds. Drain and then immediately plunge the leaves into the bowl of ice water. Blanching and shocking the leaves preserves their green color. Drain again, then lay the leaves on a towel to dry. Place them in a blender with the olive oil and a pinch of salt; purée. Let the basil infuse the oil for about 20 minutes.

Run the contents through a strainer lined with cheese-cloth or a coffee filter (a small chinois is a useful tool here).

Refrigerate the oil in a sealed container for up to two weeks.

ROASTED CELERY LEAVES

Makes approximately ½ cup

This recipe essentially teaches a versatile preservation technique. Once you've dried your celery leaves, you can keep them whole and use them as you would a bay leaf to infuse a broth or a pot of beans. You can also grind them to a powder for use in spice rubs, compound butters, scented salts, or Celery Leaf and Duck Egg Custard (see page 51).

2 cups lightly packed celery leaves (or however many celery leaves need preserving)

Preheat the oven to 300°F. Wash the leaves well; drain and lay them out on dishtowels to dry (or use a salad spinner).

Line a sheet pan with parchment paper and spread out the dry leaves in one even layer. Bake for 10 to 12 minutes, or until dehydrated. Repeat with any remaining leaves. Cool the leaves to room temperature.

Alternatively, place the leaves in a dehydrator or an oven with the pilot light on for 6 to 8 hours. The slow route preserves their integrity a bit more.

Use a coffee grinder or mortar and pestle to crush the toasted leaves into a coarse powder. Store in an airtight container in a cool, dark place for up to one month.

LITTLE GEMS IN CELERY LEAF GREEN GODDESS

Makes 6 servings

Many a cook has written rhapsodic recipes for green goddess dressing, so perhaps mine is unnecessary. Yet a good thing is a good thing. Here is my take on a glorious classic, in which celery leaves add an appreciated bitter edge to a rich dressing.

GREEN GODDESS DRESSING

1 egg, at room temperature
1 teaspoon Dijon mustard
3 tablespoons fresh lemon juice
1 garlic clove, finely chopped
1 salt-packed anchovy, rinsed, deboned, and finely chopped
¾ cup grapeseed oil
2 tablespoons extra virgin olive oil
½ ripe medium avocado
1 cup chopped celery leaves
1 small shallot, finely chopped
½ cup buttermilk
Freshly ground black pepper
Fine sea salt

SALAD

8 red radishes, scrubbed
4 medium-ripe avocados (they should be soft at the stem, while the flesh is still somewhat firm)
Juice of ½ lemon
Coarse sea salt
Freshly ground black pepper
2 pounds little gem lettuce or baby romaine, cut or torn into 2-inch pieces
2 cups roughly torn celery leaves
Fine sea salt

First, make the mayonnaise base. Pulse the egg, Dijon mustard, lemon juice, garlic, and anchovy in a blender until well combined. With the machine running, gradually add the grapeseed oil, drop by drop at first, and then—after an emulsion has begun to form—in a steady stream. Once all the grapeseed oil has been added, gradually add the olive oil.

To make the celery leaf green goddess dressing, add the avocado, celery leaves, shallot, buttermilk, a pinch of fine sea salt, and 2 grinds of black pepper to the blender. Blend until completely smooth. Taste, and adjust the seasoning, adding more salt, pepper, and/or lemon juice as needed. Chill the dressing for 15 to 20 minutes while you prepare the salad (this allows the flavors to meld, and the slightly colder temperature of the dressing seems right for the crispy lettuce and spicy radish).

Thinly slice the radishes by hand or using a mandoline. Cut the avocados in half lengthwise, and remove the pits. Now quarter them lengthwise, and the skin should peel right off without damaging the delicate flesh. Season the avocado with lemon juice, coarse sea salt, and black pepper.

In a large bowl, toss the lettuce with a bit of the green goddess dressing. Scatter one layer of dressed lettuce onto a platter or in a shallow serving bowl; layer on top half of the seasoned avocado, sliced radish, and torn celery leaves. Repeat this layering once more.

CELERY LEAF AND DUCK EGG CUSTARD

This recipe is inspired by a dish I had at a tiny joint in Osaka. It was one of at least twelve dishes served in traditional Japanese fashion. The custard came plain—not everything needs a garnish, but if that mood isn't right for you, plate it up with torn celery leaves, chive blossoms, coarse sea salt, and freshly ground black pepper.

1 teaspoon finely ground Roasted Celery Leaves (see page 49)

¾ cup half-and-half

⅓ cup heavy cream

2 duck eggs, lightly beaten

1 tablespoon unsalted butter, melted

Fine sea salt

Preheat the oven to 300°F. Place the ground celery leaves, half-and-half, cream, and eggs in a blender and purée until smooth.

Put a kettle of water on to boil. Lightly brush four ramekins (approximately 3 inches wide and 1½ inches high) with the melted butter. Ladle about ¼ cup of the egg custard into each ramekin.

Transfer the ramekins to a roasting pan. Place the pan in the oven, then add about 1 inch of hot water to pan. If you cook the custard longer at a relatively low heat, the eggs gently coagulate, producing a silky result. Bake the custards until just set (there will still be a slight movement in the center of each), 30 to 35 minutes. Carefully remove the ramekins from the roasting pan, and allow the custards to cool to room temperature.

If you'd like to release the custards, slide a thin offset spatula between each custard and its ramekin, and run the spatula all the way around. Gently pull the custard away from the edge to break the suction. Place a plate on top of the ramekin and invert it to release the custard. Alternatively, serve the custards in the ramekins.

CELERY LEAF SALMORIGLIO

Makes approximately 1½ cups

A Sicilian sauce typically made with parsley, "salmoriglio" is fun to say (sahl-moh-REE-lyee-o). I prefer to make it with celery leaves, and I find the stuff addictive. While it is commonly used as a condiment for seafood, my batch often ends up on medium-rare steaks.

¼ cup extra virgin olive oil

4 tablespoons unsalted butter

¼ teaspoon chile flakes

Fine sea salt

3 tablespoons fresh lemon juice

2 garlic cloves, minced

1 cup finely chopped celery leaves

¼ cup finely chopped oregano leaves

¼ teaspoon fish sauce (optional)

Zest of 1 lemon

Place a medium bowl over a small saucepan of simmering water, creating a double boiler. To the bowl, add the olive oil, butter, chile flakes, and a pinch of sea salt. Whisk the mixture constantly until heated through. Gradually whisk in the lemon juice, garlic, celery leaves, and oregano. It should appear emulsified. Cook, whisking constantly, for 2 to 3 minutes more.

Remove the bowl from the double boiler and stir in the fish sauce (if using) and the lemon zest. Refrigerate in an airtight container for up to three days; bring to room temperature before serving. Taste, adding more salt or lemon juice to suit your palate.

DAIKON RADISH

That white root vegetable the size of a kid's baseball bat? Get that. Its crisp texture and pearly white color make it one of the most elegant vegetables to plate. It can be puréed in a soup, shredded into a slaw, sautéed, roasted, glazed, shaved, or pickled. It is both sweet and pungent. It stimulates energy, decongests sinuses and lungs, and aids in digestion.

Like most radishes, the daikon radish is available all year. Search for roots that are heavy (a lack of weight can indicate a pithy interior); hard (flabbiness is a sign of age); and free of blemishes or wet spots. If the daikon still has its perky green leaves, all the better—cook them as you would Mustard Greens with Potatoes and Whole Spices (see page 152). Wrap the root in plastic wrap and refrigerate for up to five days.

Throughout restaurants in both the United States and Asia, you'll see daikon in many forms:

- Shredded and pan-fried into a little savory pancake (with soy dipping sauce)
- Braised in a Japanese curry with beef (accompanied by steamed white rice)
- Simmered and served in dashi
- Fried in tempura batter
- Pickled
- Folded into a cabbage kimchi
- Grated into a condiment and mounded in small balls on a plate (much like wasabi)

DAIKON SLAW WITH SHIO KOJI

Makes 4 to 6 servings

This salty, tangy, peppery slaw is good on top of a bowl of steamed rice, alongside a whole roasted fish or grilled pork chop, or as part of a picnic spread. Also eating it atop a bacon sandwich (thick slices of toasted pullman, buttered on one side) made me question the legitimacy of the iconic BLT. If there are only a few bacon sandwiches in one's life, they should be the best bacon sandwiches, and perhaps those include daikon slaw with shio koji. (See pictured on page 54.)

½ head savoy cabbage
 (approximately 12 ounces)
Fine sea salt
1 medium daikon radish
 (approximately 12 ounces)
4 green onions
1 tablespoon shio koji
1 teaspoon brown rice vinegar
1 teaspoon fresh lime juice
¼ cup extra virgin olive oil
2 handfuls daikon sprouts
 (optional)
Freshly ground black pepper

Shave the cabbage into thin strips using a sharp knife; place in a medium bowl and toss with a few pinches of sea salt. Set aside for 20 to 30 minutes, so the leaves will release their water now and not when you want them coated with the shio koji. Drain the cabbage, then lay it out on a clean kitchen towel to dry even more.

Meanwhile, cut the daikon radish into matchsticks, approximately ⅟₁₆ inch thick and 2 inches long (once again, a mandoline is useful but not necessary). Cut the green onions in half crosswise; slice each half lengthwise into thin strips.

In a small mixing bowl, whisk together the shio koji, brown rice vinegar, lime juice, olive oil, and a few grinds of black pepper. Place the drained cabbage, daikon, and onion in a large bowl, and toss with half of the dressing. Taste, and adjust the seasoning, adding more dressing as needed. If you are using them, gently fold in the daikon sprouts.

> Shio koji is a fermented mixture of rice inoculated with *Aspergillus oryzae* (koji) and sea salt (shio). It is rich in umami, and can be used in salad dressings, brines, and marinades.

TWO RADISH SALADS

Makes 4 to 6 servings

At my local market, I can find at least a dozen varieties of radish. Radish salads are a perfect way to showcase the wide spectrum of shapes and colors. Here are two great examples of a simple snack being a special treat.

RADISH SALAD WITH MINT

2 pounds mixed radishes, such as daikon, Easter egg, black, watermelon, or green elephant

1 tablespoon fresh lemon juice

1 teaspoon fish sauce

Fine sea salt

¼ cup extra virgin olive oil

Handful of baby mint leaves

Coarse sea salt

Slice the radishes about ⅛ inch thick on a mandoline or by hand.

In a medium bowl, whisk together the lemon juice, the fish sauce, a pinch of fine sea salt, and the olive oil. Toss the radishes in the vinaigrette and plate. Garnish with the mint leaves and coarse sea salt.

RADISH SALAD WITH PRESERVED LEMON AND SPROUTS

2 pounds mixed radishes, such as daikon, Easter egg, black, watermelon, or green elephant

1 Preserved Lemon (see page 282)

1 tablespoon fresh lemon juice

Fine sea salt

¼ cup extra virgin olive oil

1 pint labne

Handful daikon (or other radish) sprouts

Coarse sea salt

Slice the radishes about ⅛ inch thick on a mandoline or by hand.

Use a sharp knife to separate the rind of the preserved lemon from the flesh. Save the flesh for another use; julienne the rind, then cut it into a 1/16-inch dice. Place the rind in a medium bowl and add the lemon juice, a pinch of fine sea salt, and the olive oil. Toss the radishes in the vinaigrette.

Spoon the labne onto a plate or platter, and use the back of the spoon to swiftly smear it across the plate. Garnish with the sprouts (if using) and coarse sea salt.

SPRING ROLLS WITH DAIKON, YUBA, AND SPROUTS

Makes 6 to 8 servings

Spring rolls may be made six hours ahead and chilled, wrapped in a dampened towel in a sealed container. Bring the rolls to room temperature before cutting in half and serving.

Yuba is dried tofu skin that can be found in co-op markets and specialty food stores (Hodo Soy makes a great product). If you can't find yuba, you can use extra-firm tofu instead.

DIPPING SAUCE

1 tablespoon fresh lime juice

1 tablespoon brown rice vinegar

1 tablespoon soy sauce (I use a white shoyu.)

1 serrano chile with seeds (or without, depending on your preference), minced

1 large shallot, finely chopped

One 2-inch piece of ginger, peeled and minced

¼ cup sesame seed oil

Fine sea salt, to taste

SPRING ROLLS

6 ounces rice noodles

8 ounces yuba (or firm tofu)

Fine sea salt

20 rice paper rounds

1 medium daikon radish, cut into matchsticks approximately 1/16 inch thick and 2 inches long

Daikon, buckwheat, or sunflower sprouts (see page 238 to make your own)

In a small bowl, mix all the ingredients for the dipping sauce; set aside.

Bring a kettle of water to a boil. Cover the rice noodles with boiling water and soak for 8 minutes; drain in a fine-mesh strainer, rinse under cold water, then drain once more.

Meanwhile, slice the yuba into ¼-inch matchsticks and place in a small mixing bowl. Toss the yuba with a pinch of sea salt and a spoonful of the dipping sauce; set aside.

Put a plate or cutting board on a work surface, and fill a shallow pan or bowl with warm water (I like to keep a towel handy for soaking up excess liquid). Soak 1 rice paper round (discard any with holes) in warm water until pliable, about 30 seconds, then transfer to your work surface. In the bottom center of the circle, make a small, tight mound of noodles, yuba, daikon matchsticks, and sprouts. Roll the rice paper tightly around the filling and, after rolling halfway, fold in the sides and continue rolling (think: baby burrito). Transfer the spring roll to a plate and cover with a clean towel or plastic wrap (rice paper becomes rubbery with prolonged exposure to air). Repeat with the remaining ingredients. Serve the rolls alongside the dipping sauce.

DAIKON BRAISED IN BLACK CARDAMOM GHEE

Makes 3 to 4 servings

A few ingredients can combine to create a product exponentially greater (or "better") than you might expect. Here, peppery daikon and its slightly bitter leaves soften in sweet butter infused with aromatics. The disparate flavors meld into an amalgam both plain and alluring; heat is the magical catalyst.

Served alongside steamed rice and a bowl of lentils or beans, this is a meal in itself.

1 pound daikon radishes, with greens attached

3 tablespoons Black Cardamom Ghee (recipe follows)

2 garlic cloves, minced

Two ½-inch slices of ginger

Fine sea salt

Cut the daikon radish into a 1-inch dice, and roughly chop and wash the greens. Heat the ghee in a 12- or 14-inch sauté pan over moderately high heat. Add the garlic, ginger, daikon, daikon greens, and 2 pinches of sea salt. Reduce the heat to medium-low and cover; cook, stirring occasionally, until the daikon is tender, about 20 minutes. Taste, and add more salt if needed.

BLACK CARDAMOM GHEE

Louella Hill is the San Francisco Milk Maid and has a cookbook of her own. She astounds me with her playful teaching and skill for making some of the best homemade cheeses I've tasted. She has graciously contributed this unique ghee recipe, and it is one of the most soothing and delicious ingredients imaginable. The black cardamom adds an intoxicatingly bright, smoky spice, although you could certainly omit it.

Makes approximately 2 cups

4 cups unsalted organic butter
2 teaspoons black cardamom
  seeds, roughly crushed

Place the butter and cardamom seeds in a medium-size cast-iron or stainless steel pot. Place the uncovered pot in a 225°F oven for six to ten hours. After the butter melts, a layer of white foam appears on top the liquid. Over time, it becomes golden and may sink to the bottom. Do not stir the ghee during this time.

After several hours in the oven, you will notice a distinct "toasted" aroma. Use a spoon to bring some of the sediment from the bottom of the pot up and check the color—it should be light brown. These toasted milk solids flavor the ghee. Take care they don't become dark, or your ghee will not taste good. When the sediments are the right color and the ghee is richly aromatic, remove the pot from the oven.

Carefully ladle the ghee into a colander lined with very fine cheesecloth (I use a double layer of a clean old T-shirt) set over a bowl. The ghee that collects in the bowl will be clear and bright yellow. The straining may take 30 minutes; slower straining means less sediment in the ghee.

Transfer the filtered ghee to clean jars and store in the fridge for up to three months. Ghee can also be kept at room temperature for two to three weeks.

DANDELION

I grew up picking dandelions. Much to my mother's dismay, I'd pop those beauties (and other found oddities) straight into my mouth.

The dandelion grows wild throughout much of the world, where it is simultaneously treated as a pesky weed and esteemed as a nutritious ingredient. Together, the roots and leaves are reputed to heal most common ailments (viruses, acne, high blood sugar, bloating, and inflammation, to name a few). It is extremely high in vitamins A and C and is an excellent source of calcium and potassium.

Dandelion greens are certainly bitter, and therefore they have an affinity for sweet, salty, fatty things (such as dried fruit, salted nuts, crispy pork, aged cheese, and olive oil). They are available year-round, although they are sweetest in the spring and early summer. Wrap the leaves loosely in paper towels and refrigerate in an airtight container. Wash them only when you're ready to use them.

Here are a few simple techniques for preparing dandelion greens:

· Blanch them in boiling water for 2 minutes; drain and toss with lemon juice and olive oil (1 part acid to 3 parts oil).

· Cut them into a thin chiffonade and sauté in drippings remaining from a pan-grilled steak or roast chicken.

· Juice them with celery, apple, and lemon.

BABY DANDELION SALAD WITH FRESH FIGS AND PANCETTA

Makes 6 servings

I can eat this salad by the mixing bowl. If you'd prefer to make it without pancetta, I recommend adding another crispy or crunchy food, because such textural contrast vastly improves a heap of raw greens and fresh fruit (think about roughly chopped toasted hazelnuts or torn pieces of bread that have been shallow fried in olive oil). Endive or lamb's quarter would both work well here in place of the dandelion greens.

6 ounces pancetta,
sliced ¼ inch thick

1 tablespoon sherry vinegar,
divided

Fine sea salt

1½ tablespoons extra virgin
olive oil

8 ounces baby dandelion
greens

14 ripe figs, stemmed and
cut in half

Coarse sea salt

Freshly ground black pepper

4 ounces pecorino romano

Preheat the oven to 400°F. Place the pancetta slices on a sheet pan lined with parchment paper. Roast for approximately 15 minutes, or until the pancetta is brown and crispy; remove from the oven and drain on paper towels. Reserve 2 tablespoons of the warm pancetta fat.

In a small bowl, whisk together ½ tablespoon of the sherry vinegar and a pinch of fine sea salt. Add the olive oil and 1 tablespoon of the pancetta fat; whisk to combine. Place the dandelion greens in a medium mixing bowl and toss with half of the vinaigrette; add more, if needed, taking care not to overdress the leaves. Transfer the greens to a platter. Gently toss the figs with the remaining sherry vinegar and pancetta fat, half a pinch of coarse sea salt, and some black pepper; scatter the figs across the greens, leaving any excess dressing behind. Top the salad with broken shards of the crispy pancetta and shavings of pecorino romano.

EGGS BAKED WITH DANDELION AND CREAM

Makes 3 to 4 servings

If you ever find yourself needing to cook brunch for a crowd, this recipe could be your savior. It scales up easily and forgives you if you walk away from the stove. If you can't find dandelion greens, spinach or spigarello make good substitutes. Spigarello is a dark green cruciferous plant native to Campania, Italy. It tastes like wild broccoli and has a texture similar to that of kale, only more succulent. It is an interesting and lovable green, and one that I think will be on more plates in the coming years.

2 bunches dandelion greens (about 1 pound)

3 tablespoons extra virgin olive oil

2 shallots, finely chopped

Fine sea salt

1 scant tablespoon water

½ cup heavy cream

Freshly ground black pepper

2 tablespoons unsalted butter, softened

6 eggs

½ cup crème fraîche

Coarse salt

Preheat the oven to 375°F. Slice the dandelion leaves into ¼-inch ribbons.

Heat the olive oil in a large sauté pan over moderate heat; add the shallots and a pinch of fine sea salt. Sweat the shallot for 5 to 6 minutes. Add the dandelion greens, another pinch of salt, and the water; cover. Cook the greens, stirring a few times, until wilted, about 5 minutes. Remove the lid and cook, stirring occasionally, until any excess liquid has evaporated. Add the heavy cream and a few grinds of black pepper. Simmer, stirring occasionally, until the cream thickens slightly, about 3 minutes. Taste, and adjust the seasoning, as needed.

Meanwhile, butter a shallow, medium-size Dutch oven, stainless steel pan, or skillet. Scatter the dandelion greens across the bottom of the pan, and make six little wells throughout. Carefully crack an egg into each well; top each egg white with a tablespoon of crème fraîche, making sure not to disturb the yolk. Top each yolk with a sprinkling of coarse sea salt. Bake until the whites are just set, about 15 minutes.

MEATBALLS, SUMMER SUNDAY SAUCE, AND DANDELION GREMOLATA

I love this dish: I love its name, its provenance (ingenuity born of thrift), and how I feel after I eat it. It is a real treasure.

There is a lot of meat in this recipe, so make plans according to the number of people you're feeding and the amount of time you've allotted for the meal. (This should be a leisurely, multihour affair; it is a Sunday sauce, after all.) You can serve the meatballs alongside ribs or as a first course. Or the ribs can be refrigerated and reserved for another meal entirely. In any case, a big salad of bitter greens—thinly sliced wild arugula, endive, radicchio—is a welcome companion.

SUNDAY SAUCE

6 pounds St. Louis pork ribs, patted dry

Fine sea salt

Freshly ground black pepper

4 pounds cherry tomatoes, stemmed and divided in half

1 cup water

4 garlic cloves (fresh or smoked)

2 red onions, thinly sliced

¼ cup extra virgin olive oil

2 tablespoons unsalted butter

2 oregano sprigs

2 rosemary sprigs

2 basil sprigs

1 bay leaf

2 chiles de arbol (or 1 fresh serrano chile), cut in half

¼ pound pork salumi (I use Nostrano.)

¼ pound pancetta

2 Parmigiano-Reggiano rinds, each 3–4 inches long

Season the ribs liberally with sea salt and lightly with black pepper; refrigerate overnight. Bring them close to room temperature before proceeding with the recipe.

Preheat the oven to 275°F. Place 2 pounds of the cherry tomatoes in a blender. Add the water, garlic, onions, olive oil, 3 pinches of salt, and a few grinds of black pepper. Purée until smooth. Strain the sauce through a fine-mesh strainer (I use a chinois) into a 12- or 14-quart Dutch oven or stockpot; add the butter. Bring the sauce to a simmer over moderately high heat.

Lay a large piece of cheesecloth on a work surface. Pile the herbs, chiles, salumi, pancetta, and cheese rinds on top; use kitchen twine to tie it up into a tight bundle. Add this bundle to the simmering sauce.

Heat a large skillet over moderately high heat and add enough olive oil to coat the bottom of the pan to ⅛ inch. Add half the ribs, fat side down, and leave them to brown for approximately 8 minutes (the more you poke and prod and peek, the less browning you'll get). When they release from the bottom of the pan with the slightest touch of the tip of your tongs, they are ready to be turned. Brown the other side, 6 to 8 minutes more. Repeat this process with the remaining ribs, adding them to the pot of simmering sauce as they are cooked. Once all of the ribs have been browned and added, cover the pot. Place in the oven and stew for two and a half hours. Reserve the skillet you used to brown the ribs for the meatballs.

MEATBALLS

1 pound ground pork
(shoulder or butt)

1 egg, beaten

¾ cup fresh breadcrumbs

¼ cup grated Parmigiano-
Reggiano

Fine sea salt

Freshly ground black pepper

Extra virgin olive oil

Dandelion Gremolata (recipe
follows)

While the ribs cook, make the meatballs. Place the ground pork in large bowl, and break it up into small chunks. Add the egg, breadcrumbs, cheese, ¼ teaspoon sea salt, and 3 grinds freshly ground black pepper, mix with a fork to combine. Chill this mixture for 15 to 20 minutes. Roll the meat mixture into golf ball–size balls; cover and chill again for at least 15 minutes (and up to 12 hours).

Remove the pot from the oven and use tongs to test the ribs; if the meat separates easily from the bone, they are ready. If the meat resists, return the pot to the oven for 30 minutes more and test again. Once the ribs are ready, transfer them to a platter and keep them warm in the oven. To the sauce, add the remaining 2 pounds of cherry tomatoes, and set the pot over moderately high heat. Simmer the sauce for 20 minutes, or until the fruit begins to burst. Remove and discard the cheesecloth bundle. Taste the sauce for seasoning, adding more salt, if necessary.

Return the skillet from the ribs to moderately high heat and add enough olive oil to coat the bottom of the pan to ⅛ inch. Fry the meatballs for 2 to 4 minutes on each side; their entire circumference should be a deep, golden brown. Use a slotted spoon to add the browned meatballs to the simmering sauce. Reduce the heat, cover, and simmer until the meatballs are cooked through, 5 to 7 minutes. Serve the meatballs topped with the gremolata, as the course before the ribs; alternatively, refrigerate the ribs for another use.

DANDELION GREMOLATA

Gremolata is a fresh herb condiment that usually contains citrus zest and garlic. It can be made using a variety of herbs and greens, but the bitterness of dandelion is welcome when it accompanies something as rich as meatballs in meat sauce.

Makes 1½ cups

1 cup finely chopped
dandelion greens

¼ cup finely chopped parsley

2 tablespoons finely chopped
thyme

1 tablespoon finely chopped
rosemary

1 clove garlic, minced

Zest of 1 lemon

Zest of ½ orange

Pinch of coarse sea salt

Mix all the ingredients in medium bowl. Store at room temperature for up to two hours, covered with a slightly damp paper towel.

SEMOLINA BREAD WITH DANDELION AND GREEN OLIVES

Makes 4 to 6 servings

This bread is akin to focaccia; it bakes up bubbly and golden brown, studded with briny olives, sliced chiles, and greens doused in a garlic vinaigrette. Like all yeast breads, you'll need to start this recipe a few hours before you plan to serve it.

If you have a stake in convincing a young person that vegetables are fun and good, invite him or her to participate in the cooking! A recipe as interactive as this is a perfect place to start.

8 ounces dandelion greens

Extra virgin olive oil

1 recipe Semolina Dough (see page 285)

½ teaspoon red wine vinegar

1 garlic clove, minced

1 or 2 chiles de arbol, thinly sliced

Fine sea salt

1 cup pitted Cerignola, Sevillano, or other green olive, cut in half

2 tablespoons rosemary leaves

Coarse sea salt

Bring a large pot of salted water to a boil. Blanch the dandelion greens for 2 minutes; drain well on a kitchen towel and set aside. Use about a tablespoon of olive oil to coat a 10- or 11-inch cake pan or casserole with 2-inch sides.

Preheat the oven to 500°F. Oil your hands. Punch down the semolina dough and transfer to the greased pan. Oil your hands again, and press and shape the dough to fill the pan. Cover the pan with oiled plastic wrap, and let the dough rest for 30 to 40 minutes in a warm spot.

Roughly chop the dandelion greens and place them in a small bowl; toss with 2 tablespoons olive oil, the red wine vinegar, the garlic, one chile de arbol, and a pinch of fine sea salt. Spread this mixture on the flatbread dough. Garnish with the olives, rosemary sprigs, coarse sea salt, and another chile (if you'd like more heat). Drizzle 1 tablespoon olive oil over it all. Bake the bread for 35 to 40 minutes, or until golden brown. Let the bread rest for 10 minutes before cutting; it is perhaps even better when served at room temperature.

DATES

I love dates; I eat them practically every day. And while they are one of the more common ingredients in this book, I decided to include them because I think many folks don't seek out some of the more exciting varieties, and because this desert berry deserves more range. I most often see dates eaten out of the hand or blended with ice cream; but they are highly versatile, offering a complex sweetness from which many dishes can benefit.

Out of the foods people consume regularly, the date is one of the most ancient. It thrives in subtropical regions—the Middle East, North Africa, Southern California, parts of Asia—where the tree's beautiful palms provide much-needed shade.

Dates are sweet and soothing. They are good sources of niacin (B complex), iron, and potassium. They are also high in natural sugars, which makes them a good snack for busy days, arduous hikes, and long trips. Dates should be consumed in moderation by anyone struggling with high blood sugar, respiratory infections, or damp conditions (such as a yeast overgrowth or a sinus infection).

Fresh dates are classified by their degree of dehydration. I've tried to simplify the categories for cooking; they range greatly in moisture content but only slightly in flavor:

- *Moist* (for purées, batters, drinks, stuffing, and snacks)—brown Barhi, Medjool
- *Soft* (for all uses)—yellow Bhari, Khadrawy, Amber
- *Dry* (for garnishes, relishes and chutneys, pies, and salads)—Deglet

I've tried to include a variety of preparation methods in this chapter so that regardless of which type you prefer, you'll have a recipe to try. Refrigerating dates prevents fermentation and eases the work of chopping, so that's how I store them. In addition to the recipes in the chapter, here are a few more ideas and techniques:

- Black coffee; a plate of dates and almonds (This is my breakfast many days of the year.)
- Brown Barhis or Medjools mashed and spread on warm buttered toast
- Brown Barhis or Medjools mashed with almond butter, argan oil, and honey, then spread on warm buttered toast
- Ambers or Deglets diced as a garnish for porridge, rice pudding, or sweet polenta. Specifically, favorite oatmeal cooked in water with a good pinch of salt then left to rest for 10 minutes; topped with a spoonful of tahini, a spoonful of honey, several chopped dates, and toasted sesame seeds.

BASMATI PILAF WITH DATES AND DUKKAH

Makes 6 servings

This rice pilaf is strongly spiced and imbued with the sweetness of fresh dates. I use Deglets for this dish, but any firm variety will do; cutting them while they're cold prevents them from sticking to the knife. To make the dish a main course, follow the dukkah with layers of cooked chickpeas, lentils, or lamb.

2 cups basmati rice

Fine sea salt

8 ounces dates, refrigerated

2 tablespoons olive oil

6 tablespoons unsalted butter, divided into 1 tablespoon pieces

¼ cup boiling water

¾ cup Hazelnut Dukkah with Hazelnut Oil (recipe follows)

Approximately 2 cups parsley leaves, roughly chopped

Place the rice in a medium saucepan; cover with water to 4 inches or so, and use your hand to swirl it around (this releases the starch). Let the rice settle to the bottom, then pour off the starchy water. Repeat this process of filling, swirling, setting, and pouring three more times, or until the water runs clear. Cover the rice with water once more and soak for at least 30 minutes, or up to overnight. Strain the rice and set aside.

Fill the same saucepan with water; add 3 pinches of sea salt. Bring to a boil over high heat. Add the rice and parboil for 5 minutes. Strain the rice again. Meanwhile pit the dates and chop them into a ¼-inch dice.

Bring a kettle of water to a boil. Return the saucepan to moderate heat and add the olive oil. Cover the base of the pan with a thin layer of rice; season with sea salt and add 1 tablespoon of the butter. Scatter a spoonful of chopped dates and dukkah over the rice base. Continue to layer the remaining rice, salt, butter, dates, and dukkah, building the mixture into a pyramid in the pan.

Once all of the rice has been mounded, use the handle of a large wooden spoon to poke holes in the pyramid. Gently pour the boiling water over it. Cover the pan and cook over low heat for 20 minutes.

Remove the pan from the heat. Remove the lid, place a clean tea towel over the pan, and cover it once more. Let the rice rest for 15 minutes before serving (the towel will absorb any extra moisture). Use a fork to gently fluff the rice. Spoon the rice onto a platter and top with the chopped parsley.

HAZELNUT DUKKAH WITH HAZELNUT OIL

Dukkah is an Egyptian spice blend. I suggest incorporating this particular version into dishes of rice, beans, chicken, or lamb. Without the hazelnut oil, it will keep in an airtight container at room temperature for up to one month.

Makes approximately ¾ cup

½ cup hazelnuts

¼ cup unsweetened, dried, shredded coconut

¼ cup coriander seeds

3 tablespoons cumin seeds

3 tablespoons sesame seeds

3 tablespoons black sesame seeds

¾ teaspoon fine sea salt

½ teaspoon freshly ground black pepper

2 teaspoons hazelnut oil (or olive oil)

Preheat the oven to 375°F. Place the hazelnuts in a skillet or on a sheet pan—make sure they are in one even layer. Toast the nuts for approximately 15 minutes, or until they are a deep golden brown. Cool to room temperature.

Spread the coconut on a sheet pan and toast in the oven for 5 to 8 minutes, or until a light golden brown (keep an eye on it; it can burn in no time). Meanwhile, place the coriander, cumin, and both kinds of sesame seeds in a medium skillet and toast, stirring constantly, until fragrant, about 3 to 4 minutes. Let the coconut and spices cool to room temperature, then transfer to a spice grinder, or use a mortar and pestle. Grind them into a coarse powder; transfer to a small bowl.

Place the hazelnuts in the spice grinder or a food processor, or use a mortar and pestle; pulse or pound the nuts until roughly chopped; combine with the ground coconut and spices, sea salt, black pepper, and hazelnut oil. Stir to combine.

PARSNIP, DATE, AND OLIVE OIL TEACAKES

Makes 1 loaf (8 to 10 servings) or 18 small muffins

This recipe is not about sneaking vegetables into a child's mouth behind a veil of sugar. This is about cake—a good cake. The parsnips add earthy intrigue and texture; the dates bridge the not-too-wide gap between the sweet roots and sugar.

Using two different sweeteners, whole cane sugar and maple syrup, adds dimension and prevents either ingredient from overpowering the subtle flavor of the parsnip. There are two domestically available whole cane sugars, rapadura (Rapunzel is my favorite brand) and sucanat, both of which are 90 percent crystalline sucrose and 10 percent trace minerals.

4 ounces walnuts (about 1 heaping cup)

1 cup stone-ground whole-wheat flour

1 cup all-purpose flour

½ cup whole cane sugar

1 teaspoon baking soda

1 teaspoon baking powder

1 teaspoon fine sea salt

1 teaspoon cinnamon

½ cup extra virgin olive oil, plus extra for the loaf pan

2 tablespoons walnut oil (or extra virgin olive oil)

½ cup Grade B maple syrup

1 teaspoon pure vanilla extract

2 large eggs, beaten

8 ounces parsnips (about 3), washed and grated

8 ounces pitted Medjool dates, chopped

Preheat the oven to 350°F. Use a paper towel dipped in a bit of olive oil to grease a 9-inch loaf pan; line the pan with parchment paper (trim the paper to fit), and oil the paper as well. Spread the walnuts on a baking sheet and bake until toasted, about 9 minutes. Remove from the oven, cool, and chop coarsely.

In a large bowl, whisk together the flours, cane sugar, baking soda, baking powder, sea salt, and cinnamon.

In a medium bowl, whisk together the olive oil, walnut oil, maple syrup, vanilla, and eggs.

Add the wet ingredients to the dry ingredients, and stir with a spatula until just combined. Add the grated parsnips, chopped dates, and walnuts; stir until everything is evenly incorporated.

Pour the batter into the prepared loaf pan; bake for 50 to 60 minutes, or until a skewer inserted in the center comes out clean. Remove from the oven and let cool completely before unmolding.

Alternatively, this batter can be baked as muffins. Line 18 muffin cups with paper liners, and spray or brush with extra virgin olive oil. Spoon the batter into the lined muffin cups, filling each three-quarters full (I use a medium ice cream scoop for consistency and speed). Bake, rotating the pan halfway through, until the muffins are golden and a toothpick inserted in the center of one muffin comes out clean, about 25 minutes. Remove from the oven, and cool on a rack until room temperature.

Store bread or muffins in an airtight container at room temperature for up to four days.

JT BREAKFAST BARS

Makes 12 to 16 bars

We spotted big lizards and small lizards, jackrabbits, giant beetles, and too many kangaroo mice. The ocotillo cacti were flowering. Bees blanketed the surrounding bushes. The sunsets were shades of dusty purple and brilliant pink. It was a place that felt both ominous and alluring, surreal and exceptional.

It was Joshua Tree National Park in California. And although we cooked dinner over a campfire each night (kielbasa, trout, green onions, premade sides), the mornings called for something fast and filling. Having spent the prior weeks testing granola bars for some high school students' snack project, I had just found a formula for a chewy granola bar that didn't fall apart. Along with a thermos of homemade iced coffee, it was the perfect fuel for the long, hot days. Even while hiking ten-plus miles a day, I never once needed lunch.

For my camping needs, I baked these bars in two small loaf pans to yield even thicker cuts. I've also found that baking them in two small pans (instead of one 8-inch square pan) helps the bars hold their shape even better.

1⅔ cups rolled oats

¼ cup wheat bran

¼ cup freshly ground (golden or brown) flax seeds

1 scant cup maple sugar

½ teaspoon fine sea salt

¼ teaspoon ground cinnamon

1 pound dried fruits and nuts (chopped dates, sunflower seeds, sesame seeds, pumpkin seeds, raisins)

⅓ cup unsalted almond butter

7 tablespoons organic coconut oil, plus more for the pan

⅓ cup raw honey

Preheat the oven to 365°F. Rub two 9-inch loaf pans with coconut oil. Cover each pan in one direction with parchment paper, allowing it to hang over the sides. Lightly grease this paper, then cover the pan in the other direction, letting the second piece hang over the other two sides. Grease this second sheet. Set the pans aside.

In a large bowl, stir together the oats, wheat bran, flax seeds, maple sugar, sea salt, cinnamon, and dried fruits and nuts.

Set a small saucepan over moderate heat, and add the almond butter, coconut oil, and honey. Simmer for a minute or two, whisking occasionally (the ingredients should emulsify completely).

Toss the wet ingredients with the dry ingredients, making sure every morsel is coated. Divide the mixture evenly between the two loaf pans. Spread (I use an offset spatula) and press firmly (if the mixture sticks to the spatula, wet your hands a bit and use them instead).

Bake the bars for 30 to 35 minutes, or until they are golden brown around the edges. Remove from the oven and cool completely before unmolding. Stored in an airtight container, these bars keep for up to five days at room temperature.

CASHEW MILK WITH FRESH DATES, BANANA, AND OATS

Makes 2 to 3 servings

This thick, sweet drink invokes a childlike spirit. Think: slurping sounds, liquid mustaches, and sitting cross-legged on the kitchen countertop. It provides the simple joy of a milkshake with none of the sugar and cream.

1 cup raw cashews, soaked overnight in water

3 cups filtered or spring water, cold

2 tablespoon rolled oats

9 Medjool dates, pitted

2 frozen bananas

Scant pinch of fine sea salt

Drain the cashews and add them to a high-speed blender; add the water. Blitz for a full minute, or until the nuts are pureed. Add the remaining ingredients and blend until thoroughly combined; thin with a tablespoon or two of cold water, if desired.

This beverage keeps for a day without any loss in flavor; simply refrigerate it in a sealed container (the blender works), and shake well before serving.

EDIBLE ORNAMENTALS

Graced with the task of helping to plan, build, and maintain a garden at a local high school, I enrolled in permaculture training on a stunning farm near the Sonoma coast. For five days, I spent mornings walking the grounds, plucking buds and the berries, and popping them into my mouth.

There is a wide range of flavors in the edible ornamental family. Some are so peppery or bitter that the tongue perceives them as toxic (and some flowers are). However, many are enormously enjoyable and beautiful, and they add magic to other food. My favorites are described here.

Borage is an herb with star-shaped, purple flowers. It tastes of hay and cucumber. It cools the body and calms the nervous system. The greens of the plant can be used as an herb; for example, add a handful to Forager's Soup with Ham Hock and Mint (see page 208) or to Eggs Baked with Dandelion and Cream (see page 65).

Tiny white and yellow *chamomile* flowers have a perfume like hot apple pie. Most people are aware of chamomile's soporific effect; it also eases headaches and can be used in a poultice to promote the healing of broken skin.

Hibiscus tastes sour, astringent, and pleasantly floral. The petals are cooling and incredibly high in antioxidants (evidenced by their purplish red hue) and vitamin C. Look for dried hibiscus flowers in the bulk or spice section of your natural foods store or high-end grocer. Use them to flavor teas, kantens (a Japanese jelly), gelatins, ices, and even savory sauces.

Marigolds are bright yellow; their wispy petals make a wonderful garnish, and their mild, pleasantly bitter flavor enables them to take more prominent roles in a filling for omelets, a cold potato and caper salad, a topping for a crispy semolina flatbread, and so on.

In my mind, the vivid oranges and reds of *nasturtium* petals hint at the flower's peppery bite; this heat helps to balance the cold nature of a bowl of raw, summer salad greens.

Nigella is most often sold as a seed. Its ebony color and exotic flavor make it an easy favorite (see page 174). The blossoms of this plant, have a delicate and allium-like flavor.

Buy only organic edible flowers, then get a bit fanciful and have some fun:

· Fry them in a thin, sweet or savory batter; garnish with powdered sugar or coarse sea salt.

· Use them, as you would herbs, to infuse vinegar (see page 9).

· Brew them in cordials and syrups.

SUMMER LETTUCES, BLUE CORNFLOWERS, NASTURTIUM, AND ALMONDS IN ALMOND OIL

Makes 4 servings

When you are cooking with something as delicate as tiny petals, be mindful of how you use them: steer away from complicated ideas, heavy seasonings, and rough hands. I like to serve this salad next to a simple main dish, such as roast chicken, fish grilled on a cedar plank, or Sautéed Ramps, Lemon, and Bottarga (see page 209).

1 tablespoon finely chopped shallot

1 teaspoon sherry vinegar

Fine sea salt

½ tablespoon extra virgin olive oil

1 tablespoon almond oil

8 ounces summer lettuces

1 pint edible flowers (such as blue cornflower and nasturtium)

½ cup Almonds in Almond Oil (recipe follows), roughly chopped

In a large salad bowl, whisk together the chopped shallot, sherry vinegar, and a pinch of sea salt; let sit for 5 minutes so the shallot can mellow and infuse the vinegar.

Gradually add the olive and almond oils, whisking constantly. Add the spring lettuces to the bowl and season with another pinch of salt. Gently toss the mixture using clean hands. Top with the edible flowers and almonds. Serve immediately, as the flowers wilt quickly.

ALMONDS IN ALMOND OIL

Almond oil is relatively rare and expensive, so if you can't find it, you can substitute a mild extra virgin olive oil here. The goal is to add enough fat of a delicate flavor so that the salt adheres to the toasted nuts.

Makes 2 cups

2 cups raw almonds

2 tablespoons almond oil

½ teaspoon fine sea salt

Preheat the oven to 400°F. Spread the almonds on a baking sheet and roast for 10 to 12 minutes, or until a deep golden brown. Remove from the oven and allow to cool slightly. While they are still a bit warm, toss the almonds in a bowl with the almond oil and sea salt. Lay out to cool completely on a pan lined with paper towels, which will absorb any excess oil and salt. Once they have reached room temperature, store the almonds in an airtight container for up to two days.

HIBISCUS AND LIME ICED TEA

Makes 1 quart

This tea is perfect on a fiery hot day or next to a plate of fiery hot food. Hibiscus really cools things off. And it grows in climates where folks need it: Egypt, Morocco, Sudan, and Mexico.

1 ounce fresh or dried hibiscus flowers

3 cups boiling water

3 tablespoons wildflower honey

¼ cup freshly squeezed lime juice

Put the flowers in a small saucepan and pour in the boiling water; stir in the honey. Cool to room temperature, then refrigerate overnight. Strain the liquid; add the lime juice and stir or shake to combine. Refrigerate for up to four days.

RED CLOVER BLOSSOM TEA

Makes 6 servings

This flower tea alleviates indigestion, calms the nervous system, and can provide pain relief for women experiencing menopausal symptoms or premenstrual cramps (I drink it on an empty stomach three to four times a day). With plenty of sleep, occasional short periods of fasting (sixteen to eighteen hours, including time asleep), and some simple aids like this, the body can recover from ordinary daily strains without needing to rely on long-term "detox diets."

1 cup fresh (or ½ cup dried) red clover blossoms

One 2-inch piece of ginger, thinly sliced

4 strips lemon peel

1 burdock root, scrubbed and thinly sliced

½ teaspoon angelica root

6 cups water

Raw honey, to taste (optional)

Place all the ingredients in a medium saucepan. Bring to a boil, then lower the heat and simmer for 15 minutes. Strain. Serve with honey, if desired. Refrigerate leftover tea in an airtight container for up to three days; reheat before serving.

POACHED STONE FRUIT
WITH CHAMOMILE SYRUP

I rarely poach fruit, as I'd rather eat it fresh or dried straight out of my hand, in a salad, or baked in a cake with a slightly coarse crumb. However, I do have exceptions: poached pears in cognac, figs in port, rhubarb in red wine, and this particular combination—made with blush-colored nectarines and flower-infused syrup.

2 cups fresh Chamomile Syrup
   (recipe follows)

3 cups water

¼ cup granulated sugar

1 vanilla bean, cut in half
   lengthwise and seeds
   scraped out

Fine sea salt

1 pound stone fruit (such
   as nectarines, peaches, or
   apricots), pitted and cut
   in half

SERVING SUGGESTIONS

Shortbread and/or
   Whipped Crème Fraîche
   (see page 284)

Bring the chamomile syrup, water, sugar, vanilla bean and seeds, and a pinch of sea salt to a simmer in a large pot, stirring until the sugar is dissolved. Add the fruit, and lower the heat slightly. Cover the mixture's surface with a round piece of parchment paper, and poach the fruit until it is tender when pierced with the tip of a knife. The cooking time can vary widely depending on your choice of fruit, its size, and its ripeness; my nectarines took 10 to 12 minutes.

Use a spider strainer or slotted spoon to gently lift and transfer the poached fruit to a serving dish. Bring the poaching liquid back to a boil and cook until reduced to 1½ cups; strain. Let the fruit and syrup cool to room temperature before serving.

CHAMOMILE SYRUP

Makes approximately 2 cups

2 cups water

2 cups unrefined sugar

1 cup fresh chamomile flowers

Combine the water and sugar in a small saucepan set over high heat; simmer until the sugar is dissolved. Add the flowers to the syrup, remove from the heat, and cover. Steep for 30 minutes. Strain and allow the mixture to cool. Refrigerate in an airtight container for up to two weeks.

SPRING FLOWER AND LAVENDER JELLY

Makes three to four 8-ounce jars

Shakirah Simley is a friend and fellow teacher at 18 Reasons. She is a gracious, gorgeous woman with a potent sense of precision. When planning one of her four-hour, hands-on canning intensives, she'll wait until the very last minute to plan a menu and write recipes so she knows what exciting and wondrous produce will be harvested that week. One spring, she developed this delicious flower jelly a few days after our florist announced she was about to receive a crate of organic blooms.

INFUSION

4½ cups water

2 cups tightly packed fresh lavender buds, calendula, and salvia (include the leaves and stems)

JELLY

4 cups herbal infusion

½ cup lemon juice

2 cups sugar

4 teaspoons Pomona's Universal Pectin powder

4 teaspoons calcium water (packaged with the pectin)

Place a spoon or small plate in the freezer. To make the infusion, bring the water and flowers to a boil in a medium saucepan set over high heat. Turn off the heat, cover, and steep for 20 minutes. Strain the flowers through a fine-mesh strainer or chinois, and return the infusion to the pan—this is the base for the jelly.

Add the lemon juice to 4 cups of the infusion. In a small bowl, whisk together the sugar and pectin powder.

Bring the infusion to a rolling boil. Add the sugar mixture, whisking vigorously for 1 to 2 minutes to dissolve the pectin. Once the jelly returns to a boil, remove it from the heat. Add the calcium solution. Skim and discard the foam that rises to the top.

To check the jelly for doneness, place a few drops on the frozen spoon or plate; if it sets, the jelly is ready. If not, boil for 1 to 2 minutes more, then test again.

Ladle the hot jelly into hot, sterilized jars. Wipe the jar rims clean. Center the lids on the clean jar rims, screw the lid down until you meet resistance, then give it another quarter turn. Place the jars in a canner, ensuring that all jars are covered by at least 1 inch of water. Cover the canner and bring the water to a boil over high heat; process for 5 minutes.

Remove the canner lid, wait 5 minutes, then remove the jars without tilting. Let the jars cool, upright and undisturbed, for 8 to 12 hours. Store in a cool, dark, dry place for up to two years. Once you open a jar, you must refrigerate it.

FAVA LEAVES

Fava leaves are ubiquitous on small farms throughout the country. As a cover crop, they help fix nitrogen and restore depleted soil. The plant must be harvested before pods form, and this means there is an abundance of fava greens close to year-round. While I adore the big, broad springtime legume, these pale silver-green leaves of fall are just as sweet yet also inexpensive and easy to use.

Store them as you would any delicate greens: refrigerate them, lightly packed with paper towels, in an airtight container. Fava greens start to get slimy after about three days, so plan to use them quickly. I think washing the leaves really bruises them, and they're rarely sandy, so I generally don't bother; if water is needed, use gentle hands.

The flavor of fava leaves is so complete, they need little doctoring to taste good and balanced. They can be served raw as a salad green or garnish, sautéed, stir-fried (especially when large), added to soups, or pounded into a paste. If you can't find fava leaves, lamb's quarter, chickweed, and even baby spinach can be used ounce for ounce in the recipes that follow.

GRILLED QUAIL WITH TREVISO AND FAVA LEAVES

Makes 4 servings

While fresh fava beans and fava leaves are generally springtime treats, there is a time in the fall when farmers harvest their cover crops, and the sweet, gray-tinged greens make a second big appearance. When they do, I tend to make this earthy dish.

4 quail, patted dry

5 tablespoons extra virgin olive oil, separated

Coarse sea salt

1 teaspoon Shallot Vinegar (see page 222)

Fine sea salt

2 heads Treviso radicchio (or other chicory), sliced 1 inch thick

2 cups lightly packed fava leaves

Crushed chile de arbol

The night before you plan to serve them, cut the backbones out of the quail; salt them well on both sides. Refrigerate overnight.

Set the quail out at room temperature a good hour before you plan to cook. Preheat your grill. Massage 1 tablespoon olive oil into each quail, coating both sides. Grill skin-side down for 4 minutes; turn and grill 2 to 3 minutes more. Before serving, let the birds rest for 5 to 8 minutes at room temperature. Season each with a bit of coarse sea salt.

Meanwhile, mix the vinegar with 2 pinches of fine sea salt and the remaining tablespoon of olive oil in a medium mixing bowl. Gently toss the Treviso and fava leaves with the vinaigrette. Put the salad on plates or a serving platter, and top with the quail. Serve with a small bowl of crushed chile de arbol, for those who like a little heat.

EARLY SPRING MINESTRONE

Makes 6 servings

The inspiration for this soup was spartan: a hunk of cheese, two lemons, a homemade kombu stock, and a container of leftover mixed vegetables. The kitchen cabinets offered little more than salt, olive oil, beans, and a few grains. With these basic provisions, I made this humble yet cheerful soup.

½ pound cannellini beans, soaked in water overnight

One 3-inch piece of kombu

1 Parmigiano-Reggiano rind

2 chiles de arbol

2 fennel stalks (leaves included)

2 thyme branches and a few parsley stems, tied with twine

Extra virgin olive oil

Fine sea salt

4 green garlic stalks, white and pale-green parts only, thinly sliced

2 green onions, thinly sliced

1 fennel bulb, cut into ¼-inch dice

1 bunch (10 to 12) baby carrots

4 ounces arborio rice (or small pasta, such as canestrini)

3 cups loosely packed whole baby fava greens (or large leaves sliced ½ inch thick)

½ lemon

2 ounces Parmigiano-Reggiano

Freshly cracked black pepper (or thinly sliced chile de arbol)

Drain and rinse the soaked beans, then place them in a small pot with enough water to cover them by 3 inches. Add the kombu, cheese rind, chiles de arbol, fennel stalks, tied herbs, 1 tablespoon olive oil, and 2 pinches of sea salt. Place the pot over high heat and bring to a boil; reduce the heat until the water is at a simmer. Cook the beans for approximately 40 to 50 minutes, or until just tender (the amount of time this takes depends largely on the age of your beans). Remove and discard the kombu, rind, chiles de arbol, fennel stalks, and tied herbs. Taste the cooking liquid and add more salt, if needed—this is the broth for your soup.

When the beans are almost done, heat a large pot over moderately low heat and add enough olive oil to coat the bottom. Sauté the green garlic, onions, and diced fennel with a pinch of salt for 5 to 7 minutes. Add the beans and their liquid, the carrots, and the rice. Simmer over moderately low heat for 10 to 12 minutes, or until the carrots are almost tender and the rice is almost al dente.

Stir in the fava leaves, and cook 3 to 4 minutes more. At this point, the carrots should be cooked, and the pasta should be done. Turn off the heat and let the soup rest for 10 minutes before serving. Serve in shallow bowls topped with a squeeze of fresh lemon juice, a drizzle of olive oil, a grating of Parmigiano-Reggiano, and a pinch of cracked black pepper.

BURRATA, FAVA BEANS, AND FAVA LEAVES

Makes 2 to 3 servings

This is a recipe for the tiniest, most tender favas you can find. The sweet, grassy flavor of the beans is balanced by the richness of the cheese, and the coarsely ground black pepper prevents either from becoming cloying by the third bite.

1 pound Caña de Oveja or burrata cheese

2 cups unpeeled baby fava beans

Coarse sea salt

2 teaspoons fresh lemon juice

2 tablespoons extra virgin olive oil

1 cup loosely packed baby fava leaves

¼ cup fava flowers (optional)

Coarsely ground black pepper

Divide the cheese among two or three plates. In a small bowl, toss the fava beans with 2 pinches of sea salt, the lemon juice, and the olive oil. Spoon the dressed beans on top of the cheese; top each serving with a scattering of baby fava leaves. Drizzle a little of the remaining vinaigrette around the perimeter of the plate, and garnish it all with a pinch of coarsely ground black pepper.

Caña de Oveja is a soft-ripened sheep's milk cheese from Spain that is at once creamy and flaky, buttery and tangy. It is exceptional alongside spring produce, especially fava beans.

ROASTED ASPARAGUS WITH FAVA LEAVES, RADISH, AND GREEN GARLIC VINAIGRETTE

Makes 4 to 6 servings

This dish comes together in twelve minutes and couldn't be a more beautiful and refreshing springtime side.

2 bunches green asparagus, trimmed of tough ends and peeled, if necessary

Fine sea salt

⅓ cup extra virgin olive oil

3 green garlic stalks, white and pale-green parts only, thinly sliced

1 tablespoon fresh lemon juice

2 cups loosely packed baby fava leaves

6 pink radishes, sliced ¹⁄₁₆ inch thick

Coarse sea salt

Preheat the oven to 450°F. Line two sheet pans with parchment paper. Divide the asparagus between the pans and toss each batch with 2 pinches of fine sea salt and 1 tablespoon of the olive oil. Spread the spears in an even layer; roast for 8 minutes, or until tender and lightly browned. Remove from the oven, and let the asparagus rest at room temperature for 5 minutes before plating.

Meanwhile, in a small mixing bowl, whisk together the green garlic, lemon juice, 2 pinches of fine sea salt, a few grinds of black pepper, and the remaining olive oil. Taste, and adjust the acid-to-oil ratio to suit your palate.

Lay a handful of asparagus spears on a platter; top with the fava leaves, radish, a pinch of coarse sea salt, and a drizzle of the green garlic dressing. Repeat this layering process until all of the ingredients have been used.

FENNEL FRONDS, FLOWERS, AND POLLEN

In the small town of Panzano in Chianti, I had my first taste of fennel pollen. It is there that Tuscany's most famous butcher, Dario Cecchini, spoils his guests with course after course of expertly prepared dishes. Although his specialty is meat, and he is a master of his craft, the way in which he served a little glass of raw vegetables was noteworthy. He took almost all of the herbs and spices that speckle the Tuscan hills, pounded them into a powder with sea salt and, using a celery stick, stirred them into a bowl of local olive oil. As I chatted with strangers in broken Italian and Spanish, I dipped raw crudités and bread into that highly aromatic mixture—the perfect start to a long, rich meal.

In the United States, fennel pollen is relatively expensive and rare. You can harvest your own, but the yield per plant is quite small (see page 9 for instructions). I still seek it out, but I use it sparingly.

Fennel fronds are the natural extension of the fennel bulb and, as such, are inexpensive and widely available. They are also very versatile; they have a soft texture, and their delicate, sweet, slightly spicy licorice flavor pairs incredibly well with a wide range of foods:

- Pound them into a host of green pastes: salsa verde, pesto, pistou, compound butter, and curry.
- They quickly elevate the quality of any homemade stock, especially one made with fish bones.
- They can be cooked like other mild, soft greens (such as spinach). Try sautéing them in olive oil infused with chile and lemon zest and serving them with a poached egg and grilled bread.
- They are delicious in herb frittatas.
- Chew on them raw when you need a potent palate cleanser.
- Brew them as a tisane for one of the best natural digestive aids. Pound ¼ cup fronds to release their essential oils, then steep in just-boiled water for 5 to 7 minutes before straining.

CHIANTI-STYLE SPRING VEGETABLES

Makes 6 to 8 servings

The scent of fennel pollen transports me back to that white-walled den where an Italian butcher wielded a machete-like knife, sang the words of Dante, and served enough food and wine to turn a room full of international strangers into best friends for a night.

Without the olive oil, this is also the perfect rub for practically all meats and, when used with a very light hand, for several fish (such as swordfish). You can also spoon it on top of a crostini with ricotta and lemon zest; use it to spike a tomato sauce; infuse butter with it (think about drizzling it over popcorn); fold it into your favorite grain salad; and sprinkle it on a bowl of plain white beans served with a pile arugula.

1 cup lightly packed fennel fronds, finely chopped

2 tablespoons fennel pollen

3 tablespoons finely chopped thyme

2 tablespoons finely chopped rosemary

1 tablespoon juniper berries, lightly crushed

¼ teaspoon dried lavender

2 bay leaves, crumbled

½ chile de arbol, thinly sliced

Fine sea salt

Freshly ground black pepper

½ cup (or more) extra virgin olive oil

TO SERVE

Trimmed crudités (such as celery with leaves, fennel bulbs, baby carrots, baby turnips, radishes, and little gems cut in quarters)

Put all the herbs and spices, 2 pinches of sea salt, and a few grinds of black pepper in a food processor; pulse until finely ground. Alternatively, use a mortar and pestle as directed for Fennel Frond Salsa Verde (see page 95).

Spoon the spice mixture into a dipping bowl; use a celery stick or carrot to stir in enough olive oil to make a loose, pesto-like consistency. Serve with crudités.

FENNEL FROND SALSA VERDE

Makes approximately 3 cups

This recipe is not precise and is all the better for it. Salsa verde should be made deftly and frugally, relying on whatever green things you need to use. You can increase or decrease the more potent ingredients—garlic, capers, anchovies, and chile—based on your general like or dislike of one or the other.

You will surely think of many things you can spoon this under, over, and beside. I've enjoyed it on boiled potatoes, under fried quail eggs, alongside grilled beef tenderloin, stirred into a vinaigrette for wild spring greens, and slathered on the best roast chicken sandwich I've ever eaten.

1 or 2 garlic cloves, smashed

¼ cup salt-packed capers, soaked and rinsed

2 salt-packed anchovies, rinsed and fileted

½ chile de arbol, thinly sliced

2 cups finely chopped fennel fronds

1 cup finely chopped parsley leaves

2 tablespoons finely chopped rosemary leaves

Fine sea salt

Zest of 1 lemon

2 tablespoons fresh lemon juice

Approximately ½ cup extra virgin olive oil

Finely chop the garlic, capers, anchovies, and chile de arbol; place them in a mortar (or bowl) and pound them with a pestle until a rough paste forms. Add the finely chopped fennel fronds, parsley, and rosemary to the mortar; pound and grind a bit more. Alternatively, pulse everything in a food processor.

Add a pinch of sea salt, a few grinds of black pepper, and the lemon zest; stir until combined. Slowly stir in ½ cup olive oil until you achieve your desired consistency (consider your end use, and how loose or dry you want the mixture to be).

Stir in the lemon juice. Taste, and adjust the seasoning. Use immediately or store, spooning enough olive oil on top to cover by ½ inch (this creates an air barrier and prevents browning); cover tightly and refrigerate for up to four days.

SARDINE PÂTÉ WITH FENNEL POLLEN

Makes 6 servings

This silky smooth pâté is inexpensive and simple to make. The pronounced flavor of sardines is mellowed by the fat and milk sugars in the butter. I like to serve this with a crisp olive oil flatbread.

PÂTÉ

8 ounces sardines in olive oil, drained

Zest and juice of ½ lemon

Fine sea salt

3 tablespoons unsalted butter, at room temperature

SEAL

2 tablespoons unsalted butter, melted

⅛ to ¼ teaspoon fennel pollen

Coarse sea salt

Place the sardines in a food processor. Add the lemon zest and juice, season with 2 pinches of fine sea salt, and process until completely smooth. Taste, and adjust the seasoning as needed.

With the machine on, add the butter, 1 tablespoon at a time, until it is completely incorporated. Scrape the pâté into three or four ramekins. Press a piece of plastic wrap directly on the surface of the pâté and refrigerate until firm.

Finish the pâté with a seal: spoon a thin layer of the melted butter on top of each ramekin; sprinkle with the fennel pollen and coarse sea salt. Refrigerate until firm. Remove from the refrigerator 20 minutes before serving.

FIG LEAVES

There are many odes to the fig tree: fables and folklore, poems and paintings, myths and miracles. The genus *Ficus* is revered around the world.

My relationship to figs began as a pretty banal one. I grew up eating Fig Newton cookies, snacked on dried Smyrnas during college study sessions, and saw the fresh fruit on salads in my first restaurant stint. It wasn't until I encountered the fig's leaf that my orientation became more romantic. I suddenly saw more clearly what all of the philosophical fuss was about.

I was on a cute, sweltering hot farm just south of Atlanta. I'd been tasked with harvesting okra all afternoon and had taken shade under a fruiting fig tree. After snacking on what was ripe, I plucked a leaf and rubbed it between my fingers before lifting it to my nose. It smelled of coconut, peat, vanilla, and green walnuts. I was instantly enamored and convinced it was useful. The owner let me harvest a few dozen, and I returned home eager to search for recipes. I found only two: wrapped fish and wrapped cheese. I made the first, and it was very good, served with Olio Verde and a lemon confit.

Since that first encounter, I've found many ways to highlight the singular flavor of these dark green beauties, available from midsummer through late fall. I've included a few of my more unusual recipes in this chapter, and I do hope you'll enjoy the play (store them like all leaves: wrapped lightly in paper towels, sealed, and refrigerated). Here are a few other ideas that didn't make the cut:

· Infuse vinegar (see page 9).
· Steep them in a simple syrup (1 part hot water to 1 part sugar) destined for cocktails, lemonade, or cordials.
· Cook them with a cup of blackberries and a few tablespoons of sugar until the mixture is thick enough to coat the back of a spoon. This is quick jam.
· Use them as a "lid" for fermenting fruits or vegetables.

CHICKEN THIGHS BRAISED WITH FIG LEAVES, WHITE BEAN AND YOGURT PURÉE

Makes 6 to 8 servings

This is one meal with many tricks. In a single recipe, you can learn to brine, sear, braise, infuse, simmer, season with acid, and compose a dish with complementary textures. Figs, beans, yogurt, and mint could place you in many parts of the world—Egypt, Turkey, Iran, Morocco, Israel—so if you're planning a bigger meal, choose where you'd like to take it. I imagine introducing the meal with a mezze platter of a chopped tomato and Marash chile salad (with red wine vinegar and olive oil), black olives, rusks, and feta. Finish with bowls of fresh dates and a pot of black tea.

As with most braises, it is best to start this dish a night or two before you plan to serve it.

CHICKEN

10 chicken thighs

Fine sea salt

Extra virgin olive oil

4 fig leaves

2 to 3 green onion tops

1 bunch cilantro stems, tied with twine

1½ quarts chicken stock

4 garlic cloves

WHITE BEAN AND YOGURT PURÉE

1 cup dried white beans

Fine sea salt

1 tablespoon extra virgin olive oil

½ cup plain whole milk yogurt (I prefer sheep's milk)

1 garlic clove, roughly chopped

2 teaspoons fresh lemon juice

TO SERVE

Cores and small leaves of little gem lettuce (optional)

Mint leaves

Cilantro leaves

Extra virgin olive oil

Urfa, Marash, or Aleppo chile

Coarse sea salt

Lemon wedges

Place the chicken thighs in a large bowl and pat them dry with a paper towel. Season well with sea salt (about 2 tablespoons). Cover and refrigerate for at least 4 hours, and preferably overnight. This is a dry brine, and it makes the meat juicy and delicious.

Soak the beans overnight in a medium saucepan filled with water. When you are ready to prepare them, drain the beans and return them to the pot; cover with fresh water by 2 inches, and add 2 pinches of salt and 1 tablespoon olive oil. Bring to a boil over high heat; lower the heat and simmer until the beans are completely tender, approximately 45 to 55 minutes, depending on the age of your beans.

Preheat the oven to 300°F. Remove the chicken thighs from the refrigerator 30 minutes to an hour before cooking. If the skin is wet, pat it dry. Stack the four fig leaves; lay the green onion tops and cilantro stems on top. Roll the fig leaves around the aromatics to form a tight bundle, and tie tightly with kitchen twine.

Heat a large sauté pan or Dutch oven over high heat for a full 1 to 2 minutes. Add enough olive oil to coat the bottom of the pan. When the oil is very hot (on the verge of smoking; you'll see wisps of smoke leaving the sides of the pan), place the chicken thighs in the pan,

skin-side down, and cook 8 to 10 minutes, until the skin is a deep golden brown. Do not overcrowd the pan; you will likely need to brown the chicken in batches. When the thighs release easily from the bottom of the pan with a mere nudge of the tongs, they are ready to be turned. Cook for 2 to 3 minutes on the other side. Turn off the heat, remove the chicken, and discard all but 1 tablespoon of the fat.

Return the pan to the heat, add the chicken stock, and scrape with a wooden spoon to release the crispy bits stuck to the bottom. Add the fig leaf bouquet, garlic, and a pinch of salt. Bring to a boil, then reduce the heat to achieve a simmer. Return the thighs to the pan. This is important: they should fit snugly, and the liquid should come just above halfway up the sides of the meat (the skin should not be submerged). If you need to change pans or alter the amount of liquid, do so. Leave the pan uncovered, and place it in the oven. Braise the chicken for approximately 1 to 1¼ hours, or until it is almost falling off the bone.

Meanwhile, drain the beans, reserving the liquid. Put the beans and ¼ cup of their cooking liquid in a blender or food processor, and purée with the yogurt, garlic, olive oil, lemon juice, and 2 pinches of fine sea salt. If the mixture is too thick, add more bean liquid. (It should be thinner than hummus but thicker than soup.) Return the purée to the sauce- pan, cover, and keep warm over low heat until ready to use.

Place about a cup of the bean purée on a warm platter; use the back of a serving spoon to spread it out slightly. Spoon a small amount of the braising liquid around and arrange, in a few layers, several chicken thighs, a few little gem wedges (if using), and a scattering of herbs. Drizzle the gems with olive oil, and give it all a hit of Urfa chile and coarse sea salt. Serve with lemon wedges.

EGYPTIAN RICE WITH FIG LEAVES

Makes 6 servings

Ashrf Almasri sells clay cookware in his amazing shop in Sonoma. He's the kind of shop owner who smiles continuously, slips you a bag of lime green–flecked eggplants from his garden, and enthusiastically shares his family's recipes. His Egyptian rice is made without fig leaves and eggs and is always baked in a clay vessel called a *bram*. Ashrf is also a man of strong opinions, so I hope he'll excuse my adaptations.

3 cups whole milk

2 egg yolks

1 teaspoon fine sea salt

2 fig leaves

1½ cups short-grain rice (such as bomba or arborio)

3 tablespoons butter

Freshly ground black pepper

Preheat the oven to 385°F. In a large bowl, whisk together the milk, egg yolks, and sea salt; stir in the rice.

Place the fig leaves on the bottom of a medium *bram* or a 4-quart Dutch oven. Gently pour over the rice mixture. Distribute the butter in thin shavings over the surface. Cover with a lid or foil, and bake for 30 minutes. Uncover and bake for about 1 hour more, or until a rich, golden brown crust has formed on the top and perimeter of the rice. Most of the milk should have been absorbed. Remove from the oven and rest at room temperature for 10 minutes before serving. Top with a few grinds of black pepper.

FIG LEAF PANNA COTTA

The fat in the cream absorbs subtle flavors from the fig leaf—coconut, peat, and vanilla—without any heating or blending. This is the perfect dessert for feeding a crowd: simple, elegant, and easy to serve.

6 fig leaves

6½ cups heavy cream

2 cups whole milk

⅔ cup granulated sugar

¼ teaspoon fine sea salt

2 tablespoons unflavored gelatin

The day before you plan to prepare the panna cotta, place the fig leaves in the cream; refrigerate for 24 hours (or up to 48).

Have ten to twelve 4- to 6-ounce ramekins, custard cups, or glasses on hand. Strain the cream into a large saucepan. Add 1⅓ cups of the milk, along with the sugar and sea salt. Heat over moderately low heat, stirring occasionally, until steaming hot. Remove from the heat.

Meanwhile, in a small bowl, sprinkle the gelatin over the remaining ⅔ cup milk; set aside for 10 minutes.

Add the milk and gelatin mixture to the warm cream. Reheat to steaming hot, stirring to dissolve the gelatin. Strain through a chinois into a large liquid measuring cup or jar. Divide the mixture evenly among the ramekins. Set the ramekins on a tray, cover with plastic wrap, and chill for at least 6 hours (preferably overnight) and up to three days.

FIG LEAF SPICE BLEND

========= *Makes approximately ½ cup* =========

Inspired by Tunisia's tabil, this spice blend is well suited to fish, lentils, lamb, savory yogurt drinks, and roasted vegetables—especially cauliflower, carrots, and pumpkin.

5 fig leaves

3 tablespoons coriander seeds

2 tablespoons cumin seeds

1 tablespoon caraway seeds

1 chile de arbol

Wash and dry the fig leaves; place them on a rack to dry at room temperature for about a week until they are dry and brittle. Strip out the stems, and crush the leaves with your fingers.

Toast the coriander seeds, cumin seeds, caraway seeds, and chile de arbol in a small skillet, tossing occasionally. Watch them carefully so they don't burn. Remove the pan from the heat, and cool the spices to room temperature. Transfer to a spice grinder along with the crushed fig leaves. Grind to a powder. Spice mixture can be made two months in advance. Store in an airtight container in a cool, dark place.

SMOKED FIG LEAVES

Smoked fig leaves can be used in spice blends; brewed with tea leaves (my favorite pairing is Golden Yunnan); or added to soups, stews, or braises. Once smoked, fig leaves smell less verdant and bright and more like burning Palo Santo, the South American wood that perfumes my house most mornings and evenings. After making my first batch, I kept a capped copper container of them on my desk for months; occasionally, when I needed a momentary release, I'd remove the lid and inhale the unique scent.

Fig leaves

Small smoker (see page 289)

If you rinsed your fig leaves, make sure they are dry before proceeding. Place the fig leaves on the smoker's rack in an even layer. Smoke them for 15 to 20 minutes, or until dry and brittle. Cool completely before storing in an airtight container.

SMOKED FIG LEAF COOKIES

Makes approximately 16 cookies (if baked in a tart mold)

This recipe was inspired by my first batch of smoked fig leaf sugar, a creation born of playful experimentation. That sugar ended up in all sorts of places: chocolate cakes and glazed roots, simple syrup, and macaroons. Yet it was this simple, coarse-crumbed cookie that best presented the seductive and subtle notes of incense, musk, and mint.

11½ tablespoons unsalted butter, melted

3 Smoked Fig Leaves (see page 105)

1 cup (8 ounces) granulated sugar, divided

2 cups (9 ounces) all-purpose flour

1 cup (5 ounces) brown rice flour

½ teaspoon baking powder

¼ teaspoon baking soda

½ teaspoon fine sea salt

2 eggs, beaten

Brush a round or rectangular tart pan with ½ tablespoon of the melted butter; place the pan on a baking sheet lined with parchment paper.

Strip the smoked fig leaves from the stem; discard the stem and rub the leaves between your fingers to crush slightly. Use a mortar and pestle or a spice grinder to pulverize the crushed leaves. Add half the granulated sugar and continue to pulse until the fig leaves are incorporated, taking care not to powder the sugar (there will still be tiny bits of leaves here and there; that is fine). Add the rest of the sugar, and stir to combine well.

Put all but 2 tablespoons of the sugar in a large bowl and whisk in the all-purpose flour, brown rice flour, baking powder, baking soda, and sea salt. In a small bowl, combine the remaining 11 tablespoons of melted butter and the eggs. Add the wet ingredients to the dry ingredients, and use a spatula to combine. Spread and pat the dough evenly in the prepared pan; coat the top with the reserved 2 tablespoons of sugar. Let the dough rest for at least 2 hours, or up to overnight (this time is important for both the relaxation of the all-purpose flour's gluten and for the hydration of the brown rice flour, which can be too gritty otherwise).

Preheat the oven to 365°F. Bake the dough for 30 minutes. Remove from the oven, and let it rest for 10 minutes, then carefully remove from the pan. Use a sharp knife to cut the plank into 2-inch rectangles or wedges. Some of the sugar coating will naturally tap off, and that is fine. Place the cookies on the baking sheet and return the pan to the oven for approximately 12 minutes, or until the top and edges are golden brown.

Remove from the oven. Once cooled to room temperature, the cookies can be kept in an airtight container for up to seven days.

VARIATION: DROP COOKIES

Instead of pressing the dough into a tart pan, you can make round cookies. Gently roll a walnut-sized ball of dough in your palms, then roll it in the reserved granulated sugar. Place on a cookie sheet and press down slightly; the cookie will be about 2 inches in diameter. Repeat with the remaining dough, leaving 2 inches between cookies. Let the cookies rest for 1 hour, or overnight. Bake for 12 to 14 minutes, or until golden brown.

GOOSEBERRIES AND GROUND CHERRIES

I'm fond of England, and I'm particularly smitten with the cafés that line its small parks and grand gardens. The menus are always a blast to read—linguistic theater at its finest—and deliver surprisingly good food: bloom bread with cheese, bubble and squeak, jacket potatoes with salad garnish, sprats on buttered toast, chargrilled gammon with chips, hot bap of the day, and so on. They also have an impressive display of sweets: fools; Eccles cake; chocolate pots; rice kheer; knickerbocker glory; scones with double cream and a dark purple damson jam; and many a classic tea cake, including Victoria, lemon, vanilla sponge, and gooseberry.

My first slice of gooseberry cake is still clear in my mind: simple syrup–soaked genoise layered with whipped cream and a tart gooseberry jam at teatime. I had just finished a long walk with family through the woods next to the Midlands Art Centre in Birmingham, in the British Midlands. We had wandered off the path, stumbling upon a community garden and an old stone house that triggered stories of youth spent playing among cows and bramble bushes and trading heads of cabbage for dozens of eggs.

Fresh gooseberries are in the currant family and are not to be confused with cape gooseberries, which are kin to ground cherries (described later). They are available in the United States for only a few months in the late summer. There are several great mail-order companies that ship them frozen by the pound year-round (see the Sources section, page 297). When purchasing fresh gooseberries, you may notice a range of colors, from pale ivory to light green and even purple; they all share a high degree of tartness, so purchase whichever shade you desire in your finished dish. Stem (I top and tail with a pair of small scissors) and rinse them before using.

Ground (or husk) cherries are a fancy fruit, tiny and golden, enclosed in a delicate paper lantern. They are more closely related to the tomatillo than the gooseberry, yet their seasons are similar. Plus, gooseberries and ground cherries are interchangeable in the recipes that follow unless otherwise noted. Look for fruit that is a deep yellow-orange, and refrigerate them in a paper bag, removing their husks right before use. Be aware that they are a member of the nightshade family, so while (as their color indicates) they are high in vitamin A and iron, people with calcium imbalances should moderate their consumption.

Here are a few ideas for making the most of these fruits:

· Ground cherries, with their husks just slightly peeled back, make a wonderful garnish for any cake.

- Make jam with a fruit-to-sugar ratio of 1:1; cook it with a vanilla bean and finish with a hit of fresh lemon juice.
- Use a big jar of gooseberry jam to make a jam tart: roll out kamut pastry (see the recipe for Huckleberry Hand Pies on page 130) and use it to line a tart pan; fill it with the jam. Refrigerate for 20 minutes, then bake at 400°F until the pastry is golden brown. Cool to room temperature and top with meringue that you brown with a torch or under a broiler.
- Make a condiment of cherry tomatoes and gooseberries to top a side of salmon grilled on a cedar plank. Fry sliced garlic with 1 teaspoon crushed coriander seeds in a mixture of olive oil and butter; add a pint of both fruits with a pinch (teaspoon) of both sugar and salt. Simmer for 10 minutes, or until the tomatoes have just burst and the gooseberries are soft. Cool to room temperature.
- British chef Nigel Slater recommends a gooseberry and juniper relish for pork chops. Crush a few juniper berries; stew them with a few cups of gooseberries and a splash of water until the berries collapse and thicken.

GOOSEBERRY, POLENTA, AND YOGURT CAKE

Makes 8 to 10 servings

I am partial to barely sweet, coarse-crumbed cakes, and this is a favorite. Seek out the best medium- to fine-grained yellow polenta you can find; once ground, the corn can turn rancid relatively fast. I love Anson Mills, which grinds each batch to order.

GOOSEBERRY FILLING

3 cups fresh (or defrosted) gooseberries

⅓ cup granulated sugar

A pinch of fine sea salt

CAKE BATTER

1 cup polenta

1⅔ cups all-purpose flour

1½ teaspoons baking powder

½ teaspoon fine sea salt

¾ cup granulated sugar, plus 2 tablespoons for topping the cake

1¼ cups unsalted butter, cut into ¼-inch cubes and chilled

2 large eggs

½ cup whole milk plain yogurt

½ teaspoon vanilla extract

Line a 9-inch loaf pan or a 9-inch round springform pan with parchment paper; butter the paper liberally. For cakes that have thick batters, the easiest way to line a springform pan is to take a square of parchment paper and lay it across the base of the separated pan. Simply clasp the springform round on top (there will be an overhang, and that's fine). This method ensures that you can spread the batter evenly across the base of the pan without a circle of parchment moving around. To line a loaf pan, grease it first—this helps the paper stick to the pan—then cut two rectangles of parchment paper, one to cover the pan lengthwise and the other to cover it crosswise.

Preheat the oven to 400°F. In a medium bowl, combine the gooseberries, granulated sugar, and salt; set aside. Put the polenta, flour, baking powder, ½ teaspoon sea salt, and ¾ cup granulated sugar in the bowl of a food processor. Add the diced butter and pulse for a few seconds, or until the mixture resembles coarse, wet breadcrumbs.

Break the eggs into a small bowl, and use a fork to whisk in the yogurt and vanilla. Add this mixture to the food processor and pulse until the batter forms a soft, misshapen ball of dough. Don't overmix, or the all-purpose flour will develop its gluten and produce a bread-like texture.

Press about two-thirds of the polenta mixture into the cake pan, pushing the batter about an inch up the sides with a floured spoon or offset spatula. Use a slotted spoon to give the gooseberries a quick toss and then to spread them on top of the batter, leaving much of their liquid behind. Crumble the remaining polenta mixture over the fruit with your fingertips, and don't worry if there are a few gooseberries peeking through—the dough will spread as it bakes. Sprinkle the remaining 2 tablespoons of sugar on top. Bake for 60 to 70 minutes, or until golden brown. Remove from the oven. This cake is very fragile when warm, so let it cool completely before serving.

GROUND CHERRY FOOL

Makes 3 to 4 servings

A fool is a traditional British dessert and a treat whose beauty belies its simplicity. I vary this recipe with the seasons, maintaining the proportion of cooked fruit to rich dairy but adjusting the sugar based on the sweetness of the fruit. In the early spring, it may be roasted rhubarb accented with rose water and in the fall, plums simmered with a few Tellicherry peppercorns. In the summer, it has to be sharp ground cherries or similarly tart plums.

8 ounces ground cherries
  (or gooseberries)
¼ cup granulated sugar
1 vanilla bean, cut in half
  lengthwise and seeds
  scraped out
Fine sea salt
1¼ cup heavy cream, cold
½ cup whole milk yogurt (I use
  the sheep's milk variety.)

Place the fruit in a small saucepan and toss with 2 tablespoons of the granulated sugar, the vanilla bean and seeds, and a small pinch of sea salt. Bring to a simmer over moderate heat. Cook, stirring occasionally, until the fruit bursts and reduces to a jam-like consistency, about 10 to 12 minutes. Set the mixture aside to cool to room temperature (or refrigerate overnight).

Whip the heavy cream, adding the remaining sugar by the tablespoon, until the cream forms soft, wet peaks. Fold in the yogurt. Fold in the fruit ever so slightly, leaving streaks of pale orange or green and bright white visible throughout.

The fool can be made up to 3 hours in advance; chill until ready to serve.

VARIATION: ETON MESS

Eton mess is named for the school's annual cricket match against Harrow at which it is traditionally served. It is made by mixing smashed sugared fruit (often strawberries), whipped cream, and crushed meringue. What sweet, delicious mayhem!

2 to 3 plain meringues,
  store-bought or homemade,
  lightly crushed

Follow the recipe for Ground Cherry Fool, but as a final step, gently fold in the crushed meringues.

FARMER'S CHEESE, HONEYCOMB, GROUND CHERRIES, AND ENNIS HAZELNUTS

While there is comfort in rhythm and routine, rote habits can become dull and calculated, even first thing in the morning. When I start to notice the need for inspiration, I like to start my day with a quaint breakfast like this, in which rich and creamy cheese acts as a foil for sweet and slightly chewy honeycomb; tart fruits; and crunchy, salty hazelnuts.

¼ cup farmer's cheese (such as fromage blanc) or whole milk ricotta

½ cup fresh ground cherries (or gooseberries)

2 to 3 tablespoons solid honeycomb, in pats

¼ cup chopped roasted Ennis hazelnuts (or your favorite variety)

¼ teaspoon hazelnut oil (or extra virgin olive oil)

Coarse sea salt

Toast, for serving (optional)

Spoon the cheese onto a small plate or into a shallow bowl; use the back of the spoon to make a slight indentation in the middle. Spoon the fruit and honeycomb on top. Toss the hazelnuts with the oil and a pinch of coarse sea salt. Scatter the hazelnuts on top of the honeycomb and cheese. Serve with a thick piece of golden brown toast, if you'd like.

GREEN GARLIC

I once left a student horror-struck in a basic knife skills class. I stated that I rarely cook with minced garlic, declaring, "I think garlic, like black pepper, is overused and too overpowering for most foods." The man to my right barely moved his body but contorted his face into confusion and disgust. When finally able to speak, he firmly replied, "Why in the world would someone want to deprive themselves of using metric tons of garlic?"

I understand that his opinion is shared by many, but I still often omit garlic or use it sparingly, whole or sliced. I'll mince it or add it in quantity in a few circumstances: when excessive brightness must be balanced (as in the Six Citrus Rice Salad on page 18); when it is a main seasoning in an otherwise one-tone dish (as with Squash Blossom Flatbread with Anchovy Butter and Arugula on page 253); when it can truly mingle with ingredients that can hold their own in the face of it (dandelion, mustard, or radicchio); or when it is used as medicine.

Green garlic is different. It is the adolescent stage of the same plant, ready for harvest the moment winter begins its transition to spring (in the Bay Area, this can be as early as late January). Green garlic is tender and mild and has a long, slender shape that makes it easy to use in a broad range of recipes. It has the characteristic essence of garlic but is sweet—even in raw form—and far less pungent.

Like aged garlic, the young stuff has antibacterial and antifungal properties; at the first sign of sinus trouble, I halve and pop cloves like pills. Garlic is very warming, a boon for folks with ice-cold constitutions. (If you run hot or suffer from hot conditions, consider limiting your use of it and the entire allium family.)

Green garlic can be stored at room temperature for a day or two, but it will begin to dry out and yellow after that. To prolong its vibrancy, wrap it in paper towels and refrigerate in an airtight container for a week or more. Before using green garlic, trim the roots and the very tips of the relatively tough, dark green ends and rinse well.

Green garlic can be used in just about any recipe that calls for garlic, baby leeks, or (when thin and tender) green onions. For the few months it is around, I use metric tons of the stuff.

GRILLED GREEN GARLIC
WITH ROMESCO BREADCRUMBS

Makes 4 to 6 servings

This dish makes a good starter to any summer meal. If there are any leftovers, fry them in a hot pan with olive oil and an egg for a strong breakfast.

ROMESCO BREADCRUMBS

2 tablespoons extra virgin olive oil

½ cup Romesco (recipe follows)

1 cup fresh breadcrumbs

Fine sea salt

GRILLED GREEN GARLIC

12 green garlic stalks, white and pale-green parts only

3 tablespoons extra virgin olive oil

Fine sea salt

½ lemon

Preheat the oven to 400°F. Heat a medium, ovenproof frying pan over moderately high heat; add the 2 tablespoons of olive oil. Fry the romesco for 2 minutes, stirring constantly with a spatula, until it begins to sputter and has turned a shade darker. Add the breadcrumbs and a pinch of sea salt; stir to combine, then spread evenly in the pan. Transfer the pan to the oven, and bake the breadcrumbs until they are dry and a deep, burnished red hue, about 7 minutes.

Meanwhile, preheat the grill. Toss the green garlic with the 3 tablespoons of olive oil and a pinch of sea salt. Grill for 5 to 6 minutes on each side, or until tender. Season with a squeeze of lemon, and top with the romesco breadcrumbs.

ROMESCO

This is my easy take on a classic Spanish condiment. It's delicious on potatoes, under fish, in a sauce, and by the spoon!

½ pound sweet red peppers (such as Jimmy Nardello)

1 chile de arbol

2 garlic cloves, roughly chopped

Fine sea salt

¼ cup almond flour

¼ cup hazelnut flour

2 tablespoons red wine vinegar

1 tablespoon tomato paste (I prefer the stuff sold in tubes)

1 teaspoon smoked paprika

½ cup extra virgin olive oil

2 tablespoons hazelnut oil

Char the sweet peppers over a direct flame, on a grill, or under a broiler. Once the skin blisters, put them in a saucepan with a tight-fitting lid; add the chile de arbol and garlic, and cover. Allow these ingredients to steam together for 20 minutes.

Remove from the heat. Stem and seed the sweet peppers and chile de arbol. Place them in a food processor along with the garlic, pinches of sea salt, and the remaining ingredients; purée until smooth. Thin the romesco with a bit of water if the batch is too thick to purée completely. Season to taste with more salt. Refrigerated in an airtight container, romesco keeps for up to a week.

WHOLE ROASTED FISH STUFFED WITH GREEN GARLIC, ROSEMARY, AND LEMON

Makes 4 to 6 servings

This version of roasting is a fast and easy way to cook fish. I serve this alongside a salad of wild arugula and shaved fennel, sometimes with roasted potatoes or steamed rice.

Although it may seem odd to keep fish at room temperature, all proteins should have time between cold storage and a hot pan. This facilitates even, efficient, and more predictable cooking.

---

1 whole fish (about 3½ pounds), cleaned and scaled

Extra virgin olive oil

Fine sea salt

3 green garlic stalks, white and pale-green parts only, thinly sliced

1 rosemary sprig, torn in two

1 chile de arbol

½ lemon, thinly sliced

1 lemon, cut into wedges and seeded

Coarse sea salt

Preheat the oven to 500°F. Let the fish sit at room temperature for 20 to 30 minutes. Pat the fish dry and place in a large roasting pan. Rub the entire exterior and cavity with olive oil and fine sea salt. Stuff the cavity with the green garlic, rosemary, chile de arbol, and sliced lemon. Roast for 25 minutes, or until the flesh is slightly firm and the eyes have turned white. Remove the fish from the oven and let it rest for 10 minutes before filleting and serving.

Season each serving with a spoonful of accumulated pan juices, a slight squeeze of lemon (then serve the half-used wedge on the plate for diners who want more), a drizzle of olive oil, and a pinch of coarse sea salt.

GREEN GARLIC HOT SAUCE I (ZHUG)

Makes approximately 2 cups

Zhug is a Yemeni condiment that too few people are enjoying. This version, made with green garlic and green chiles, is a perfect complement to just about any foodstuff from the Middle East. I reach for a jar when serving lamb; grilled octopus; fatty fish; and simple vegetarian rice pilafs.

½ Preserved Lemon (see page 282)

10 green garlic stalks, white and pale-green parts only, thinly sliced

3 serrano chiles, thinly sliced

3 cups cilantro leaves, roughly chopped

1 cup mint leaves, roughly chopped

1 teaspoon freshly ground toasted cumin seeds

2 teaspoons lemon juice

¼ cup extra virgin olive oil

Fine sea salt

Use a sharp knife to separate the rind of the preserved lemon from the flesh; reserve the flesh. Cut the rind into a julienne, then into an ⅛-inch dice. Place in a blender with the remaining ingredients and 2 pinches of sea salt; blitz until smooth. Taste, and add a bit of the Preserved Lemon flesh, if you need more salt.

Use immediately, or store in an airtight container. Spoon enough olive oil on top to cover by a ½ inch (this creates an air barrier and prevents browning), cover, and refrigerate for up to four days.

GREEN GARLIC HOT SAUCE II

Makes approximately 2 cups

This hot sauce undergoes a slight fermentation. It is well suited to beef, eggs, beans, grilled summer vegetables, and avocado sandwiches.

½ Preserved Lemon (see page 282)

12 green garlic stalks, white and pale-green parts only, thinly sliced

8 serrano chiles, thinly sliced

1 tablespoon freshly ground toasted pumpkin seeds

1 cup white vinegar

1½ tablespoons fine sea salt

Use a sharp knife to separate the skin of the preserved lemon from the flesh. Discard the flesh. Cut the skin into a julienne, then into an ⅛-inch dice. Place in a blender with the remaining ingredients; blitz until smooth. Transfer the mixture to a jar and seal; leave at room temperature for four to five days. Strain the sauce through a fine-mesh strainer into a well-sealed, sterilized container, and refrigerate. Because it is fermented, this hot sauce keeps well; it will last a year or more.

SHELLING BEAN SALAD WITH GREEN GARLIC AND WALNUTS

Makes 4 to 6 servings

My friend Liana was very pregnant at the height of a Los Angeles summer. We had been grilling meat and vegetables over a fire pit we'd built on her concrete patio. While the meat was resting, I wanted to rest too. As I sat down with a cold Russian beer, Liana exclaimed she had forgotten a salad: "*Mishka! Salat!*" In her house, you must always have a salad (often three); it's Azerbaijani tradition. She grabbed me by the wrist and waddled into the kitchen. She cracked open a can of red kidney beans, chopped some green onions, and reached for the plate of soaked walnuts (always on hand). "Red chile flakes, never black pepper," she mumbled to me, always the teacher. The following recipe is my adaption on a Liana classic.

1 cup walnuts

Fine sea salt

2 pounds shelling beans (such as cranberry or Dragon Tongue)

6 green garlic stalks, white and pale-green parts only

A handful of cilantro stems, tied with twine

1 tablespoon red wine vinegar

3 tablespoons extra virgin olive oil

Mild red chile flakes, such as Aleppo or Marash

To remove the bitterness from the walnuts, place them in a bowl, add a pinch of sea salt, and cover with hot water. Soak for 1 hour, or up to overnight. Before serving, drain and rinse the nuts until the water runs clear. Pat dry with a kitchen cloth.

Shell the beans. Combine with a stalk of green garlic and the cilantro stems in a medium pot; cover with water by 2 inches, and season with 2 pinches of salt. Bring to a boil over high heat; lower the heat and simmer for 20 to 30 minutes, or until the beans are just tender. Remove from the heat and strain; remove and discard the aromatics.

Meanwhile, thinly slice the remaining green garlic. Place it in a mixing bowl and add the beans, a pinch of salt, the red wine vinegar, and the olive oil. Add a pinch or more of mild red chile. Let the beans cool to room temperature. Fold in the soaked walnuts.

GARLIC SOUP

Makes 4 to 6 servings

Oh, this soup is delicious medicine. Forget caramelized onion with cheesy croutons and that potato-leek madness. Make garlic soup with not one but three types of garlic, and finish it off with Green Garlic Hot Sauce (see pages 119).

Black garlic is fermented garlic; it adds richness and tones of molasses and licorice to an otherwise simple soup. It can be found in specialty shops and online, or you can make your own by placing whole heads of garlic in a rice cooker on the warm setting for two to three weeks.

12 black garlic cloves

5 cups chicken stock

2 tablespoons rendered chicken (or pork, or bacon) fat

4 baby leeks, cut in half lengthwise and thinly sliced

Fine sea salt

24 green garlic stalks, white and pale-green parts only, thinly sliced

8 garlic scapes, thinly sliced

½ cup white wine (or verjus)

1 to 2 teaspoons (or more) Green Garlic Hot Sauce I or II (see pages 119)

Chive blossoms, for serving

Purée the black garlic and chicken stock in a blender; set aside. Heat a medium pot over moderate heat and add the chicken fat. Add the leeks and sweat with 2 pinches of sea salt for 3 to 4 minutes. Add the green garlic and garlic scapes, and cook for 5 to 7 minutes more. Add the wine; bring to a boil over high heat, and cook until the liquid has almost entirely evaporated, about 4 to 5 minutes. Add the black garlic chicken stock and 2 pinches of salt; bring to a boil. Lower the heat and simmer for 30 to 35 minutes. Remove from the heat and stir in 1 teaspoon of the hot sauce. Taste and add more salt or hot sauce, as needed.

Ladle the soup into bowls and garnish with chive blossoms, and even more hot sauce, if you'd like.

HORSERADISH

Some folks consider horseradish root a real irritant to their nasal passages and eyes. The root's essential oil is toxic in large quantities, so if you are sensitive to its fumes, I won't dare try to convince you to use it. However, if you look forward to the sensation of your sinuses clearing and your nervous system buzzing, get on with this chapter!

You can likely find whole horseradish root year-round and occasionally the plant's big leaves as well. Purchase firm, plump roots that show no sign of dampness. Wrap them in paper towels, and refrigerate in an airtight container for up to a week. Peel before using. If you don't have a Microplane, this is an ingredient that should motivate you to get one; all of the recipes in this chapter require it. Cooking destroys the flavor of fresh root, but there are many ways to use it raw. Here's a menu of options:

· A side of cold salmon, shaved onion, grated horseradish, dill, and capers
· Pork dumplings, pea leaves, and horseradish
· Green beans, brown butter, lemon, and horseradish
· Toast with lardo (or butter) and horseradish
· Endive with apples, walnuts, and horseradish vinaigrette
· Cucumber, avocado, and horseradish sushi

If you've purchased a horseradish root that is starting to look limp, it is easy to preserve. Grate enough fresh root to fill a jam jar, sprinkle with 1 teaspoon salt and 1 teaspoon sugar, top up with cider vinegar, and seal with a lid. Refrigerate for up to one month.

OPEN-FACED SANDWICH OF DANISH RYE, BEET RELISH, AND HORSERADISH CRÈME FRAÎCHE

Rugbrød (Danish rye bread) is a dense, dark, sour loaf that is sturdy on the plate but crumbles in your mouth. I use Anna's Daughters' rye, which is made in San Francisco, but there are other similar breads in health food stores and online. If you do find yourself a favorite loaf, do a little research into the myriad ways Danes take pleasure in the stuff: layered in trifles, crumbled in cakes, and boiled with beer in breakfast porridge. (Yes, beer for breakfast. *Skål!*)

BEET RELISH
(Makes approximately 4 cups)
2 pounds beets, scrubbed
2 tablespoons extra virgin olive oil, plus extra for cooking
⅓ to ⅔ cup Shallot Vinegar (see page 222)
Fine sea salt

SANDWICH
Danish rye bread (see headnote), sliced ¼ inch thick
Horseradish Crème Fraîche (recipe follows)
Crispy Shallots (see page 225)
Fresh dill
Coarse sea salt
Freshly ground black pepper

Preheat the oven to 400°F. Trim the beet greens from the root, saving them for any preparation calling for spinach or chard. Place the beets in a medium saucepan, drizzle with a little olive oil and a splash of water, then cover. Roast the beets for approximately 1 hour (or less, if you found some small ones), or until they are easily pierced with the tip of a paring knife. Remove from the oven. While they are still warm, peel the beets by rubbing them with a cloth. When they are cool enough to handle, cut them into a ¼-inch dice and place them in a small bowl; toss with the vinegar and fine sea salt to taste. Add the olive oil and toss again. This relish can be refrigerated in an airtight container for up to four days; bring it to room temperature before serving.

Spread the rye bread with the crème fraîche. Top with a layer of the beet relish; follow this with the shallots, dill fronds, coarse sea salt, and black pepper.

HORSERADISH CRÈME FRAÎCHE

Horseradish crème fraîche keeps for up to three days in the refrigerator. The mixture will thicken slightly, and the mustardy bite will become a bit more pronounced.

Makes approximately 1 cup

One 6-inch piece of horseradish
8 ounces crème fraîche
Fine sea salt

Use a Microplane to grate the fresh horseradish into a small mixing bowl. Whisk in the crème fraîche with a pinch of sea salt. Taste and add more salt, if necessary. Refrigerate until you are ready to use. It will keep in the refrigerator for four to five days.

ROASTED BROCCOLI
WITH GRATED HORSERADISH

Makes 4 servings

Members of the cabbage family have a natural affinity for horseradish. Try this basic roasting technique with trimmed whole Brussels sprouts, wedges of cabbage, or cubes of kohlrabi. If you have some horseradish preserved in vinegar (see page 123), you can use it here: stir a teaspoon of the preserve into 2 tablespoons olive oil or melted butter, and spoon it on top of the roasted greens in place of the final step.

1 pound broccoli (tender cores and florets), cut into 3-inch pieces

¼ cup extra virgin olive oil

Fine sea salt

One 6-inch piece of horseradish

1 lemon

Coarse sea salt

Preheat the oven to 475°F. On a rimmed baking sheet lined with parchment paper, toss the broccoli with the olive oil and a pinch of fine sea salt to coat. Roast until tender and slightly brown, about 15 to 20 minutes.

Remove from the oven and cool slightly. While the broccoli is still warm, shower it with horseradish and lemon zest grated with a Microplane; garnish with coarse sea salt. Taste, and add a dash of fresh lemon juice and more salt or horseradish, if desired.

POTATO SALAD WITH GREEN GARLIC AND FRESH HORSERADISH

Makes 6 servings

My favorite potato salad doesn't include mayonnaise or capers or herbs. Instead it features the more potent flavors of fresh lemon juice, green garlic, and just-grated horseradish. Like all potato salads, this version keeps well for a few days and is delicious cold or at room temperature.

3 pounds whole new potatoes

Fine sea salt

2 tablespoons lemon juice

Freshly ground black pepper

3 green garlic stalks, white and pale-green parts only, thinly sliced

¼ cup extra virgin olive oil

One 4- or 6-inch piece of horseradish

Coarse sea salt

To parboil the potatoes, place them in a large pot with 2 pinches of fine sea salt and cover with cold water by 1 inch. You are starting the whole potatoes in cold water so they cook evenly from the center out. Bring them to a boil over high heat; reduce the heat to a simmer and cook for approximately 15 to 20 minutes, or until a paring knife inserted in them meets only slight resistance. Remove from the heat, drain, and cool to room temperature.

Meanwhile, whisk together the lemon juice with 2 pinches of fine sea salt and a few grinds of black pepper. Add the green garlic and olive oil; whisk to combine.

Once the potatoes have cooled completely, slice each into ¼-inch rounds. Layer the potatoes, dressing, a generous grating of fresh horseradish (as much or as little as you like), and coarse sea salt. Repeat until all of the potato slices have been used.

HUCKLEBERRIES

Huckleberries helped ease my transition into the Bay Area. I was missing New York terribly but was intent on giving the West Coast a go. Aware of my tender spots, I hurried to a farmers' market for an experience to convince me that I was home. There I felt the cold summer air, smelled fresh lavender mingling with rotisserie chicken, saw white egg-like eggplants and piles of fig leaves, tasted chilaquiles and canelés, and purchased my first bag of wild huckleberries. I was giddy—and I was hungry. I christened my new kitchen with a brunch of sautéed mushrooms, poached eggs, chervil, and a huckleberry and buttermilk coffee cake (sliced, toasted, and topped with butter and a pinch of coarse salt).

Since then, I've moved away from the obvious (cake) and experimented using huckleberries in a variety of applications. Wild berries are one of the greatest edible treasures; their flavor is more concentrated than their domesticated successors and more nuanced as well (inky, earthy, and herbaceous).

Huckleberry season peaks in late summer. While they may be difficult to find fresh (especially on the East Coast), they can be shipped frozen nationwide. Great mail-order options abound, and I've included a few of my favorites in the Sources section (page 297) .

Like blueberries, huckleberries are a great source of vitamin C, and their dark purple color indicates medicinal pigments that are especially healing for the blood and circulatory system. They are worth seeking out for their flavor alone. They can be used pound for pound in any recipe that calls for dark, jammy fruit:

· Included as the base for crisps, cobblers, and buckles
· Preserved with sugar and herbs, then slathered on toast
· Layered in a cornmeal or coffee cake
· Folded into pancake batter

HUCKLEBERRY HAND PIES

Makes 10 to 12 servings

For folks who fear making pies, I urge you to start here. This kamut dough is incredibly forgiving, thanks to the nature of the grain and the addition of baking powder, which creates tiny gas bubbles during mixing and baking, resulting in a relatively flaky texture. Rolling the dough into small circles and forgoing the pie plate further vanquishes the fear of making crust.

FRUIT FILLING

1 pound huckleberries

¼ cup granulated sugar

2 teaspoons cornstarch

Fine sea salt

PIE DOUGH

1¼ cups kamut flour

1 cup all-purpose flour, plus more for dusting

½ cup granulated sugar, plus more for garnish

½ teaspoon baking powder

½ teaspoon fine sea salt

1 cup unsalted butter, cold

6 to 7 tablespoons ice water

1 egg, beaten

Melted unsalted butter, for brushing

Cold crème fraîche, for serving (optional)

Toss the huckleberries with the ¼ cup granulated sugar, cornstarch, and a pinch of sea salt; set aside.

In a large bowl, whisk together the flours, granulated sugar, baking powder, and sea salt. Using a pastry cutter or a fork and clean hands, cut the butter into the flour mixture until the texture resembles coarse, wet breadcrumbs; tiny pieces of butter should be visible but no larger than small peas. Add the water, 1 tablespoon at a time, and mix with a fork just until the dough pulls together. Transfer the dough to a work surface, pat into a ball, and flatten into a disk. Use a bench scraper or knife to cut the dough into two pieces; form each piece into a disk.

Lightly flour the work surface. Flatten one disk with six to eight gentle taps of a rolling pin. Lift the dough and give it a quarter turn. Lightly dust the top of the dough or the rolling pin with flour *only when needed*. Roll the dough into an 11-inch circle, about ⅛ inch thick. Repeat with the other disk. Use a cookie cutter to cut out 5- or 6-inch circles. Take half of the circles (destined to be the top crusts) and roll them to be slightly (about ¼ inch) larger than the others. Use a pastry brush to gently sweep away excess flour.

Transfer the smaller dough circles (the bottom crusts) to a baking sheet lined with parchment paper, leaving 2 inches between each. Brush (or rub) the edges of these circles with a bit of beaten egg (you can also use your finger for this). Place 2 tablespoons of the huckleberry mixture in the center of each circle; top with the reserved pieces of dough, pressing with the tines of a fork to seal. Brush the pies with melted butter and top with a pinch of granulated sugar. Use kitchen shears to snip the center of each pie so steam can escape while they bake. Ideally, chill these prepared pies for at least 1 hour (and up to overnight) before baking.

Preheat the oven to 425°F. Bake for approximately 30 minutes, or until golden brown. Serve with crème fraîche alongside or poured on top.

HUCKLEBERRY MOSTARDA

Makes 2 cups

I learned to make mostarda while wielding a 4-foot wooden spoon in a 60-quart stockpot. I was volunteering in the *laboratorio* of a tiny but ambitious family farm near Montferrat, Italy. Rapha, the matriarch and cook, ran a restaurant, an inn, and an all-women farmers' market where she sold an amazing array of homegrown and homemade condiments. Her use of mustard powder in recipes was surprising and revelatory.

A jar of huckleberry mostarda next to a roast loin of pork, a pile of lightly dressed arugula, and an aged cheese is easy and elegant and just the sort of thing I want on a cool, gray, autumn day. Blackberries, cherries, and cranberries all make good alternatives if you can't find huckleberries.

1 pound huckleberries

1 cup white wine

½ cup granulated sugar

1 bay leaf

Fine sea salt

1 teaspoon dried mustard powder

1 teaspoon red wine vinegar

In a wide, shallow saucepan (this shape will facilitate fast evaporation) over moderately high heat, combine the huckleberries, sugar, white wine, bay leaf, and a pinch of sea salt; bring to a boil. Reduce the heat and simmer, stirring occasionally, until the huckleberries have softened and the liquid coats the back of a spoon like a thin syrup, about 8 to 10 minutes. Remove from the heat, and discard the bay leaf.

In a small bowl, dissolve the mustard powder in the red wine vinegar; stir this mixture into the warm huckleberries. Taste, and adjust the seasoning, adding more salt, sugar, vinegar, or mustard powder to suit your palate; keep in mind that all flavors (sweet, salty, acidic, and hot) will mellow as the mixture cools.

Cool the mixture to room temperature, then cover and refrigerate overnight. Refrigerated in an airtight container, this mostarda keeps for up to one week.

HUCKLEBERRY SHRUB

Makes approximately 1 cup (undiluted) or 3 to 4 servings (diluted)

I lose my mind at the sight of wild berries and always purchase more than I can eat. When I'm left with a pint on the verge of turning, I make a shrub. Shrubs are flavored drinking vinegars, and variants are made across the globe to preserve fruit as a refreshing beverage.

This recipe can easily be adapted to account for the amount of huckleberries you need to preserve. Only the ratio of ingredients matters: 1 part berry to ½ part vinegar to ¼ part sugar. The bay leaf is entirely optional, and thyme rosemary both would make a similar contribution.

SHRUB

1 cup fresh (or frozen and defrosted) huckleberries
½ cup red wine vinegar (I use Banyuls)
¾ cup granulated sugar
1 fresh bay leaf

TO SERVE

Ice cubes
Sparkling water
Gin (optional)
Simple syrup (optional)

Place the huckleberries in a glass jar that holds at least a pint; make sure it has a tight seal. Use the back of a fork to lightly crush the huckleberries until they release a bit of their juice. To the jar, add the red wine vinegar, granulated sugar, and bay leaf; stir with the fork. Seal the jar and refrigerate the shrub mixture for at least five days (or up to seven).

Place a chinois or fine-mesh strainer over a jar or liquid measuring cup. If you want a perfectly clear shrub, line the strainer with a large piece of cheesecloth. Strain the shrub mixture; press on the berries with a wooden spoon until no juice remains. Discard the remaining pulp.

Now make yourself a drink. Add ¼ cup of the shrub to a glass with a few ice cubes; add 1 cup sparkling water and stir. Or try a cocktail: stir together 2 ounces gin, 1 ounce huckleberry shrub, ½ ounce simple syrup, and (perhaps) a splash of sparkling water.

KOHLRABI

Alien-like with its bright purple skin, circumferential ridges, and antennae-like leaves, kohlrabi has a flavor reminiscent of sweet earth and mild mustard. Unlike its leafy relatives in the cabbage family, kohlrabi's texture is somewhere between starchy potato and water chestnut (firm, crisp, and juicy), making it perfect for shaving and serving raw, caramelizing in a hot oven, stir-frying until tender, or simmering into a silky soup.

You can find kohlrabi at farmers' markets, co-ops, and Asian grocers from November through April. They range greatly in size, so if they're destined for a purée, purchase the larger ones, which make peeling and chopping a breeze. Otherwise, opt for smaller specimens, whose insides are less likely to be pithy or fibrous. The different colors of the kohlrabi varieties are only skin deep; the flesh's white hue and delicate flavor remain the same.

I've eaten kohlrabi in restaurants, homes, and street stalls all over the world, and I suspect that its ubiquity across cultures speaks to its affinity for a wide range of ingredients. During a vacation in Budapest, I found kohlrabi in several incarnations: stuffed with its own leaves and ground pork; stewed with chicken, apples, and potatoes in a fiery broth calmed with the coldest of cultured cream; and shaved in a salad with onions, herbs, and fried goose skin.

At home I enjoy preparing kohlrabi with simpler techniques:

· Quarter and roast it alongside a pork loin, juniper salt, and thyme.
· Slice it thin and bake with crème fraîche and Comté (aged Gruyère) cheese.
· Dice and sautée it with bacon and spring onions, then adorn with a fried egg.
· Leave it whole and caramelize with butter, maple syrup, and black pepper.
· Braise it with coconut oil, turmeric, mustard seeds, and bolting cilantro.
· Shave it over a pizza with walnuts and blue cheese.

TORN LEAF SALAD WITH
SHAVED KOHLRABI AND LABNE

Makes 4 to 6 servings

As a little girl, the only salad I knew of consisted of packaged, precut iceberg lettuce and carrots drowned in a few glugs of so-called French dressing. It wasn't until college, when I had my first encounter with a farm stand, a salad spinner, and a squeeze of fresh lemon juice, that I learned a salad is a thing to love. Now there is rarely a day that I don't tear, toss, and tuck into a bowl of dressed, seasonal vegetables.

The key to creating a good salad is using contrasting textures, flavors, and temperatures. Raw, thinly sliced kohlrabi is sweet and mildly pungent and is accented by briny olives and the tart, wonderfully funky flavor of preserved lemon. As always, the sharpness of fresh lemon juice brings flavors into focus. And everything is brought together and softened by rich, creamy labne.

---

3 small kohlrabi (1 pound total)

1 Preserved Lemon (see page 282)

2 tablespoons fresh lemon juice

Fine sea salt

¼ cup extra virgin olive oil

1½ cups green olives (such as Cerignola), pitted (a cherry pitter does a nice job)

6 ounces mixed greens (such as gem lettuce, arugula, fava leaves, pea shoots, and chickweed)

1 pint labne

Coarse sea salt

Freshly ground black pepper

Peel the kohlrabi and cut it in half lengthwise. Slice it thin (about ¹⁄₁₆-inch thick) on a mandoline or with a sharp knife.

Use a sharp knife to separate the rind of the preserved lemon from the flesh, and discard the flesh or reserve for another use. Cut the rind into matchsticks; line up the matchsticks, and cut them crosswise into a ¹⁄₁₆-inch dice. In a large mixing bowl, whisk together the preserved lemon, lemon juice, a pinch of fine sea salt, and the olive oil. Cut the green olives in quarters and add them to the bowl. Add the kohlrabi and toss gently.

Tear or chop the greens into approximately 2- to 3-inch irregular pieces; add to the vinaigrette with a pinch of fine sea salt and toss gently. Place the kohlrabi and olives on a serving platter in a somewhat even layer; spoon quenelles of the labne on top. Top with the torn leaves, with a drizzle of the remaining vinaigrette, a pinch of coarse sea salt, and a few grinds of black pepper.

KOHLRABI SOUP WITH ORCHARD FRUIT AND WALNUT OIL

Makes 4 to 6 servings

I first made this soup for Thanksgiving and have returned to it over and over. It is silky, rich, white, and warming. Its elegant appearance and subtle flavor make it suitable for the start of a celebratory meal or—alongside a pull of good, rustic bread—a simple weeknight supper. Like most soups, it gets better on days two and three.

4 tablespoons unsalted butter

4 large shallots, thinly sliced

Fine sea salt

3 large kohlrabi (2½ to 3 pounds total), trimmed, peeled, and diced

1 small apple (any crisp, tart-sweet, white-fleshed variety will do), peeled, cored, and diced

½ small ripe pear, peeled, cored, and diced

3 cups water

¼ cup crème fraîche

TO GARNISH

1 to 2 cups Butter-Glazed Kohlrabi (recipe follows)

A handful of radish or kohlrabi sprouts

Walnut oil

Coarse sea salt

Freshly ground black pepper

Warm the butter in a heavy-bottom pot over low heat; add the shallots and a pinch of fine sea salt. Cook the shallots for approximately 8 minutes, or until translucent. Add the kohlrabi, apple, pear, and another good pinch of salt. Add 2 cups of the water, and bring the mixture to a simmer. Cover and cook for approximately 30 minutes, or until the kohlrabi is completely tender.

Remove from the heat, and purée the soup in a blender until very smooth (depending on the size of your blender, you may need to do this in batches). Blend thoroughly; this can take a full minute or even two. If needed, you can add more stock or water to achieve a desirable consistency (for me, this means something like pancake batter—not too thick, not too thin). Taste, and adjust the seasoning; I almost always need to add salt at this stage.

Return the soup to the pot and reheat on low. Stir in the crème fraîche and turn off the heat. Let the soup sit for 10 to 15 minutes before serving; it will thicken, and the flavors will meld and settle. Serve each bowl with a spoonful of glazed kohlrabi, a few radish sprouts, a drizzle of walnut oil, a pinch of coarse sea salt, and some black pepper.

BUTTER-GLAZED KOHLRABI

Makes 4 to 6 servings (as a side)

If I am not braising kohlrabi and glazing it in butter, I am likely making soup with it, and I often top it with these rich, earthy, faintly sweet morsels. This recipe makes a good-size batch and is a wonderful side to a grilled steak, roast chicken, or salad of bitter greens. There are only a few ingredients, but they create alchemy in the pan.

2–3 kohlrabi (2 to 2½ pounds), peeled and cut into ½-inch dice

4 tablespoons unsalted butter

⅔ cup water

½ teaspoon granulated sugar

¾ teaspoon fine sea salt

¼ to ½ teaspoon apple cider vinegar

Coarse sea salt

Place the kohlrabi in a single layer in a 12- or 14-inch sauté pan. Add the butter, water, sugar, and fine sea salt. Bring the mixture to a gentle simmer over moderate heat. Cook until the kohlrabi is tender to the core but not at all mushy, approximately 20 to 25 minutes. The right cooking time can only be ascertained by tasting for texture.

Toward the end of cooking, when the liquid has evaporated halfway, occasionally shake the pan and gently turn the kohlrabi with a wooden spoon or flexible spatula (metal is too strong here). Continue to simmer until the liquid reduces to a thin glaze and the kohlrabi begins to caramelize. In the final minutes, the dish needs a patient, watchful eye—things can go from golden brown to black pretty quickly.

Remove from the heat, and stir in the apple cider vinegar. Add a pinch of coarse sea salt. Taste, and adjust the seasoning as needed.

KUMQUATS

At the end of every season, it happens. Suddenly it dawns on me that I have overlooked an ingredient, a special fleeting something that, in a few weeks' time, will be no more until next year. Since kumquats arrive in mid-December, I tend to ignore them in favor of more exotic mandarin oranges, Barhi dates, and pomelos. When I finally realize that eight weeks of kumquat season have passed without a single sweet, tart, orange jewel entering my kitchen, I'm likely to purchase pounds and commence candying, slicing, and dicing kumquats for weeks thereafter.

This tiny fruit is eaten and used whole. It is bold, so popping one in your mouth could deter you from purchasing more, if you are not into the sour taste. Used in cooking, kumquats do what all good citrus does—balances, brightens, and enlivens.

The kumquat, however, is not a true citrus; while considered a member of the broader citrus family, many botanists place it in a genus all its own. It grows on a tree that pollinates the blossoms of citrus, thereby creating crosses with ridiculous names such as "limequats," "mandarinquats," "sunquats," and so on.

Kumquats are native to China, and their name comes from the Cantonese *kam kwat*, which means "golden orange." They are a symbol of prosperity and a traditional gift at Lunar New Year, which is why they are a common sight in Chinese households and shops at that time of year.

Purchase kumquats (or any "-quats") that are plump and firm. There are at least six species available at my local market, and they differ slightly in tartness and size. Refrigerate them in a brown paper bag and use within a week. Slice them for salads, purée them for cakes, braise them with meats, and simmer them in tea. After deseeding, you can also do the following:

· Slice and toss them with sugar and a vanilla bean, then simmer into marmalade.
· Mince and fold them into softened buttered with a pinch of salt; use this compound butter on a whole roasted fish.
· Finely chop and cook them with shallots, star anise, salt, black pepper, and just enough water or salt to prevent scorching. This chutney is particularly good with duck and pork fermented into kvass (follow the instructions for Fermented Citron and Honey Tea on page 24).

SPRING LETTUCE, AVOCADO, AND SHAVED KUMQUAT WITH BUTTERMILK VINAIGRETTE

Makes 4 to 6 servings

You'll need the firmest fruit for this salad, since you'll be slicing it thin. Also, this recipe yields more vinaigrette than the salad needs. Since it requires a blender and a good amount of resting time, it's nice to make extra for a later use. You could certainly make this salad again, but the buttermilk vinaigrette is also delicious on top of plain boiled potatoes, a puréed vegetable soup, escarole salad with bacon, or leftover cold chicken.

BUTTERMILK VINAIGRETTE
1 egg, at room temperature
1 tablespoon lemon juice
1 small shallot, finely chopped
Fine sea salt
¼ cup extra virgin olive oil
⅔ cup buttermilk

SALAD
4 small heads tender
  green-leaf lettuce
2 avocados, ripe but semifirm
Coarse sea salt
Freshly ground black pepper
8 kumquats, thinly sliced
  and seeded

Place the egg, lemon juice, shallot, and 2 pinches of fine sea salt in a blender. While processing at low speed, gradually add the olive oil in a slow, steady stream; follow with the buttermilk. Taste, and adjust the seasoning. Cover and chill the vinaigrette for at least 3 hours, or up to 2 days; this allows all the flavors to meld. Let it stand at room temperature for 20 minutes before serving.

Pull off and discard any wilted outer leaves from your lettuce. Wash the lettuce gently and lay it out on a kitchen towel to dry. Cut the avocados in half lengthwise; remove and discard the pits. Cut the halves lengthwise into quarters; peel off the skin. Season the avocados with coarse sea salt and black pepper.

Place the lettuce and avocados in a large, shallow serving bowl; scatter the kumquats on top. Use your hands to toss the salad very gently; do not break up the avocado. Shake the dressing well, and drizzle it over the salad (you will not need all of it; reserve the remainder for another use). Finish with a bit more black pepper, if you'd like.

PRESERVED KUMQUATS

Extend the kumquat harvest by preserving them in salt. After a few months, the bright, slightly funky rind will be ready. I recommend folding them, finely chopped, into a fried rice with duck egg, scallions, peanuts, and sesame. Add a handful of preserved fruit cut in quarters to a roasting pan for a pork shoulder.

3 pints kumquats, rinsed and dried

¼ to ½ cup fine sea salt

Freshly squeezed citrus juice (I use lemon) or whey, as needed

Cut the kumquats into quarters, removing as many of the seeds as you can. Put a thin (about a 1/16-inch) layer of salt in the bottom of a jar, followed by a layer of kumquats, and another layer of salt. Continue filling the jar and pressing the fruit down to eliminate air pockets and to release the juice. If there is not enough liquid to cover the final layer by at least 1 inch, add additional citrus juice or whey; leave 1 inch of air space between the liquid and the lid. Cover the jar and store at room temperature, away from direct sunlight.

For the first week of fermentation, open the jar every day and press the kumquats down so the liquid rises to cover them. If small amounts of white or light green mold form on the surface, simply remove it with a spoon. You'll see the fruit start to change character after a week or two, and the flavor will continue to evolve for a year or more. Taste after a month or two, and decide whether you'd like the fermentation to continue. When you are ready to halt the process, refrigerate the kumquats; at this point, they can be kept for several years.

KUMQUAT AND GINGER TEA

Makes 2 servings

Kumquats are warming and a significant source of vitamin C. Some folks believe that they relieve colds and coughs, and in my experience, they certainly do help. Sip this tea a few times a day as long as symptoms persist.

10 kumquats, cut in quarters

One 2-inch piece of fresh ginger, thinly sliced

2 cups water

Put the kumquats and ginger in a small saucepan, and cover with the water. Simmer over low heat for 15 minutes. Remove from the heat, strain, and sip.

SHORT RIBS WITH KUMQUAT AND KOMBU

Makes 6 servings

I hadn't planned on ever writing a recipe for these short ribs, but when my mother requested it for Christmas dinner one year, claiming she craves it often, I reconsidered. Alongside steamed jasmine rice, a salad of sliced chicories, a plate of lime wedges, and Salt-Baked Sweet Potatoes, Alliums, and Bean Sprouts (see page 242), these ribs are worthy of a holiday feast.

DRY BRINE

Four 8-ounce pieces bone-in beef short ribs

¾ teaspoon fine sea salt

Freshly ground black pepper

1 tablespoon vegetable oil

BRAISE

2 medium carrots, rinsed and cut into 2-inch pieces

1 yellow onion, cut in quarters

4 green onions

1 serrano chile

8 kumquats

5 garlic cloves

One 2-inch piece of ginger

One 14-ounce can whole San Marzano tomatoes in juice, puréed in a blender with juice

2 cups Kombu Stock (see page 281)

2 tablespoons tamari or shoyu

1 teaspoon fish sauce

1 tablespoon red wine vinegar

Fine sea salt

The night before you plan to cook them, season the ribs with about ¾ teaspoon sea salt and some black pepper. Cover and refrigerate overnight.

Put a rack in the lower third of the oven, and preheat to 250°F. Pat the beef dry. Heat the olive oil in a wide 3- to 5-quart heavy pot over moderately high heat until hot but not smoking. Without overcrowding the pan (you may need to do this in batches), brown the ribs on both sides; don't turn the meat until it releases easily from the pan. If you give the ribs a poke with tongs and they don't give, they're not brown enough on the first side; this step can take up to 10 minutes, depending on your pan. Transfer the ribs to a plate as they finish browning.

Add the chopped carrots, yellow and green onions, chile, kumquats, garlic, and ginger to the same pan; cook over moderate heat, uncovered, stirring and scraping the bottom of the pan with a wooden spoon. Once the vegetables and kumquats have begun to caramelize, about 10 minutes, stir in 2 cups of the puréed tomatoes along with the kombu stock, tamari, and fish sauce (reserve the remainder of the tomatoes for another use); bring to a boil over moderately high heat.

Lower the heat and add the beef, along with any juices that have accumulated on the plate. Transfer the pot to the oven and braise until the beef is very tender, about 4 hours. Remove from the oven and let the beef cool in the braising liquid; refrigerate overnight.

The next day, skim the solidified fat from the surface of the meat. Reheat gently over medium-low heat or in a 275°F oven. Remove from the heat, transfer the ribs to a plate, and strain the sauce; discard the vegetables. Return the sauce to the pot and bring to a boil over high heat; reduce until thickened, about 12 minutes. Return the ribs to the pot and braise until warmed through.

KUMQUAT, ALMOND, AND POPPY SEED CAKE

Makes 6 servings

I pretty much only eat cake as breakfast. After a meal, I rarely want more food, and I am too satisfied to crave sugar. But I do love small, mildly sweet breakfasts, and a slice of this fits the bill perfectly.

CAKE

7 ounces kumquats, rinsed
   and dried
3 large eggs
1 cup (4 ounces) almond flour
½ cup (2½ ounces) white rice
   flour
¼ cup (1 ounce) buckwheat
   flour
½ cup plus 2 tablespoons
   (5 ounces) granulated sugar
2 tablespoons poppy seeds
¾ teaspoon baking powder
⅛ teaspoon fine sea salt
½ tablespoon softened or
   melted unsalted butter,
   for greasing the pan

CANDIED CITRUS

10 to 12 ounces citrus fruit
   (kumquats, blood oranges,
   mandarinquats, and/or
   Page mandarins)
½ cup granulated sugar
¼ cup water

Preheat the oven to 375°F. Butter an 8-inch square baking pan, line with parchment, then butter that too.

Place the kumquats in a medium saucepan with enough cold water to cover by 2 inches. Bring to a boil over high heat; lower the heat and simmer the kumquats for 35 minutes, or until tender. Remove from the heat and drain the kumquats; cool to room temperature. Cut each kumquat in half, and remove any seeds with the tip of a paring knife. Add the seeded fruit (flesh and rind) to the bowl of a food processor; purée the mixture until a rough paste forms.

In a large bowl, beat the eggs and kumquat purée until combined. In a small bowl, whisk together the almond flour, rice flour, buckwheat flour, sugar, poppy seeds, baking powder, and sea salt. Add the almond mixture to the eggs and stir with a spatula until combined. Let the batter sit for 20 to 30 minutes.

Meanwhile, prepare the candied citrus. Cut the citrus fruit into ⅛-inch slices, removing seeds as you go. In a small saucepan over moderate heat, dissolve the sugar in the water. Add the sliced citrus and lower the heat; poach for 12 to 15 minutes. Remove from the heat and cool slightly.

Arrange the candied citrus in the bottom of the prepared pan. Slowly pour the batter over the fruit, disturbing your arrangement as little as possible. Use an offset spatula to gently spread the batter evenly across the pan. Bake for 35 to 40 minutes, or until the cake is golden brown and has pulled away from the sides of the pan. Remove from the oven.

Strain the citrus syrup and return it to the saucepan. Bring it to a boil and let it reduce until it coats the back of a spoon. Allow cake to cool completely before brushing the syrup on top.

Stored in an airtight container at room temperature, this cake keeps for up to four days.

MUSTARD GREENS

Mustard greens are the black sheep of this book. The ruffled leaves are unequivocally peppery and pungent, and just the word *mustard* connotes harshness and fire. I see countless shoppers walk right by these greens at the market.

I will start their defense by stating that mustards are superior to other leafy greens both biochemically and energetically. I once worked with an oncologist to devise a series of cooking classes for a group of women recently diagnosed with cancer, and at the top of the list of therapeutic ingredients sat mustard greens (along with fresh turmeric). In addition to disease-mitigating glucosinolates, these greens have significant amounts of folate as well as vitamins K, C, E, and A. They warm a cold constitution, dispel dampness (such as sinus infections and wet coughs), and move stagnant or contractive energy. These remarkable effects can be immediately noticeable. Even when I'm well, I feel more sprightly and stimulated after a fork full of Preserved Mizuna (see page 153) or a bowl of Mustard Greens with Potatoes and Whole Spices (see page 152).

There are numerous subvarieties of mustard greens, and they range in pungency and heat. At many farmers' markets, you can taste before you buy. Most mustards are available in all seasons, and I favor Japanese mizuna and komatsuna gai choy, and purple mustard. These greens will yellow and rot more quickly than other brassicas (such as kale, cabbage, or collards), so you'll need to refrigerate them in an airtight container lined with a paper towel and use them within three days.

Mustard greens give rise to vivid yellow flowers, which are especially wonderful when blanched for 30 seconds and used instead of dandelion greens for the Semolina Bread with Dandelion and Green Olives (see page 69), sautéed for Pasta with Brassica Flowers and Ricotta (see page 155), stirred into Poached Chicken and Burdock Broth (see page 28); scrambled with eggs, or pan-fried in duck fat for a bowl of rice.

ROASTED WINTER SQUASH WITH PURPLE MUSTARD AND PANTALEO

Makes 4 to 6 servings

Mustard greens harvested while they're the length of a pinky are still peppery and pungent but can be eaten raw. They are quite unlike the fully grown plant, which is woodsy and—when not fully cooked—can wreak havoc on your gastrointestinal tract. Mustard's characteristics balance the contractive energy and sweetness of roasted winter squash and stand strong against the bold flavors of minced garlic, crumbled chile, rosemary, and butter. Pantaleo is a phenomenal goat's milk cheese from Sardinia, and I recommend asking around for it, but any hard, aged cheese will serve this salad well.

½ cup hazelnuts

1 teaspoon hazelnut oil, plus more for drizzling

Fine sea salt

1 (or 2 small) rugosa or butternut squash

Extra virgin olive oil

4 tablespoons unsalted butter

1 medium shallot, diced

2 garlic cloves, minced

2 rosemary sprigs

1 chile de arbol, thinly sliced

1 teaspoon red wine vinegar

8 ounces baby purple mustard greens (about 4 to 5 cups)

5 ounces panteleo, pecorino romano, or Parmigiano-Reggiano

Preheat the oven to 400°F. Toast the hazelnuts for 10 to 12 minutes. Cool slightly, roughly chop, then toss the hazelnuts with a drizzle of hazelnut oil and a pinch of sea salt.

Increase the oven temperature to 450°F. Peel the squash and remove the stem and root end. Cut it in half crosswise where the neck meets the base. Cut the base in half and remove the seeds with a spoon. Cut the base and the neck into 1-inch-thick wedges and half-moon slices, respectively. Toss the squash with enough olive oil and salt to coat, and spread the pieces across two sheet pans lined with parchment paper. Roast for approximately 35 minutes, or until caramelized, turning the pieces once to ensure that both sides brown.

Meanwhile, heat the butter in a small saucepan over moderately high heat; using stainless steel pans enables you to watch the butter and make sure it doesn't burn. To the butter, add the shallot, garlic, rosemary, chile de arbol, and a generous pinch of salt. Cook until the butter begins to brown, watching it carefully so it doesn't burn. Once the butter has browned and the aromatics have softened, add the red wine vinegar, 1 tablespoon of the olive oil, and the teaspoon of hazelnut oil. Remove and discard the rosemary sprigs. Taste, and adjust the seasonings.

In a wide serving bowl or platter, make a base of half the roasted squash; top with two handfuls of mustard greens, a drizzle of the warm vinaigrette, shavings from the cheese (I use a Swiss peeler), and the hazelnuts. Maintain the integrity of each ingredient, avoiding any tossing, smashing, or even mixing. Repeat the layers once more. In this manner, each bite will be a bit of surprise and different from the last.

Refrigerated overnight, this salad is still delicious the next day; the mustard greens and cheese both wilt slightly, but I don't mind at all.

MUSTARD GREENS WITH POTATOES AND WHOLE SPICES

Makes 4 servings

Just the aroma of smoky, sour, sweet black cardamom pods makes me happy. This dish showcases whole spices, and I leave them in when I serve it. If you are feeding kids or sensitive eaters, go ahead and remove them before plating.

4 medium potatoes

Fine sea salt

3 bunches mustard greens (2 pounds), tough stems removed

6 tablespoons unsalted butter

One 3-inch piece of ginger, thinly sliced

2 chiles de arbol

1 cinnamon stick

2 black cardamom pods

½–⅗ cup water

SERVING SUGGESTIONS

Perfect Steamed Rice (see page 286)

1 bunch washed cilantro, stems attached, dried on a towel-lined plate

1 bowl plain yogurt

A plate of thinly sliced yellow onions and green chiles (jalapeño or serrano)

Place the potatoes in a large pot; cover them with cold water by 1 inch, and add 2 pinches of salt. By starting the whole potatoes in cold water, you ensure that they cook evenly from the center out. Bring the pot to a boil over high heat. Reduce the heat to a simmer and allow the potatoes to cook for approximately 20 to 30 minutes, or until a paring knife inserted in several of them meets only slight resistance. Remove from the heat and drain. Once the potatoes have cooled, cut them all in half or in quarters, if large.

Meanwhile, bring another large pot of salted water to a boil. Add the mustard greens and cook for 2 to 3 minutes; remove from the heat, drain the greens, and return the pot to moderate heat. Transfer the greens to a cutting board and finely chop.

Return a pot to low heat. Add the butter ginger, chiles de arbol, cinnamon, black cardamom pods, and a pinch of salt; cook for 2 to 3 minutes to toast the spices. Add the mustard greens and ½ cup of the water; cook for 15 minutes more. Add the potatoes and another pinch of salt. Stir with a wooden spoon to combine gently, adding more water, as needed, to achieve a stew-like consistency. Taste, and adjust the seasoning. Remove the whole spices before serving, if you'd like.

PRESERVED MIZUNA

Makes 3½ to 4 quarts

There are some nights when, after a long day of work, I don't really want food but need something nourishing and elemental. A small bowl of steamed brown rice and preserved vegetables is just the thing. If I sense I need protein, I'll add a steamed or soft-boiled egg.

Preserved mizuna is shockingly delicious and can serve as a meal's main attraction or a pickle on the side. It improves digestion and overall vitality, and a single chopped spoonful makes a dish refreshing and complex.

2 bunches mizuna or purple mustard greens (approximately 2 pounds), tough stems removed

Fine sea salt

8 to 10 cups rice soaking water (see page 286)

¼ cup rice wine vinegar

One 8-inch piece of kombu

Wash the mizuna until the water runs clear. Soak the greens in a bowl of water with a handful of sea salt overnight. This wet brine helps neutralize a lot of bitterness while softening and seasoning the leaves.

The next day, drain the mizuna; spin dry. In a large bowl, whisk together 8 cups rice soaking water with 1 tablespoon salt, the rice wine vinegar, and the kombu. Let this sit at room temperature for 30 minutes. The kombu will expand.

Sterilize a 48-ounce jar with boiling water; allow to dry. Pack the greens in the jar; pour the brine on top, leaving 1 inch of space between the top of the liquid and the lid. Fold the soaked kombu and use it to submerge the top leaf completely under the brine. Add more water, if needed.

Allow the mizuna to sit at room temperature for one to two weeks, checking the jar periodically to make sure the liquid has not evaporated. If you find a bit of mold on the surface, simply skim it off with a spoon. As needed, add a few tablespoons of a simple brine (a 1:1 ratio of salt to water) just to keep everything submerged.

Taste your preserved mizuna after a week or so, and decide if you'd like to let it go longer (think about your sauerkraut preference), or if you'd like to slow the fermentation by sealing and refrigerating your jar. Once you're happy with it, refrigerate and use within one year.

PASTA WITH BRASSICA FLOWERS AND RICOTTA

Makes 4 to 6 servings

When I'm making vegetarian pasta, I almost always reach for orecchiette. Those little ears cup the braised vegetables, and their texture is relatively meaty. If you can't find mustard flowers, you can use chopped broccoli rabe, kale, or even diced roasted pumpkin (but skip the wilting step).

1 pound orecchiette

¼ cup + 2 tablespoons extra
   virgin olive oil, plus more
   for serving

2 tablespoons unsalted butter

3 large garlic cloves, sliced

2 chiles de arbol, cut in half

2 pounds mustard flowers (or
   kale and/or broccoli flowers)

Fine sea salt

Zest of 1 lemon

1 to 2 tablespoons fresh
   lemon juice

Crushed chile de arbol
   (optional)

1 pound fresh ricotta (I adore
   the sheep's milk variety.)

Bring a large (6- to 8-quart) pot of salted water to a boil. Cook the orecchiette according to the package instructions (my favorite brand recommends boiling for 9 to 11 minutes).

Meanwhile, place a 14- to 16-inch skillet over moderately high heat; add ¼ cup olive oil, butter, garlic, and chiles. Cook for about 2 minutes; the garlic and chiles will infuse the warm fat with their pungency and heat. Add about half the mustard flowers to the pan with a pinch of sea salt, then toss them until they begin to wilt. Add the remaining flowers and another pinch of salt; toss. Cover the pan and cook for 5 minutes, or until all of the flowers appear wilted and bright.

Drain the pasta and add it directly to the sautéed flowers, adding a splash of the pasta water to the pan as well. Turn the heat to low, and toss everything together with a wooden spoon (using metal here can cut the pasta and mash the flowers); cook for a minute or two, then remove from the heat. Discard the chiles. Stir in the lemon zest, the remaining 2 tablespoons of olive oil, and a squeeze of lemon juice. Taste, and add more salt, lemon juice, or crushed chile, if needed.

Spoon the ricotta onto warmed plates; use the back of a spoon to sweep the creamy mixture across into a thin, asymmetrical base. Top with the pasta and a drizzle of your favorite olive oil.

NETTLES

My first introduction to nettles was on a sheep-dotted scree slope in Wales. I was hiking and slipping and unknowingly grabbed the nearest bush to stay upright. The little hairs of those nettle leaves sent an electric-like sting across every cell they touched. Moments after that, lost in the drizzle and feeling stuck, my skin turned red as my histamine levels rose. Luckily, I became reacquainted with nettles in a more hospitable circumstance, one involving pizza and wine.

Nettles contain more vitamins and minerals than just about any other food. They help regulate blood sugar and build energy and a sense of vitality (you literally feel this when you eat them, like with mustard greens). Their deep green color is an indication that they are very alkalizing to the system.

Tasting of chlorophyll and minerals, nettles' green flavor is so intense that I sometimes find it overpowering. But with a little enrichment, especially in the form of fat and acidity, they quiet and nourish. They can feel both healthy and indulgent, a lovely dichotomy.

Nettles are a fast-growing weed available January through June, almost anywhere fertile soil is moist. Try to find young plants that haven't flowered; older leaves contain calcium oxalate that feels sandy and gritty in the mouth. Always wear dishwashing gloves while handling them. Pull off any large, woody stalks; wash them in a big basin of cold water; then blanch the leaves in salted water. The blanching water can be reserved and chilled, and you can drink it for a mineral-rich boost. Once boiled, their stinging powers are neutralized, and you can touch them with your bare hands.

Blanched nettles are almost as versatile as cooked spinach and can be used in many preparations:

· Chop them finely and fold them into softened butter (to finish a steak or elevate grilled bread).

· Toss them with al dente trofie, crumbled chile de arbol, the zest of a lemon, more olive oil than you think you need, and freshly shaved pecorino romano.

· Spoon them into ramekins and top them with a freshly cracked egg, cream, coarse salt, and freshly cracked pepper; bake until the egg is set.

NETTLE SOUP WITH WHIPPED CRÈME FRAÎCHE AND CHIVE BLOSSOMS

Makes 6 to 8 servings

This soup boasts a brilliant shade of green and packs more vitamins and minerals than a big bowl of kale chips. It is easy to prepare and impressive to present. Like most soups, it improves after an overnight rest; it is also very good chilled, so let the weather dictate your decision to reheat. (Note that the flavors of any cold dish will be more mellow than its warm version.)

½ pound nettles

1 tablespoon unsalted butter

1 tablespoon extra virgin olive oil

2 small leeks (or 1 large leek), cut in half lengthwise and thinly sliced

3 green garlic stalks (or 2 garlic cloves), thinly sliced

Fine sea salt

Freshly ground black pepper

2 Yukon Gold potatoes (or another starchy variety), peeled and diced

1½ quarts vegetable stock, chicken stock, or Kombu Stock (see page 281)

4 ounces crème fraîche, cold

½ cup heavy cream, cold

3 tablespoons roughly chopped thyme leaves

Zest of 1 lemon

1 bunch chives (preferably with blossoms)

Don some dishwashing gloves. Pick over the nettles, removing any large woody stalks, and wash them thoroughly. Bring a large stockpot full of salted water to a boil over high heat. Blanch the nettles for 1 minute in the boiling water. Drain and set aside.

Dry the pot and return it to moderate heat. Add the butter and oil. When the foam from the butter subsides, add the leeks, garlic, 2 pinches of sea salt, and a few grinds of black pepper. Cover and sweat the alliums gently for 10 minutes, stirring a few times, until the leeks are soft but not brown. Add the potatoes and the stock, and raise the heat to high. Bring to a boil, then reduce the heat and simmer for 20 minutes. Stir in the nettles and simmer for 10 to 15 minutes more, or until the potatoes and any tough nettle stalks are completely tender. Remove from the heat and purée the soup thoroughly (depending on the size of your blender, you may have to do this in two batches). Return the soup to the pot (reheat if necessary), stir in 3 ounces of the crème fraîche, and taste. Add more salt, if needed.

Whip the cream until it forms soft peaks. Gently fold the remaining ounce of crème fraîche (you don't really need to weigh it; eyeball it as a large spoonful or two) into the whipped cream; refrigerate until ready to use.

Ladle the soup into oven-warmed bowls, topping each portion with a dollop of whipped crème fraîche, thyme leaves, a grating of lemon zest, freshly cracked black pepper, and a generous sprinkling of finely chopped chives.

NETTLES WITH COCONUT OIL
AND MUSTARD SEEDS

=== *Makes 4 servings* ===

Nettles may be at their best when sautéed in coconut oil infused with dried red chile and pungent mustard seeds. You can serve this as a main course alongside a small bowl of warm chickpeas, steamed basmati rice, and an herb salad of cilantro and fenugreek leaves.

2 pounds nettles

2 tablespoons coconut oil

1 chile de arbol

1 teaspoon brown mustard seeds

2 green garlic stalks, white and pale-green parts only, thinly sliced

Fine sea salt

1 lime

Don some dishwashing gloves. Pick over the nettles, removing any large woody stalks, and wash them thoroughly. Bring a large stockpot of salted water to a boil over high heat. Blanch the nettles in the boiling water for 1 minute. Drain, and finely chop.

In a large frying pan over high heat, warm the coconut oil. When it is hot, add the chile de arbol and fry, stirring, until it turns dark brown, about 1 minute. Add the mustard seeds, and cover the pan. When the seeds stop sputtering, about 30 seconds, uncover and add the green garlic. Cook, stirring constantly, until the garlic turns golden, about 1 minute.

Add the nettles and a good pinch of sea salt. Cook, stirring constantly, until the excess moisture evaporates, about 5 minutes. Remove from the heat and stir in the juice of half a lime. Taste and add more lime or salt, if you'd like.

NETTLE SANDWICH

Makes 3 to 4 servings

Braised greens sandwiched between garlic-rubbed bread is one of the most delicious and unexpectedly satisfying meals you can eat. If you have a child (or inner child) who refuses to eat bitter, grassy greens, try this dish. Kale, beet greens, Swiss chard, and spinach can all easily replace nettles in this recipe.

GREMOLATA
1 bunch parsley
2 tablespoons thyme leaves
1 lemon
1 orange
Coarse sea salt

SANDWICH
6 ounces nettles
Extra virgin olive oil
Fine sea salt
1 or 2 chiles de arbol,
    crumbled
2 rosemary sprigs
1 long Italian loaf or baguette
4 garlic cloves, smashed
1 pound burrata or mozzarella
    cheese

Prepare the gremolata: finely chop the parsley and thyme leaves, and place in a small mixing bowl. Stir in the zest from the lemon and the orange and a pinch of coarse salt; reserve the rest of the lemon for another use, including brightening the flavor of the nettle in a step that follows.

Don some dishwashing gloves. Pick over the nettles, removing any large woody stalks, and wash them thoroughly. Bring a large stockpot of salted water to a boil over high heat. Blanch the nettles in the boiling water for 1 minute. Drain, and cool slightly.

Roughly chop the blanched nettles (stems and all). Return the pot to moderate heat; add enough olive oil to coat the bottom of the pan. Add the rosemary and chile, and let them infuse the oil for 1 minute. Add the nettles and a pinch of fine sea salt to the pot. Cook for 3 to 5 minutes, or until the greens are fully tender and all of their bright bluish-green liquid has evaporated. Remove the chile and rosemary sprig, and add 1 teaspoon fresh lemon juice. Taste, and adjust the seasoning. Allow the greens to cool slightly before composing the sandwich.

Meanwhile, preheat the broiler or toaster oven. Cut the bread in half lengthwise and drizzle both sides with olive oil. Toast the cut side until golden. While it's still warm, rub the toast generously with the smashed garlic. Slather burrata (or lay thinly sliced mozzarella) over one side. Top the cheese with the braised nettles. Top the nettles with a sprinkling of the gremolata. Top with the other side of the bread. Slice the loaf into 3 to 4 sandwiches with a serrated knife.

PERSIMMONS

Many cultures consider the persimmon a divine fruit. It is prized for its versatility, healing properties, striking beauty, and sweet, earthy, floral taste. If you can't find this extraordinary fruit in your local market, I hope you'll still take inspiration from the recipes and photos in this chapter and apply whatever ingredient you do have; apples and pears make wonderful substitutes.

Persimmons begin appearing in markets in late September and are available through December. This brilliantly colored fruit is a phenomenal source of vitamin A and potassium; it is cooling and counters dry conditions. There are two main varieties commercially available in the United States: the acorn-shaped Hachiya and the squat, tomato-shaped Fuyu. Hachiya persimmons are incredibly astringent until they are extremely ripe or preserved as Hoshigaki, a Japanese delicacy. Fuyus look like matte orange, plastic tomatoes; they are sweeter than the Hachiya, although both taste like honey, apricot, and winter squash to me. Fuyus can be eaten while still firm, and they do not need to be peeled. Avoid any fruit with soft spots or bruises. I have found that the darker the orange, the better the flavor. Store persimmons at room temperature.

Many recipes—puddings, quick breads, ice creams, jams—use and accentuate the fruit's natural sweetness. Yet I—focused exclusively on the Fuyu variety—prefer to eat them unpeeled as handheld snacks or thinly slice them for a host of salads. In addition to the two salads in this chapter, here are a few other combinations I like, all dressed with a simple red wine vinaigrette (1 part Banyuls vinegar to 3 parts olive oil and a pinch of salt, whisked):

· Chicories, toasted pecans, and shaved Parmigiano-Reggiano
· Little gem lettuce, pomegranate seeds, and toasted walnuts
· Wild arugula with prosciutto or speck
· Lamb's quarter (or spinach), thinly sliced red onions, and feta cheese
· Barley, shallots, toasted almonds, and mint

ESCAROLE SALAD WITH FENNEL AND FALL FRUIT

Makes 6 servings

Escarole is one of the most delicious leafy greens, and this salad showcases its subtle bitterness and slightly crunchy texture alongside the sweet persimmon and apple. The goat cheese gives this dish some heft, but leave it out to enjoy a lighter version.

1 teaspoon Champagne vinegar

1 teaspoon lemon juice

1 teaspoon Dijon mustard

1 medium shallot, finely chopped

Fine sea salt

Freshly ground black pepper

¼ cup extra virgin olive oil

1 crisp apple (such as Fuji)

2 Fuyu persimmons

1 fennel bulb

1 head escarole

5 ounces semifirm goat cheese (I used Andante Crottin.)

Whisk together the Champagne vinegar, lemon juice, Dijon mustard, and shallot in a large bowl with a pinch of sea salt and a few grinds of black pepper; add the olive oil.

Use a mandoline to slice the apple $\frac{1}{16}$ inch thick, and immediately add the pieces to the vinaigrette (which prevents them from turning too brown). Thinly slice the persimmons and fennel; add to the bowl.

Chop or tear the escarole into bite-size pieces, and add it to the bowl as well; season the greens with a pinch of salt. Toss lightly.

Thinly slice the goat cheese, and scatter it on top of the salad. Lightly toss once more to incorporate the cheese, but be careful not to overmix. Serve immediately.

KOHLRABI SALAD WITH PERSIMMONS AND SHEEP'S MILK CHEESE

Kohlrabi's assertive flavor—reminiscent of cabbage, broccoli, and turnips—is surprisingly happy nuzzled up to slices of sweet persimmon. The fruit balances the deep savory flavor of the vegetable, and finding spots of tangy, salty cheese and toasted nuts keeps the palate interested.

3 small heads kohlrabi (relatively small and tender plants are required here)

2 Fuyu persimmons

1 tablespoon lemon juice

Fine sea salt

¼ cup extra virgin olive oil

½ cup coarsely chopped toasted walnuts

Freshly ground black pepper

Coarse sea salt

6 ounces sheep's milk cheese (such as manchego or pecorino sardo)

Peel the kohlrabi and cut it in half lengthwise. Slice the kohlrabi and persimmons about 1/16 inch thick using a mandoline or by hand. In a large mixing bowl, whisk together the lemon juice, a pinch of fine sea salt, and the olive oil.

Toss half the sliced kohlrabi with the lemon vinaigrette; layer half the dressed slices with half the persimmon slices, a scattering of the toasted walnuts, a pinch of coarse sea salt, and shavings of the cheese. Repeat the layers once more, finishing with shaved cheese.

FARRO WITH PERSIMMONS, ARUGULA, AND PANCETTA-FRIED HAZELNUTS

Makes 6 servings

This salad is a chorus of different flavors and textures. And these highly seasoned, crunchy pancetta-fried hazelnuts likely deserve a page of their own. Please don't let them stay buried here, hiding behind persimmons—they are very exciting and have some range. They can even be served on their own as an hors d'oeuvre (leave the hazelnuts whole).

12 ounces farro

2 garlic cloves

1 chile de arbol

A handful parsley stems, tied with twine (optional)

Extra virgin olive oil

Fine sea salt

FOR THE PANCETTA-FRIED HAZELNUTS

Four ¼-inch-thick slices pancetta

1 cup toasted hazelnuts (the Ennis variety is phenomenal here)

2 rosemary sprigs

1 garlic clove

1 chile de arbol

1 teaspoon hazelnut oil

Coarse sea salt

½ pound wild arugula, baby lacinato kale, or baby dandelion leaves

4 small Fuyu persimmons (or 2 large, cut in half lengthwise), sliced ⅛ inch thick

A splash of red wine vinegar

Place the farro in a large saucepan; add enough water to cover it by 1 inch. Add one garlic clove, chile de arbol, parsley stems (if using), a few tablespoons olive oil, and a good pinch of fine sea salt. Bring the mixture to a boil over high heat; reduce the heat and simmer for 30 to 45 minutes, or until the farro is al dente.

Meanwhile, add the pancetta to a medium skillet set over moderate heat. Cook the meat slowly, allowing it to release its fat. Cook for 8 to 10 minutes, turning once, until the pancetta is a deep golden brown and lightly crispy. Use tongs to transfer it to paper towels to drain; reserve the fat. Add the toasted hazelnuts to the pan along with one of the rosemary sprigs, chile de arbol, and a pinch of fine sea salt. Cook the hazelnuts, stirring occasionally, until they are deeply caramelized, 4 to 6 minutes. Remove the nuts from the heat; stir in the hazelnut oil and coarse sea salt to taste. Use a slotted spoon to transfer the nuts to paper towels to drain and cool. Once both have cooled to room temperature, finely chop the hazelnuts and pancetta with the remaining rosemary sprig, a garlic clove, and chile de arbol.

While the farro is warm but off the heat, toss in the wild arugula and persimmons. Taste; I often need to season the dish with more salt, olive oil, and a splash of red wine vinegar. Stir in half the hazelnut mixture; garnish with the rest.

DRIED PERSIMMON TEA

Makes 2 to 3 servings

This brew is reminiscent of chai but without sugar. Persimmons boast a natural honey-like sweetness that infuses the water and balances the heat imparted by the ginger, star anise, and cinnamon.

Dried Fuyu persimmons are available in co-op markets, health food stores, and farmers' markets, as well as online. You can also dry your own by cooking ⅛- to ¼-inch slices on a rack in a dehydrator or 200°F oven for two to three hours.

8 dried Fuyu persimmon slices

3 cups water

One 3-inch piece of ginger, peeled and sliced

1 star anise

1 large cinnamon stick

Whole milk, warm (optional)

Place the persimmon slices in a pot with the water, ginger, star anise, and cinnamon stick; bring to a boil over high heat. Reduce the heat and simmer for 20 minutes. Remove from the heat, strain the tea, and discard the persimmon and spices.

Serve this tea plain or with warmed milk, if you prefer.

POMEGRANATES

The pomegranate is a thick-skinned fruit full of juicy, crunchy, ruby-hued, edible seeds that are bright, fruity, sweet, and slightly astringent.

I had my first taste when I was in my early teens. My best friend Liana, a transplant from Baku, Azerbaijan, lived with her parents, older brother, maternal grandparents, and a very large husky. Life in that often-chaotic household revolved around meals. Mornings were met with potato pancakes, Grandma's homemade bread (which I was never allowed to cut), softened butter, and several jars of jam. Black tea, a symbol of hospitality in Azerbaijani culture, was continuously brewing. Lunch was a time for grazing on rustic dishes like sliced cucumbers; kidney bean salad; pork and potato soup; and ikra, a cold eggplant-and-bell-pepper mixture I would, and still can, eat by the quart. And, of course, more bread and butter. Supper was always an extravagant feast, and it was the meltingly tender barbecued lamb adorned with pomegranate that made the biggest impact on my palate and imagination; those bites were revelatory.

Pomegranates are in season in fall and early winter. Purchase heavy fruits with smooth skins; store them at room temperature for up to a week. As you may know, having been deemed a "superfood" by the popular media, pomegranates are high in potassium, vitamin C, and numerous antioxidants. They also reduce inflammation and promote both blood and prostate health.

To reap all of the benefits of a pomegranate, you must break it open. First, protect your clothing with an apron or cloth. Bruise the whole fruit by rolling it on a hard surface with the palm of your hand; you should hear the seeds releasing from the skin. Puncture the bud end with the tip of a knife and squeeze out the juice into a cup. Enlarge your puncture by cutting an *X* and then pry the fruit open. Many seeds will fall right out, but a few will need your help. These crimson gems can be used in one of the recipes in this chapter, consumed by the spoonful, or used as vibrant garnish to enliven everyday dishes such as the following:
- Oatmeal, granola, and muesli
- A salad of winter greens such as kale, frisée, and chicories
- Roasted cauliflower
- Baked chicken, especially when served over bulgur, under cilantro, or next to yogurt
- Rice pudding, possibly imbued with coconut milk or saffron

CARAMELIZED KABOCHA
WITH SEEDS AND SHALLOT

People really go mad for this particular combination of flavors and textures; the dark crimson of the pomegranate against the golden orange of the caramelized pumpkin is striking. I've heard many cooks say that this dish is a new classic for their winter celebrations.

1   medium kabocha squash

Extra virgin olive oil

2   chiles de arbol, cut in half

Fine sea salt

1   tablespoon fresh
     pomegranate juice

Red wine vinegar

Coarse sea salt

2   cups pomegranate seeds
     (see page 173 for instructions)

1   tablespoon finely chopped
     Preserved Lemon rind
     (see page 282)

1   tablespoon toasted white
     sesame seeds

1   tablespoon toasted nigella
     seeds

1   tablespoon toasted cumin
     seeds

1   cup small mint leaves

1   cup cilantro leaves

1   cup Crispy Shallots
     (see page 225)

Preheat the oven to 450°F. Line two sheet pans with parchment paper. Remove the stem and root end from the squash. Peel the squash and cut it in half lengthwise; remove the seeds with a spoon. Cut the squash into 2-inch wedges. Divide the pieces between the sheet pans and toss each with 3 tablespoons olive oil, 2 of the chile de arbol halves, and 2 pinches of fine sea salt; spread the squash into a single, even layer in both pans. Roast the squash for approximately 35 to 45 minutes, or until caramelized, turning the pieces once to ensure that both sides brown. Season each batch with ½ tablespoon fresh pomegranate juice, ½ teaspoon red wine vinegar, a drizzle of olive oil (or Shallot Oil, on page 225), and a pinch of coarse sea salt.

In a medium bowl, toss the pomegranate seeds with the preserved lemon rind, a few drops of vinegar, and a pinch of fine salt. Add the seeds, herbs, and shallots; toss gently. Lay the caramelized squash in an even layer on a plate or serving platter. Top with the pomegranate, seeds, and herbs; season with coarse sea salt.

LAMB MEATBALLS WITH CHESTNUTS AND POMEGRANATE

The sharp and slightly sour flavor of pomegranate seeds is a classic complement to gamy, rich lamb. The vibrant seeds make this a real showstopper, the perfect dish for feeding a crowd. It easily scales up, and much of the prep can be done in advance: the chestnuts can be roasted and peeled up to four days ahead; the raw meatballs can be refrigerated the night before and—once fried—can be kept in a low oven for up to an hour.

1 pound large fresh chestnuts

1 pound ground lamb shoulder

1 large egg

½ cup fresh breadcrumbs
   (I used half of a stale pita.)

1 tablespoon Baharat
   (recipe follows)

Fine sea salt

Extra virgin olive oil

1 tablespoon unsalted butter

1 shallot, thinly sliced (I use
   a mandoline for this.)

1 cup pomegranate seeds
   (see page 173 for instructions)

1 tablespoon pomegranate
   molasses

1 tablespoon fresh lemon juice

SERVING SUGGESTIONS

Perfect Steamed Rice
   (see page 286), lavash,
   and/or pita bread

Sheep's milk yogurt

Trimmed scallions

1 cup loosely packed leaves
   of herbs and wild greens
   (such as cilantro, mint,
   arugula, or purslane)

Preheat the oven to 425°F. Cut an X on the flat side of each chestnut; place them in an even layer on a baking sheet. Roast until tender, about 35 minutes. Remove the nuts from the oven, and cool to just above room temperature; peel off the shells and the inner skins. Set aside until completely cool. Cut the chestnuts in half crosswise.

Lower the oven temperature to 275°F. Combine the ground lamb, egg, breadcrumbs, baharat, and a pinch of sea salt in a large bowl. Mix until combined, then refrigerate for 30 minutes. Shape the chilled lamb mixture into apricot-size balls.

Heat ⅛ inch of olive oil in a large skillet over moderately high heat. Add the meatballs in one even layer, leaving about ½ inch between them; you will likely have to cook them in several batches. Use a spoon to carefully turn the meatballs, and cook until browned on all sides, about 15 to 17 minutes per batch. Use a slotted spoon to remove the meatballs; place them on a sheet pan and keep them warm in the low oven until ready to serve. Repeat this process until all are cooked. Pour the fat out of the pan; add the butter and return it to the heat.

Add the shallot to the pan; fry until golden brown. Add the chestnuts and a pinch of salt; fry until heated through. Remove the pan from the heat; add the pomegranate seeds, pomegranate molasses, and lemon juice. Mix well.

Place the meatballs on a platter; top with the chestnut, shallot, and pomegranate dressing. Finish the dish with a heavy scattering of fresh herbs, greens, and a pinch of coarse sea salt.

BAHARAT

Baharat is a spice mix with many incarnations; it crosses cultures and varies among households. This is mine. I always keep a jar in the cupboard, refreshing the mixture every three months, as the flavor of ground spices dramatically dulls over time.

½ cup cumin seeds

⅓ cup coriander seeds

3 tablespoons fresh chili flakes (I take a chile de arbol and pulse it in a spice grinder or repurposed coffee mill.)

5 tablespoons smoked paprika

2 tablespoons ground cinnamon

1 tablespoon hot paprika

½ teaspoon allspice

Set a small skillet over moderately high heat. Add the cumin seeds, coriander seeds, and chili flakes. Toast the spices, stirring constantly, until their aromas are released; be careful not to burn the spices or they will turn bitter. Pour the spices into a spice grinder, mortar, or repurposed coffee grinder, and let cool for a couple of minutes. Add the smoked paprika, cinnamon, hot paprika, and allspice; grind to a powder. The blend can be stored in an airtight glass jar at room temperature for up to three months.

FREEKEH WITH WINTER GREENS, POMEGRANATE, AND PISTACHIOS

Makes 4 to 6 servings

Freekeh is green wheat that has been toasted over fire; it is smoky and grassy and sweet. It also cooks up quite fluffy, making it perfect for grain salads like this.

1½ cups freekeh

2 tablespoons unsalted butter

4 tablespoons extra virgin olive oil

2 medium shallots, thinly sliced

Fine sea salt

A pinch of ground cumin

A pinch of ground cinnamon

1¼ cup water, Kombu Stock (see page 281), or bean stock

1 tablespoon fresh lemon juice

1 tablespoon pomegranate juice

Seeds of 1 pomegranate (see page 173 for instructions)

A few handfuls of baby wintergreens (such as kale, purslane, spinach, and mustard)

A handful of mint leaves

½ cup toasted pistachios, roughly chopped

1 tablespoon pistachio oil (or extra virgin olive oil)

Soak the freekeh in cold water overnight. The next day, drain the freekeh in a sieve, rinse, and drain well.

Heat a large pot over moderate heat; add the butter, 2 tablespoons of the olive oil, the shallots, and a pinch of sea salt. Sweat shallots for 5 to 7 minutes. Add the freekeh, cumin, cinnamon, and 2 more pinches of salt. Add the water, and bring the mixture to a boil over high heat. Reduce the heat and simmer for 15 to 20 minutes, or until all the water is absorbed. Remove the pot from the heat, cover, and let sit for 5 minutes. Uncover and add the lemon juice, pomegranate juice, and remaining 2 tablespoons of olive oil; stir and fluff with a fork. Allow the freekeh to cool to room temperature. Taste, and adjust the seasoning.

To the freekeh, add the pomegranate seeds, greens, mint, pistachios, pistachio oil (if using), and another pinch of salt. Toss gently. Taste once more, adding more salt, lemon juice, or oil, as needed.

LABNE, DATE SYRUP, POMEGRANATE, AND PUFFED AMARANTH

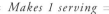

Makes 1 serving

My colleague Sarah is one of nature's cutest creatures—she is small, snarky, and incredibly generous. She finds immense pleasure in pottery classes, mounds of butter, and bike coalitions. When pomegranates are in season, she begins every day with a bowl of yogurt and a heap of their ruby red seeds. I've adapted her breakfast ritual slightly to suit my needs; with the addition of protein- and fiber-rich amaranth, this dish can keep me moving for hours, even through a multi-hour surf session on a cold autumn morning.

If you have some well-stocked Mexican groceries in your area, you can likely find puffed amaranth. It is also available online, often under the name *amaranto tostado*.

⅓ cup amaranth

⅓ cup labne

1 tablespoon fresh pomegranate juice

¼ cup pomegranate seeds (see page 173 for instructions)

1 tablespoon date syrup

1 teaspoon sesame seeds (brown or black)

Heat a large, stainless steel saucepan over high heat. Add the amaranth and stir constantly until the seeds begin to pop and puff. Approximately half of the seeds will puff into white balls; you must remove the pan from the heat before the other seeds burn. Let the seeds cool before storing at room temperature in an airtight container for up to five days.

Spoon the labne into a shallow bowl, using the back of the spoon to make an off-center indentation; fill the well with a spoonful of pomegranate juice and top with a layer of puffed amaranth, a layer of pomegranate seeds, a drizzle of date syrup, and a sprinkling of sesame seeds.

PURSLANE

On a surfing vacation to a tiny town on the coast of Mexico, six girlfriends and I ventured out for food and beer against our better instincts. After a long day of travel, we were reeling and in need of sustenance. So we all agreed to stop at the local *supermercado*, which stocked anything we might need. Among the aisles of mattresses, home hardware, tequila, and pastries, I found purslane, of all things, piled next to bunched epazote and flowering herbs. I felt both awe and appreciation for the culture whose cheap, big-box, commodity-packing department store heeded local produce and seasonality.

Purslane is a weed valued around the world as a delicious ingredient and medicinal herb. Most cuisines include it in some sort of meat stew (such as Mexico's *rebocado*, which includes pork neck and chiles), and it can also be eaten raw, pickled, and stir-fried. Although it shows up all year, it is best in the spring before it flowers. Although it would be reasonable to include purslane with the other weeds in this book (see the "Weeds We Want" chapter), I have too many enticing tips for this special and fairly prevalent plant, so it deserves its own chapter.

Purslane's addictive crisp and juicy texture and succulent-like beauty make it a crowd pleaser as does its flavor of lemon, almonds, chlorophyll, and black pepper. Purslane must be used within a few days of harvest; its own water content causes it to rot quickly. Layer it with a few paper towels in an airtight container and refrigerate; wash it only immediately before using.

CHARRED PADRÓNS, PURSLANE, AND VINEGARED TORPEDO ONIONS

Makes 4 servings

When Padrón peppers are in season, I make some version of this salad every day. The purslane's high note of lemon lifts the rich, spicy peppers away from being overwhelming, and every other bite is punctuated by sweet, tangy, pungent onion. This may appear to be a modern and sparse salad on the palate, but the flavors are unabashedly robust.

¼ cup (or more) extra virgin
    olive oil
1½ pounds Padrón pepper
Coarse sea salt
2 Torpedo onions (or 4 green
    onions), trimmed
1 tablespoon red wine or
    sherry vinegar
2 ounces purslane, cut into
    1- to 2-inch pieces

SERVING SUGGESTIONS
Good, crusty bread
Olive oil–fried egg
Thinly sliced jamón serrano
    or prosciutto
Avocado slices, seasoned with
    lemon juice and coarse
    sea salt

Heat 2 tablespoons of the olive oil in a large, wide skillet over high heat. Add half of the peppers; cook, tossing occasionally with tongs, until the skins are blistered and the flesh is softened, about 3 minutes. Remove the peppers from the heat and transfer them to a bowl; sprinkle them with sea salt, and toss to coat. Repeat the process with the remaining peppers, adding more oil to the pan, if needed.

Meanwhile, thinly slice the onions; toss with the red wine vinegar and a pinch of salt. Let the onions sit in the vinegar while you fry the peppers. This is a quick pickle.

On a platter or in a shallow bowl, layer the Padróns with the onions and purslane. Serve at once, alongside good, crusty bread or, for a complete meal, fried eggs, ham, and seasoned avocado.

PURSLANE AND HERB SALAD
WITH POTATOES AND PANCETTA

=== *Makes 4 to 6 servings* ===

This dish is a study in contrasts: succulent greens layered with soft, starchy potatoes; crispy fat; and crunchy radishes.

2 pounds baby potatoes

6 ounces pancetta, sliced ¼ inch thick

1 tablespoon fresh lemon juice

Fine sea salt

3 tablespoons extra virgin olive oil

2 bunches baby radishes, cut in quarters

4 ounces purslane, cut into 1- to 2-inch pieces

3 cups torn or roughly snipped herbs (chives, tarragon, and/ or parsley)

Preheat the oven to 375°F. Place the baby potatoes in a medium pot and cover with cold water by 1 inch (you start the whole potatoes in cold water so they cook evenly from the center out). Bring the potatoes to a boil over high heat. Reduce the heat and simmer for approximately 20 minutes, or until a paring knife inserted in several potatoes meets no resistance. Remove the potatoes from the heat, drain, and allow them to cool to room temperature. Cut them in half or in quarters, depending on their size.

Meanwhile, place the pancetta slices on a sheet pan lined with parchment paper. Roast in the oven for approximately 15 minutes, or until the pancetta is brown and crispy. Remove from the oven and drain on paper towels.

In a large bowl, whisk together the lemon juice, a pinch of sea salt, and the olive oil. Add the potatoes, radishes, purslane, and herbs. Break the pancetta into large pieces and add to the bowl. Gently toss the salad, plate, and serve at once (really, *at once*; the herbs wilt very quickly).

CHILLED CUCUMBER AND PURSLANE SOUP WITH ARGAN OIL AND PARSLEY POLLEN

Makes 4 to 6 servings

This soup is quite possibly the most refreshing meal you can eat on a hot July day. If you can't find purslane, no worries—use a handful of spinach instead.

1½ pounds Armenian
cucumber, diced

4 ounces purslane, roughly
chopped

2 cups buttermilk

½ cup water

Fine sea salt

Purslane leaves, for garnish

Parsley pollen, for garnish
(optional; see page 9)

Argan oil, for garnish

Freshly ground black pepper

Cut the cucumber in half lengthwise and slice thin. Place the cucumber and most of the purslane in a blender with the buttermilk, water, and 2 pinches of sea salt. Purée until completely smooth. Taste, and add more salt as needed. Pass the soup through a chinois or fine-mesh strainer. Soup can be made two days ahead; cover and chill until ready to serve.

Divide the soup among serving bowls. Garnish each with a few leaves of purslane, a pinch of parsley pollen, a drizzle of argan oil, and a grind of black pepper.

PURSLANE SALAD WITH PEACH, FETA, AND ALMONDS

Makes 4 to 6 servings

I served family-style platters of this salad at a private summer event. I watched guests abandon their plates and forks to pick unabashedly from the center spread. Using their hands, they'd form the perfect bite: a piece of floral and fruity peach; a shard of salty feta; half a crunchy almond; and a sprig of verdant, perky purslane.

2 teaspoons Champagne vinegar

1 tablespoon finely chopped shallot

Fine sea salt

3 tablespoons extra virgin olive oil

3 yellow peaches

4 ounces purslane

Coarse sea salt

Freshly ground black pepper

4 ounces feta cheese, thinly sliced

½ cup Almonds in Almond Oil (see page 80), roughly chopped

In a medium bowl, whisk together the Champagne vinegar, shallot, and a pinch of fine sea salt; set aside for 5 minutes or so (this mellows the shallot and dissolves the salt). Whisk in the olive oil.

Core the peaches and cut each half into ½-inch wedges. Gently toss the peaches and purslane with three quarters of the vinaigrette, a pinch of coarse sea salt, and 2 grinds of black pepper. Taste, and add more vinaigrette or salt as needed—you want the purslane to be delicious and glistening, not leaden and limp with oil. On a serving platter or in a bowl, layer the dressed ingredients with slices of the feta and a scattering of the almonds. I don't like to toss the feta, as it loses its integrity and coats everything in its milky richness (which we want, but as an accent and antidote). Serve immediately.

QUINCE

Every autumn, I keep a bowl of quince on my dining room table. The sweet, floral aroma of the ripening fruit is surprisingly soothing and uplifting, and I wake up grateful for it each day.

I'm not alone in my almost romantic notions of this fruit. In Greek mythology, the quince was the golden apple that Paris used to lure Aphrodite, and when purchasing seeds from a local grocer, I was told that giving someone a quince is "giving love and happiness."

Quince are available October through early January in most regions. Purchase firm fruits with unblemished skin, and store them at room temperature for several weeks. They are ripe when their skin is fully yellow and their fragrance fills the air.

To prepare a quince, wipe off the pretty gray fuzz. Peel the quince, but reserve the peel if you'd like to impart more color to the final dish. Using a sharp knife and your body weight, carefully but firmly cut lengthwise through the fruit and core. Remove the core and seeds, and proceed with the recipe. The white flesh turns brown quickly, so keep a bowl of lemon water nearby to catch the fruit as you cut. You can keep it submerged while you work.

Two recipes in this chapter are simple preparations for a variety of applications: puréed and poached quince. With batches of both on hand, you can easily whip up a variety of dishes:

- A crisp or cobbler—Combine 1 part quince paste with 1 part sugar; cover with your favorite topping (I am into sweet corn-flour biscuits these days) and bake.
- A wonderful condiment for basting a smoked, bone-in ham—Whisk together ½ cup quince purée, ¼ cup melted butter, ¼ cup honey or maple syrup, 2 tablespoons apple cider vinegar, and sea salt to taste.
- A cocktail with quince syrup—Shake 0.75 ounces syrup with 2 ounces gin, 0.75 ounces lemon juice, and a dash of angostura bitters.
- A quince milk drink (it sounds odd, but it's oh so good)—Blend 2 cups milk, 2 tablespoons quince paste, 2 tablespoons sugar, and 2 drops rose water together; serve chilled.

WINTER ROOT AND QUINCE TAGINE

Makes 6 servings

A recommendation: make more of this dish than you plan to serve. Purée the leftover stew, thinning it with a bit of water; rewarm and top each bowl of soup with a drizzle of yogurt and olive oil, a few tablespoons of warm couscous, and a few cilantro leaves.

Ideally the potatoes and turnips should be cut to approximately the same size as the quince, since they cook at similar rates; halve, quarter, or dice them accordingly.

1 cup chickpeas, soaked overnight

Fine sea salt

2 tablespoons extra virgin olive oil

2 tablespoons butter

1 red onion, peeled and cut into quarters

2 garlic cloves, sliced

1 small (½-pound) quince, peeled and cut into 1½-inch dice

½ teaspoon ground toasted coriander seeds

½ teaspoon ground toasted cumin seeds

1 cinnamon stick

1 chile de arbol

4 baby potatoes, scrubbed and cut in halves or quarters

6 baby turnips, scrubbed and cut in halves or quarters

2 small fennel heads, cut in quarters

15 ounces canned whole tomatoes and their juices, crushed with your hands

½ Preserved Lemon (see page 282), finely chopped

½ teaspoon saffron threads

6 baby carrots, scrubbed

TO SERVE

Extra virgin olive oil

Steamed couscous

Labne and harissa

Cilantro leaves

Drain the chickpeas; place in a pot with 2 pinches of sea salt and water to cover by 3 inches. Bring to a boil over high heat; lower the heat and simmer for 30 to 35 minutes, or until almost tender. Remove the beans from the heat and drain, reserving the cooking water for steaming couscous, if you wish.

In a 5½- to 7-quart pot, heat the olive oil and butter over moderately high heat. Add the onion, garlic, quince, coriander, cumin, cinnamon, chile de arbol, and a pinch of salt. Cook, stirring occasionally so the spices don't burn, for approximately 6 minutes, or until the onion begins to brown. Add the potatoes, turnips, fennel, tomatoes, preserved lemon, and partially cooked chickpeas, along with a cup or so of the bean cooking water (the liquid should rise halfway up the sides of the vegetables). Add the saffron and 2 pinches of salt. Bring the mixture to a boil over high heat; lower the heat and simmer for approximately 15 minutes. Add the carrots; simmer for 8 to 10 minutes more, or until all the vegetables are tender (soft enough to pierce effortlessly with tongs but not at all mushy). Taste, adding more salt if needed. Remove the dish from the oven and let it rest for 15 minutes before serving.

Drizzle in a bit more olive oil. If you'd like, serve the tagine on top of warm couscous and alongside little bowls of labne, harissa, and cilantro leaves.

POACHED QUINCE

Makes 6 to 8 servings

Poached quince can be sliced and used in galettes, tarts, and apple pies. If you'd like to serve it alone, perhaps adorned with a bit of labne or whipped crème fraîche, transfer the cooked quince to a bowl, and return the poaching liquid to a boil over high heat. Reduce the liquid until it coats the back of a spoon, about 20 minutes, and strain this reduction over the quince before serving.

6 cups water

2 cups honey

2 strips lemon rind

1 vanilla bean, split

Fine sea salt

4 small quinces (about
   2 pounds), rinsed and dried

Use a pot you're sure is large enough to accommodate the quince pieces in one even layer; add the water, honey, lemon rind, vanilla bean, and a pinch of sea salt. Bring to a boil over high heat; lower the heat and simmer until the honey has dissolved.

Peel the quinces, then cut them in half and core; reserve a few of the peels. Add the fruit and reserved peels to the syrup, and return to a simmer. Reduce the heat further, until only a few slow bubbles rise to the surface (approximately 165°F). Poach the quinces, turning occasionally, until tender, about 30 to 40 minutes (depending on their size and ripeness). Remove the pot from the heat and allow the quince pieces to cool in the poaching liquid. The quince can be made two days in advance; keep the fruit in the syrup, cover, and refrigerate until ready to use.

QUINCE PURÉE

Makes about 2 cups

This purée is easily scaled up; just maintain the ratio of quince to lemon. For homemade *dulce de membrillo*, which is a sweet, thick jelly common in Spain, reduce this purée in a saucepan with an equal volume of sugar (for example, 1 cup purée to 1 cup granulated sugar).

2 large quince (about 2 pounds), peeled, cored, and cut into 2-inch dice

2 medium lemons, seeded and cut into quarters (I prefer Lisbon lemons for this.)

Place the quince and lemon in a medium saucepan; cover with water by 2 inches. Bring to a boil over high heat; lower the heat and simmer until the quince is so soft it is collapsing, about 45 to 55 minutes. Remove from the heat and strain. Place the quince and lemon in a food processor, and purée until completely smooth. Store in an airtight container in the refrigerator for up to one week.

VARIATION: WARM QUINCE PURÉE WITH COLD CREAM

The contrast of the warm, fragrant purée and cold, rich cream seems elegant and whimsical, an effect that beguiles the truly humble nature of this dish.

Makes 2 servings

1 cup Quince Purée

Approximately ½ cup maple syrup

Fine sea salt

Cold heavy cream, for serving

1 cinnamon stick, for serving

Heat the quince purée, maple syrup, and a pinch of sea salt over moderately low heat, stirring constantly, until the mixture is warmed through. Taste, adding more maple syrup, if you'd like. Remove from the heat. Spoon into a small serving bowl and top with a spoonful of cold cream. Use a Microplane to grate a little cinnamon on top.

QUINCE 195

QUINCE VINAIGRETTE FOR BITTER GREENS

A vinaigrette for bitter greens profits from a little fruit (or an anchovy). Here, quince purée acts as an emulsifier and a soft sweetener. This recipe also works well with apple or pear purée.

1   shallot, peeled and finely
    chopped
1   tablespoon Quince Purée
    (see page 195)
1   tablespoon fresh lemon juice
Fine sea salt
3   tablespoons extra virgin
    olive oil
1   tablespoon walnut oil
Freshly ground black pepper

In a large mixing bowl, whisk together the shallot, quince purée, lemon juice, and a pinch of sea salt. While whisking, add the olive oil and walnut oil. Season with black pepper. The vinaigrette can be made up to eight hours ahead.

QUINCE, ALMOND, AND BROWN BUTTER TORTE

Makes 6 to 8 servings

This cake was my first foray into baking with quince. It happens to be gluten-free, but I chose the almond and buckwheat because their nutty and stony flavors complement the quince by grounding its tropical fruit and floral notes.

Softened unsalted butter, for greasing the pan

3 or 4 Poached Quince halves, cut into ⅛-inch slices (see page 194)

7 tablespoons (3½ ounces) Brown Butter, at room temperature (see page 287)

Approximately ½ cup plus 2 tablespoons (3½ ounces) granulated sugar

3 large eggs, at room temperature

Approximately 1¼ cups (5 ounces) almond flour

¼ cup plus 2 tablespoons (2 ounces) buckwheat flour

¼ teaspoon baking powder

½ teaspoon fine sea salt

Preheat the oven to 350°F. Line a 9-inch springform pan with parchment paper; grease the bottom and sides with softened butter.

For cakes that have thick batters, the easiest way to line a springform pan is take a square of parchment paper and lay it across the base of the separated pan. Clasp the springform round on top (there will be overhang, and that's fine). This method ensures that you can spread the batter evenly across the base of the pan without a circle of parchment moving around.

In the bottom of the pan, arrange the quince slices in two or three concentric, overlapping circles. I like to start at the perimeter of the cake and move inward.

Place the brown butter and sugar in a large food processor; pulse until combined. Add the eggs and pulse to combine. Place the almond flour, buckwheat flour, baking powder, and sea salt in a medium bowl and whisk to combine. Add the dry ingredients to the food processor; pulse until the batter is thoroughly mixed, scraping down the sides with a spatula, as needed.

Scrape the batter over the fruit; use an offset spatula or the back of a spoon to spread it evenly. Bake for about 40 to 50 minutes, until the cake is golden brown and pulling away from the sides of the pan. Remove from the oven, and cool the cake in the pan for at least 20 minutes. Release the springform pan and cool the torte completely before serving.

RADICCHIO

"Like someone has disguised an ancient household astringent as a sturdy piece of lettuce." This is one friend's first impression of radicchio.

The reaction is justifiable. Most people's first instinct is to spit out highly astringent or bitter ingredients, since these flavors are associated with poisonous plants. But there is ample evidence to support that tolerance can be acquired and that tolerance often evolves into affection. Just consider how we consume coffee, tea, dark chocolate, beer, herbal liqueurs, and dark leafy greens, and it is obvious that most experienced palates appreciate the dimension astringency and bitterness provide.

The same person who once likened this bitter vegetable to a scouring agent grew to desire it. She now reports that over time she began to appreciate that if it was balanced with other flavors, she enjoyed "the bitter bite."

Radicchio is a chicory that is easy to grow. It can be served raw, simmered, sautéed, roasted, and even grilled. When we seek to balance its intensity, we get to employ some exciting sidekicks like pork fat, preserved fish, and vinegar.

Radicchio's red color and bitter flavor indicate its ability to help cleanse the blood and lymphatic system. Like most highly pigmented leafy plants, it is a significant source of calcium and vitamins C and A.

Radicchio has a few varieties, including Treviso, Castelfranco, Chioggia, and Verona, and all of these chicories can be used in the recipes that follow. They vary slightly in flavor yet differ primarily in the waxiness and length of their leaves. You'll spot them in farmers' markets from April through December. Like all leafy greens, radicchio should be stored in the refrigerator in an airtight container lined with a few paper towels. It tends to last longer than other leafy plants; I once found an abandoned bag that had remained tucked in the crisper drawer for more than a week with little loss of quality.

One of the absolute easiest things to do with radicchio is to toss halved heads in olive oil and salt, grill them until brown, and season them with acid and a pungent, salty something (such as preserved lemon, bottarga, or fried onions). Just a little longer in prep time is a salad of thinly sliced Treviso with shaved Parmigiano-Reggiano, lemon juice, and olive oil. And if you are willing to spend even a few more minutes, try the recipes that follow.

ROASTED CAULIFLOWER, TREVISO, AND CRISPY SPECK

Makes 4 to 6 servings

Roasting cauliflower brings its inherent sweetness to the fore and dims its characteristic cabbage-like flavor. The smoky speck is an addictive surprise; I find myself seeking out little morsels among the pieces of Treviso, which keeps each bite light and refreshing. An exception to the general rule, this salad is still delicious the next day.

Fine sea salt

½ cup toasted farro

4 tablespoons extra virgin olive oil, separated, plus more for tossing

Juice of ½ lemon

2 medium cauliflower heads

2 rosemary sprigs

2 chiles de arbol, cut in half

2 teaspoons red wine vinegar

2 tablespoons fresh thyme leaves

2 radicchio heads, torn into 2-inch pieces

2 cups cooked white beans, such as cannellini

Crispy Speck (recipe follows)

Preheat the oven to 475°F. Fill a medium pot with water and add 2 pinches of sea salt; bring to a boil over high heat. Add the farro and cook for approximately 35 to 45 minutes (different brands of farro vary greatly in cooking times), or until the grain is al dente. Remove from the heat, drain the farro, and return it to the pan. Season with 2 tablespoons of the olive oil, the lemon juice, and a pinch of salt. Set aside.

Trim the base of the cauliflower and cut each head into 2-inch florets; cut the core into 2-inch pieces. Toss the florets, leaves, and core wedges with enough olive oil to coat. Add the rosemary, chile de arbol, and a generous pinch of salt; toss again. Spread the cauliflower out on a sheet pan, making sure there is 1 inch of space between the pieces. Roast for approximately 35 minutes, or until the cauliflower is caramelized. Once cooled slightly, taste, and add more salt if needed.

In a large bowl, whisk together the red wine vinegar, a pinch of salt, the thyme, and the remaining 2 tablespoons of olive oil. Toss the radicchio and beans with the vinaigrette.

In a large, wide, shallow serving bowl, layer half the caramelized cauliflower, farro, radicchio, and torn pieces of crispy speck; top with a second layer of the remaining ingredients.

CRISPY SPECK

Speck is basically smoked prosciutto. I like to eat it freshly sliced and cold, with nothing more than bread, olive oil, and a few slices of an Orange Pippin apple. Yet I also love it roasted and incorporated in pasta, in a sandwich, over braised greens, or as a garnish.

¼ pound thinly sliced speck

Preheat the oven to 400°F. Line a sheet pan with parchment paper. Lay the slices of speck across the pan in one even layer. Roast for approximately 10 to 12 minutes, or until each piece has begun to crisp at the edges. Remove from the oven and let cool slightly before using (it will continue to crisp up as it sits).

Crispy speck keeps fairly well for up to twenty-four hours. Cool completely, then store at room temperature in an airtight container lined with paper towels.

SPELT AND RADICCHIO RISOTTO

Makes 4 to 6 servings

For winter risottos, consider farro or spelt over the standard rice; the nutty, earthy flavor complements seasonal items like kale, pumpkin, and chicories. However, unlike arborio or carnaroli rice, cooking times for farro and spelt grains vary widely. When making a risotto with a new grain, keep a kettle of warm water nearby so you can continue adding extra liquid after all of the stock has been used, if necessary.

2 medium radicchio heads

3 tablespoons extra virgin olive oil

1 rosemary sprig

1 chile de arbol

Fine sea salt

Approximately 2 quarts chicken stock

5 tablespoons unsalted butter

3 shallots, finely chopped

1 cup semipearled farro or farropiccolo from Anson Mills

3 ounces Parmigiano-Reggiano or pecorino romano cheese

3 tablespoons crème fraîche

½ cup roughly chopped parsley

Freshly ground black pepper

Prepare the radicchio by cutting it into quarters through the root end and cutting away any tough core. Slice each quarter ½ inch thick from the root end to the tip.

Set a medium sauté pan over moderately high heat; add the olive oil, rosemary, and chile de arbol. Stir in the radicchio and a pinch of sea salt; cook for 5 to 7 minutes, tossing occasionally with tongs. Meanwhile, place the chicken stock in a small saucepan and bring to a simmer over moderately high heat.

Heat the butter in a medium, preferably wide saucepan over moderate heat. Add the shallots and 2 pinches of salt. Cook for 2 to 3 minutes, stirring once or twice. Add the farro and cook 2 to 3 minutes more, stirring to coat the grains in the hot butter.

Ladle the hot stock over the farro, ½ cup at a time, stirring until the liquid has been completely absorbed before adding more stock. Continue this process until the farro is tender; this may take from 20 to 40 minutes, depending on the brand you use. When the grains are al dente, stir in the sautéed radicchio. Cook 3 to 4 minutes longer, stirring well to incorporate and combine. Add more stock or water as needed; you want it slightly soupy (the farro will continue to absorb more liquid, even when you take it off the heat).

Remove the pan from the heat. Stir in the cheese, crème fraîche, and parsley. Taste, and season with salt and black pepper.

RADICCHIO AND CHICKEN SALAD WITH WALNUTS AND PICKLED GOLDEN RAISINS

Makes 4 to 6 servings

This salad is a lunchbox staple. The sturdy leaves of chicories hold fairly well, even after they have been dressed. The pickled raisins take the edge off the raw radicchio, and the abundance of walnuts makes it hard to stop eating.

2 bone-in, skin-on chicken breasts (or leftover roast chicken)

½ cup extra virgin olive oil, plus more for rubbing the chicken

Fine sea salt

Freshly ground black pepper

2 cups walnuts

1 tablespoon walnut oil

Zest of ½ lemon

2 teaspoons fresh lemon juice

2 medium shallots, finely chopped

2 large radicchio heads, leaves stacked and chopped into 2-inch dice

Approximately ½ cup Pickled Raisins (recipe follows)

½ cup parsley leaves

½ cup mint leaves, torn if large

Preheat the oven to 400°F. Rub the chicken breasts with olive oil, and season with sea salt and pepper. Place on a sheet pan lined with parchment paper (which makes for easy cleaning), and roast for 30 minutes, or until golden brown and just cooked through. Remove the chicken from the oven and cool slightly. Take the meat off the bones and chop into 1- to 2-inch pieces; set aside.

Meanwhile, spread the walnuts on a sheet pan or in a medium skillet; toast in the 400°F oven for 8 to 10 minutes, or until golden brown. Remove them from the oven, roughly chop, and toss with the walnut oil and a pinch of salt.

Add lemon zest and juice to a large bowl. Add a pinch of salt and the chopped shallots; allow the shallot to mellow in the acid for a few minutes. Whisk in ¼ cup of olive oil; taste, and add another tablespoon if the lemon's acid is still too prominent. To this vinaigrette, add the chicken, walnuts, radicchio, raisins, parsley, mint, a pinch of salt, and some black pepper; toss well. Taste, then adjust the salt, pepper, lemon juice, and olive oil.

PICKLED RAISINS

Makes ¾ cup

¼ cup honey

2 tablespoons Champagne
   vinegar (or white wine vinegar)

½ cup water

¾ cup golden raisins

1 bay leaf

1 teaspoon fine sea salt

Add all the ingredients to a medium saucepan and bring to a boil over high heat. Reduce the heat and simmer until the liquid reduces by half, about 15 to 17 minutes. Remove from the heat and let the mixture cool completely. Store the raisins in the pickling liquid in a jar with a tight-fitting lid and refrigerate for up to three days; strain before using.

RAMPS

If you are fortunate enough to encounter a display of pristine ramps, purchase them and make plans to cook them immediately. If you find a few spindly things with droopy greens and slightly wet roots, consider this purchase as well. We should buy whatever ramps there are whenever there are ramps, as long as they are not sopping wet and showing signs of rot.

Ramps are wild leeks, and that is exactly how they taste. I find them at New England farmers' markets, specialty grocers, and online dealers from April through May. Their recent surge in popularity among restaurant chefs and home cooks has led to overharvesting in some areas; I urge you to do some research on your source.

It is wise to cook ramps as soon as possible, but if you must store them, wrap them loosely in paper towels, seal them in an airtight bag, and refrigerate for a day or two.

Here are some simple techniques for preparing ramps:

· Sliced and sautéed in ample butter and good salt (a beautiful base for anything and a wonderful topping for morning toast)
· Grilled on a cedar plank
· Fried in tempura batter
· Baked in an egg dish, such as a frittata, tortilla, or kuku
· Stuffed into the cavity of a whole fish or chicken, alongside lemon slices and fresh thyme
· Thrown in the roasting pan a few minutes before the potatoes are done

FORAGER'S SOUP WITH HAM HOCK AND MINT

Makes 6 servings

If you find yourself with a bunch of wild greens with long, woodsy stems and big leaves, choose soup over salad. The stems actually add viscosity, and when blended with ramps and mint, the relatively vigorous flavor of the plants results in a more interesting and balanced bowl.

6 tablespoons unsalted butter

½ pound ramps, thinly sliced

3 starchy potatoes (such as Yukon Gold, Kennebec, and russet), cut into ¼-inch dice

Fine sea salt

1 ham hock

1 chile de arbol

4 cups Kombu Stock (see page 281)

¾ pound spicy and/or bitter wild greens (such as dandelion, cress, wild arugula), roughly chopped

½ pound bright and/or grassy wild greens (such as sorrel, chickweed, blanched nettles), roughly chopped

½ cup baby mint leaves, plus more for garnish

Zest of ½ lemon

½ teaspoon fresh lemon juice

Extra virgin olive oil

Fine sea salt

Coarse sea salt

Heat the butter in a large pot over moderate heat. When the foam subsides, add the ramps, two-thirds of the potatoes, and 2 pinches of fine sea salt. Cook, stirring occasionally, for 4 to 5 minutes. Add the ham hock, chile de arbol, kombu stock, bitter and bright greens, and a pinch of fine sea salt. Simmer over low heat for 1 hour, or until the greens are soft and the ham is beginning to fall off the bone.

Stir in ¼ cup of the mint leaves; discard the chile. Remove the ham hock and set aside; once it is cool enough to handle, shred the meat from the bone and season it with a pinch of salt. Remove the soup from the heat and pass it through a food mill or purée it in a blender. Taste, and adjust the seasoning.

Place a medium skillet over moderate heat; add enough olive oil to reach a depth of ⅛ inch. Add the remaining diced potato and 2 pinches of fine sea salt; sauté until tender and golden brown, about 9 minutes. Season the potato with the lemon zest and juice. Remove from the heat.

Pour the soup into oven-warmed bowls; top each serving with a drizzle of olive oil, a few pieces of pan-fried potato, a few pieces of ham hock, a few small or torn mint leaves, and a pinch of coarse sea salt.

SAUTÉED RAMPS, LEMON, AND BOTTARGA

Makes 6 servings

This is the dish for showing off a perfect array of ramps. Bottarga, a traditional delicacy of both Sicily and Sardinia, is salted, pressed, and dried mullet roe. It tastes strongly of fresh fish and the sea. To store leftover bottarga, rub down the cake with good-quality olive oil, wrap it first in plastic wrap and then in foil, and store it in the refrigerator. Rubbed once a week with olive oil, it should keep for at least three months. If you can't find bottarga or don't want to endure the expense (as it is costly), you can substitute Parmigiano-Reggiano here with great results.

4 tablespoons unsalted butter

24 ramps

Fine sea salt

2 ounces bottarga

1 lemon, cut into wedges

Heat the butter in a large sauté pan over moderate heat. When the foam subsides, add the ramps and 2 pinches of sea salt. Sauté, shaking the pan occasionally, until the ramps are tender, approximately 6 to 7 minutes. Remove from the heat and cool slightly; transfer the ramps to a platter. Using a Microplane, grate the bottarga over the ramps. Serve with lemon wedges.

ROASTED ARTICHOKES WITH RAMP MAYONNAISE

Makes 4 to 6 servings

Ramp mayonnaise is dangerous stuff. When I have a jar of it, I cater my cooking to meet its needs—steaks, grilled octopus, boiled potatoes, and these sweet and crispy artichokes.

24 baby artichokes

½ cup extra virgin olive oil

2 chiles de arbol, cut in half

Fine sea salt

2 to 3 teaspoons fresh lemon
juice

TO SERVE

1½ cups Ramp Mayonnaise
(recipe follows)

1 cup baby fava or mint leaves

Coarse sea salt

Preheat the oven to 450°F. Line two sheet pans with parchment paper.

Slice off the top third of each artichoke with a serrated knife, and cut off the tip of the stem. Pull off the outermost dark green leaves around the heart as well as the small leaves around the bottom.

Divide the artichokes between the two pans, and toss each pile with enough olive oil to coat, 1 chile de arbol, and a pinch of fine sea salt. Spread the artichokes into an even layer on both pans, making sure there is enough space between them for water to evaporate quickly, so the artichokes will caramelize. Roast for 20 to 25 minutes, or until a deep golden brown.

Remove from the oven, and season the artichokes with lemon juice. Serve with ramp mayonnaise, garnished with a few baby fava or mint leaves and coarse sea salt.

RAMP MAYONNAISE

Makes 1 cup

4–6 ramps, trimmed
(4 ounces total)

2 large egg yolks, at room
temperature

1 tablespoon fresh lemon juice

½ teaspoon fine sea salt

1 cup grapeseed oil

In a blender, combine the ramps, egg yolks, lemon juice, and sea salt. Mix thoroughly. With the motor running on low (so you don't get splattered), slowly add several teaspoons of the grapeseed oil, drop by drop, until the mixture begins to thicken. With the motor still running, add the remaining oil in a steady stream. Stop the motor periodically and scrape down the sides of the blender with a flexible spatula; this ensures all the bits of ramp are incorporated and puréed.

Taste for seasoning to see if you prefer more lemon juice or salt. Transfer the mayonnaise to a small container, seal, and refrigerate until ready to use. The mayonnaise can be stored, covered and refrigerated, for up to three days.

ROSE PETALS

I arrived in Marrakesh on a dark August night. The ride from the airport included a barrage of loud and foreign speech, nudged bumpers, and daring scooters. Rushing through my line of vision were women robed in turquoise, kids with balloons, blaring boom boxes, and emaciated camels. Upon entering the confines of the medina, the chaos continued. The call to prayer echoed. When I finally reached the door of the white-walled *riad* (a traditional house with an interior garden), I was greeted with the scents of orange blossoms, smoke, and baking bread. I felt especially porous.

I remained open for the remainder of the trip, especially at mealtimes. I got lost and tasted everything I could. The combinations of sweet and savory penetrated: honey with pigeon, prunes with beef, and dates with onion. Yet it was the copious and effective use of rose petals and rose water that enchanted me the most: a salad of citrus and black olives, a hot pepper relish with cumin, spiced lamb kebabs, a dessert of ground nuts and dried fruit, a cup of cold almond milk, and a mysterious brew of spiced coffee. These encounters transformed my cooking.

Spring and summer are the seasons to seek fresh roses; dried petals can be purchased year-round from specialty markets, tea shops, and online. Choose unsprayed and fragrant blooms. Keep the flowers in a vase of water, and pull petals as needed.

There are many ways to incorporate roses:

· Add fresh or dried petals to herbal tea or combine them with black tea leaves.
· Make a classic Middle Eastern dip. Combine plain sheep's milk yogurt with minced garlic, a pinch of dried mint, finely chopped Persian cucumber, soaked currants, and salt; garnish with olive oil, more currants, dried mint, and dried rose petals.
· Make Almond Picada (see page 37), but add soaked, dried rose petals and a bit more chile; serve with grilled lamb and/or grilled vegetables.
· Finely crush the petals and add to pastry or shortbread doughs; the addition is especially welcome in *maamoul*, a Middle Eastern cookie stuffed with puréed dates.
· Steep petals in warm heavy cream, then strain; the rose cream can be used for ganache, truffles, panna cotta, and crème brulée.
· Steep petals in simple syrup, then strain; the rose syrup can be used to make sorbets (especially good with strawberry, rhubarb, or raspberry), lemonade, and poached fruit.

TWELVE-HOUR LAMB SHOULDER WITH RAS EL HANOUT

Makes 6 to 8 servings

One question I'm most often asked is, "What is your favorite thing to cook?" My answer always seems too complex for such a simple inquiry. So I often do a nimble dodge: "Whatever I'm cooking in the moment is my favorite thing to cook." But my favorite thing to *eat* is always the same: this dish.

Plan to start this dish a day or two before you're going to serve it. While the actual hands-on time is mere minutes, the success of the dish depends on a long, slow preparation. I serve this with couscous or lavash and a salad of sliced radishes and herbs.

One 4-pound bone-in lamb
   shoulder, patted dry
2 tablespoons fine sea salt
¼ cup extra virgin olive oil
½ cup Ras el Hanout (recipe
   follows)
3 medium carrots, cut in half
   crosswise
1 red onion, peeled and cut
   in half lengthwise
1 fennel bulb, cut in quarters
1 garlic head, cut in half (or 3
   green garlic stalks, trimmed)
1 Preserved Lemon, cut in half
   lengthwise (see page 282)
2 tablespoons unsalted butter
2 cups water

Ideally, you'll prep the lamb shoulder the night before you plan to cook it; this presalting and prespicing is a dry brine, and it will create the best results. Place the shoulder in a large roasting pan with at least 2-inch sides. Season the meat generously with the sea salt. Rub it in olive oil and massage in the ras el hanout. Tuck the carrots, onion, fennel, garlic, and preserved lemon around the meat. Add a pat of butter on top. Cover and refrigerate the lamb overnight.

Allow the meat to come to room temperature before roasting; this step is essential and requires 1 to 2 hours. Preheat the oven to 425°F. Roast the shoulder at this heat for 20 minutes, then lower the temperature to 275°F. Add the water to the pan and cover tightly. Cook the shoulder for 12 to 16 hours. You can baste the meat a few times, or you can leave it alone completely. Braises are wonderful in this way; they don't ask for much.

During the last hour of cooking, uncover the pan; this allows some remaining moisture to evaporate, yielding a nice crust around the meat. All meat should rest before serving, and in the case of a 4-pound joint, give it a good 30 minutes. Discard the vegetables, or make An Unusual Breakfast (page 215).

DANDELION & QUINCE 214

RAS EL HANOUT

Ras el hanout means "top of the shop." Theoretically, every shop owner in Morocco has his or her own proprietary blend. This is mine. I like it on lamb; in a tagine of sardines; and as part of a marinade for grilled vegetables (particularly red peppers, red onions, and summer squash).

½ cup cumin seeds

¼ cup coriander seeds

3 tablespoons fresh chili flakes
   (I pulse a chile de arbol in
   a spice grinder.)

¼ cup dried rose petals

5 tablespoons smoked paprika

1 tablespoon black peppercorns

2 tablespoons ground cinnamon

½ teaspoon allspice

⅛ teaspoon freshly grated
   nutmeg

Set a medium skillet over moderate heat. Add the cumin, coriander, and chili flakes. Toast the spices, tossing regularly, until they release their aromas and have turned a shade darker. Be careful not to burn the spices or they will turn bitter. Remove the spices from the heat and pour them into a spice grinder, mortar, or repurposed coffee grinder; let cool to room temperature. Add the rose petals, smoked paprika, peppercorns, cinnamon, allspice, and nutmeg. Grind to a powder. The blend can be stored in an airtight container in a cool, dark place for up to three months.

AN UNUSUAL BREAKFAST

I have this little tradition that emerged in a moment when hunger converged with thrift. I had prepared Twelve-Hour Lamb Shoulder for a private client; the joint had braised in my home oven overnight. I woke to the scent of coffee and cooking bones. I was ready for breakfast but without much to eat. As I lowered the shoulder into a hotel pan for transport, I glanced at the collapsed carrots, onions, and garlic cloves that had given almost all of their flavor to the liquid. My belly was empty and hot.

I ladled the vegetables—along with a bit of the fat and broth—into a bowl and mashed them with a fork. I stirred in half a cup of leftover rice and took a bite. It needed coarse salt, so I gave it a pinch. With that and only that, I had a most nourishing and exciting breakfast.

I've continued using braised vegetables this way ever since. If I don't need the vegetables to add texture to some sauce (in which case, they make their way through a food mill and back into the pan), then they become breakfast: stirred into rice, slathered on grilled bread, or puréed into soup.

I've shared this ritual with a few others, and for some reason, I'm always a little embarrassed when I do. My friend Gabe has told me on more than one occasion that I eat like a refugee. My mother looked at me with a mix of skepticism and hopelessness right before devouring her serving and pushing me to include it in this book. Folks are just amazed at how utterly delicious mushy vegetables in animal fat seem to be. So I'm relinquishing any residue of self-consciousness. I am very happy to share this unusual breakfast with you.

BLACKBERRY, RYE, AND ROSE CAKE

Makes 8 servings

Rye flour is dark, earthy, and a little funky. The blackberries and rose petals lift and balance those qualities, and the result is a cake that is as unique as it is harmonious.

7 ounces unsalted butter, at room temperature, plus more for greasing the pan

2 tablespoons dried rose petals

About 1 cup (8 ounces) granulated sugar

About 1½ cups (10 ounces) blackberries

6 large eggs

2½ cups (10 ounces) almond flour

¾ cup (4 ounces) rye flour

1 teaspoon fine sea salt

½ teaspoon baking powder

1 batch Whipped Crème Fraîche (see page 284)

Line a 9-inch springform pan with parchment paper; butter it liberally. For cakes that have thick batters, the easiest way to line a springform pan is take a square of parchment and lay it across the base of the separated pan. Simply clasp the springform round on top (there will be an overhang, and that's fine). This method ensures that you can spread the batter evenly across the base of the pan without a circle of parchment moving around.

Preheat the oven to 375°F. Crush the rose petals with 3 tablespoons of the granulated sugar using a mortar and pestle. Toss the blackberries with 2 tablespoons of the rose sugar in a small bowl, then crush into a coarse purée using the tines of a fork (pieces of fruit should still be discernible).

Combine the butter and remaining sugar in a food processor, and pulse until combined. Whisk together the eggs and add them to the processor; pulse to combine.

Whisk together the almond flour, rye flour, sea salt, and baking powder in a medium bowl. Add the dry ingredients to the food processor, and pulse until the batter is thoroughly mixed, scraping the sides of the bowl as needed.

Spread one third of the batter into the prepared pan, then gently spoon the crushed blackberries on top. Carefully spread the remaining batter over the blackberries. Scatter the rest of the rose sugar on top (you may not use it all). Bake until the cake has set and turned a deep golden brown, 45 to 50 minutes. Remove from the oven and let it cool completely before unmolding and slicing. Serve with whipped crème fraîche. Store the leftover cake covered at room temperature for up to three days.

RASPBERRY AND ROSE KVASS

Makes approximately 1 quart

Fermented foods are an invaluable source of beneficial enzymes and bacteria. Most traditional diets tout cultured products, and there seems to be a resurgence of interest among modern foodsmiths in this country. Fermentation is having a moment, and I hope it's here to stay.

While many folks are now keeping kombucha mothers, preserving lemons, and packing jars with salted cabbage, very few people speak of kvass. Yet this Russian beverage is one of the easiest and most delicious home fermentation projects.

It is essential that you use raw honey; the microbes in an unpasteurized jar act as a starter culture. While springwater isn't a must, chlorinated tap water can slow things down.

You could easily double this recipe and make a big batch of homemade soda, but I recommend starting small until you feel confident watching the process and tasting for a mature product. If you are really excited about preservation and homemade probiotics, take a look at Sandor Katz's grand tome, *The Art of Fermentation*.

2 cups raspberries

¼ cup dried rose petals

2 tablespoons raw honey

3 cups spring water

Sterilize a 1-quart glass jar with boiling water. Set aside to dry.

Place the raspberries and rose petals in the sterilized jar; smash slightly with a fork. Add the honey and enough water to fill the jar, leaving 1 inch of space between the top of the liquid and the rim.

Tightly cover the jar with its lid, and keep it in a fairly warm spot (such as near a window). Shake the jar a few times a day (this helps prevent bacteria from forming) and look for bubbles. When you see bubbles, press on the center of the lid. After a few days, the lid will bulge, telling you it is time to carefully open it and release some of the gas.

Tighten the lid on the jar once again. In another day or two (no shaking necessary), you'll likely see bubbles in the still jar. When these bubbles become vigorous, your kvass is ready.

Refrigerate the kvass until cold. Strain it through a fine-mesh strainer or chinois. You can drink it immediately, or refrigerate it in an airtight container for up to two weeks.

SHALLOTS

I'm as shocked as some of you that shallots could be considered "an unusual vegetable." But truly, every time I teach a cooking class, there are at least a few folks who have never seen this tiny cousin of the onion and others who recognize it but consign it to vinaigrettes.

From this moment forward, I implore you never to leave a market without a few shallots in your bag. They can transform your cooking, adding allure to the most quotidian dishes.

Shallots taste like onions but are sweeter, more aromatic, and more powerful. They are crisp and juicy when raw, creamy when cooked, and crunchy when fried. They are available year-round but are fresh in spring, boasting green shoots like their garlic kin. There are several varieties of shallots—yellow, red, and gray—and while I am slightly partial to the Dutch red, any type you find can be used in the recipes that follow.

Treat spring shallots as you would green garlic (see page 115). When purchasing the adult bulbs with a thick, papery skin, give them a soft squeeze to make sure they are plump and firm; avoid any that show signs of sprouting or excessive mildew. Shallots can be stored at room temperature for two to three weeks, depending on when they were harvested. Trim, peel, and rub them clean before using.

Shallots can replace yellow onions in many recipes. I primarily use them in vinaigrettes; as a quick pickle; or as a fried, crispy garnish. But there are endless uses for them. Here are a few others:
· Finely diced and incorporated into classic sauces like tartar and béarnaise
· Finely diced and stirred into a not-so-classic sauce, such as shallot tzatziki (in winter, when cucumbers are out of season)
· Left whole, peeled, and salt-baked (see Salt-Baked Sweet Potatoes, Alliums, and Bean Sprouts on page 242); then drizzled with a bit olive oil and a squeeze of lemon to make a simple but special side dish
· Cut in half lengthwise and pan-roasted with a gastrique, a reduced syrup of equal parts vinegar and sugar (For shallots, I recommend apple cider vinegar and maple syrup.)

CRISPY EGGPLANT WITH PICKLED SHALLOTS, GREEN CHILES, AND THAI BASIL

This is my favorite late summer dish; I eat as much as my belly can stand. I especially enjoy serving it up when there is a self-proclaimed eggplant hater around—this recipe boasts a 99 percent conversion rate.

I like to serve it with steamed rice and a roasted pork loin. You can swap out the Thai basil for some fresh mint leaves and take the meal into a Middle Eastern territory with chicken baked in za'atar and frisée with pomegranate seeds.

2 pounds Japanese eggplant, sliced ⅛ inch thick

¾ cup melted virgin coconut oil

Fine sea salt

3 limes, cut into wedges

¾ cup Quick Pickled Shallots (see page 222), drained

5 green onions, thinly sliced

3 serrano chiles, thinly sliced

3 cups baby Thai basil or mint leaves (or large leaves, torn or roughly chopped right before use)

Coarse sea salt

Extra virgin olive oil

Preheat the oven to 475°F. Line two sheet pans with parchment paper. Divide the eggplant between the baking sheets and toss each with ¼ cup of the coconut oil and a pinch of fine sea salt. Use your hands to thoroughly rub the oil into the flesh, adding more oil if there are any uncoated, matte spots on the eggplant. Spread the slices in an even layer across the pans; you want a good ½ inch of space between the pieces so the water from the vegetable evaporates quickly. Roast for approximately 35 minutes, turning the slices once, or until the eggplant is dark brown and slightly crispy. Remove from the oven and allow the eggplant to cool slightly before composing the salad.

Place a single layer of crispy eggplant on a serving platter; season each slice with a squeeze of lime. Top with a thin layer of pickled shallots, green onions, chiles, and about 1 cup of the Thai basil leaves. Season with coarse sea salt, and drizzle with about 2 teaspoons of olive oil. Repeat the layers until you've used up all of your ingredients, ending with a top layer of herbs, coarse salt, and olive oil. Serve with a side of lime wedge.

QUICK PICKLED SHALLOTS
AND SHALLOT VINEGAR

Makes approximately 1 cup

This is a simple process that leaves with you two products: an enormously versatile pickle and flavored vinegar. These shallots are tangy, pungent, and slightly sweet; they brighten and complicate any dish they touch. I often have them on hand and find endless uses for them (there are five in this book alone).

10 small (or 6 large) shallots (about ½ pound)

¼ teaspoon fine sea salt

Approximately ¾ to 1 cup red wine vinegar (Banyuls is my favorite.)

Cut the shallots crosswise in $\frac{1}{16}$-inch slices; I use a mandoline for this. Toss the shallots with the salt and pack them loosely in a jar with a tight-fitting lid. Add enough red wine vinegar to cover the shallots by 1 inch (or more, if you want more shallot vinegar). Set the mixture aside for at least 30 minutes (or refrigerate for up to four days).

SHALLOT PURÉE

Makes 6 servings

This ivory purée makes a perfect bed for grilled asparagus, lentils, or wild salmon (or all three together).

---

1 pound shallots, sliced
½ inch thick

3 tablespoons Shallot Oil
(see page 225)

Fine sea salt

Bring a medium pot of salted water (approximately 5 cups) to a boil over high heat. Blanch the shallots in the boiling water for 5 minutes. Remove from the heat and drain. Return the shallots to the pot with more salted water, and return the pot to the stove; repeat the process two more times. This repeated blanching softens and sweetens the shallots.

Place the shallots in a blender with ¼ cup water, the shallot oil, and 2 pinches of sea salt. Purée until smooth, adding more water if necessary to achieve a thick purée. Taste, and adjust the seasoning. Use immediately or refrigerate in an airtight container for up to three days. Before serving, place the purée in a small saucepan over low heat, stirring constantly, until it is warmed through.

CRISPY SHALLOTS AND SHALLOT OIL

Makes approximately 2 cups

In my kitchen, pickled shallots and crispy shallots are indispensable. Crispy shallots alone appear several times in this book regularly in my kitchen. Recently, I've been grinding them into my spice blends (curry, baharat, berbere, ras el hanout) too.

My preferred method for caramelizing and crisping up thinly sliced shallots is relatively slow; it results in evenly golden, perfectly sweet little chips that keep for almost two days. You can certainly achieve consistent, thin slices with a sharp knife and a lot of practice. However, a mandoline makes it easy, delivering precision and speed simultaneously.

Approximately 3 cups grapeseed oil, pork fat, or rice bran oil (or other fat with a high smoke point)

5–6 large shallots (½ pound), cut lengthwise in ¹⁄₁₆-inch slices

Line a sheet pan with a double layer of paper towels. Set a medium saucepan over moderately high heat; I use stainless steel so I can easily determine the color of the shallots as they cook. Add enough oil to reach a depth of 2 inches. Heat the oil until it reaches 350°F; I can tell by using a candy thermometer (a handy tool, if you plan to fry regularly) or by dropping in a few shallot slices and seeing if they bubble and jump right away.

Add the shallots and give them a stir with a slotted spoon or spider strainer. Lower the heat slightly; the shallots should still be simmering. Cook, stirring once or twice, until the shallots are a light golden brown, about 15 minutes (they will continue to cook after removed from the oil). Use a spider or slotted spoon to remove them from the oil and transfer them to the paper towels to drain. Use immediately or store at room temperature in an airtight container for up to two days.

Strain the shallot oil through a fine-mesh strainer. Store at room temperature in an airtight container for up to two weeks. This delicious ingredient can be used to flavor dressings or marinades or to fry more shallots.

GREEN SHALLOTS BAKED WITH COMTÉ

Makes 6 servings

Here is an easy, gratin-like preparation that doesn't require a béchamel sauce. I like to serve these shallots with a whole roast chicken and a salad of edible flowers (see page 79).

24 green shallots

4 to 5 tablespoons unsalted butter, melted

Fine sea salt

Freshly ground black pepper

½ pound Comté cheese, grated

Bring a pot of salted water to a boil. Line a sheet pan with a clean kitchen towel. Blanch the shallots in the boiling water for approximately 5 to 7 minutes, or until the bulbs are tender enough to be pierced with the tip of a knife. Remove from the heat, drain the shallots, and immediately spread them out on the towel-lined pan to cool and dry.

Preheat the broiler. Butter a shallow baking dish just large enough to hold all of the shallots snugly. Place the shallots in the dish (I like to alternate the direction of the bulbs and greens); brush with butter and season with sea salt and black pepper. Top with an even layer of cheese and broil for approximately 5 minutes, or until the cheese is bubbly and a deep golden brown (I'm actually a fan of a few dark brown spots).

SORREL

If you've spent any time flipping through this book, my immense love for citrus and herbs should be apparent. Sorrel is basically both. It has the sharp, bright flavor of lemon and the lively, grassy, mysterious something that characterizes herbs. I'm smitten.

Some foods need acid to balance out their dominant flavor. For example, beets taste so earthy, that I won't take a bite until Banyuls red wine vinegar lifts their earthiness above ground. Yet that same vinegar is too harsh for dishes with raw fish; cocktails; or sweet, tender greens. When I want to season such foods without overpowering them, I turn to milder brighteners like citrus zest, crème fraîche, sumac, purslane (see page 183), or our star here—sorrel.

Sorrel is harvested spring through fall and must be used within a few days of purchase, so buy small amounts. It has an affinity for seafood (especially salmon), eggs, potatoes, bacon, steak, and cream. Loosely wrap the leaves in paper towels and refrigerate in an airtight container.

I use sorrel as both an herb and a vegetable. Here are a few ways to think about it:

· Add it, along with watercress, to a pea and potato soup.
· Sauté whole leaves with shallots, butter, salt, and pepper; along with a pinch of grated Gruyère, this is a fantastic filling for an omelet.
· Finely chop those same sautéed leaves, and add them to hollandaise sauce.
· The sharpness of sorrel is perfect for eggs, so make an herb frittata with chopped dill, thinly sliced sorrel, and minced chives.

BAKED OMELET WITH SORREL, DILL, AND TOASTED FENUGREEK

Makes 2 servings

Fenugreek is a classic addition to Iranian egg dishes. The combination is genius, in part because fenugreek tastes like breakfast: maple and butter and cured meat are its funkiest aromatic compounds. This crazy little legume is smaller than a peppercorn and has a pale golden hue. Toasting it whole is an important step toward understanding what it has to offer.

Sorrel, with its lemon-forward flavor, is a wonderful complement to fenugreek and a classic pairing for eggs.

¼ cup olive oil, divided

5 sorrel leaves

4 whole eggs

Fine sea salt

¼ cup finely chopped dill

½ teaspoon freshly ground toasted fenugreek

2 egg whites

Fenugreek sprouts and/or dill flowers, for serving

Coarse sea salt

Preheat the oven to 400°F. Place 2 tablespoons of the olive oil in a small baking dish or 9-inch skillet, and place it in the oven.

Stack, roll, and thinly slice the sorrel. In a medium bowl, beat the whole eggs with 2 pinches of fine sea salt; add the sorrel, dill, fenugreek, and remaining olive oil. Beat the egg whites until soft peaks form. Fold the egg whites into the sorrel and egg mixture; mix until no white streaks remain.

Remove the preheated pan from the oven; swirl the oil around so it coats the bottom and sides well. Pour the omelet into the pan and bake 20 to 25 minutes, or until it is puffy and golden brown. Remove from the oven, turn out on a plate, and garnish with the sprouts and coarse sea salt.

SALT COD FRITTERS WITH SORREL MAYONNAISE

Makes 6 servings

Salt cod is cod that has been preserved by salting and drying. It is an affordable and versatile ingredient to have in your larder. I soak more than I need for this recipe and incorporate it into a few meals throughout the week (poached and flaked into hash, risotto, pasta, or soup). You can find salt cod at some fishmongers and supermarkets, as well as at Italian delicatessens (as *baccalà*), at Mexican *tiendas* (as *bacalao*), and online. You can also make your own.

1 pound dried salt cod

1 pound starchy potatoes (such as Yukon Gold, Kennebec, and russet)

Fine sea salt

2 tablespoons extra virgin olive oil

2 eggs

1 cup almond flour

1 quart grapeseed or rice bran oil

Flaky sea salt

Sorrel mayonnaise (recipe follows)

Soak the salt cod in cold water for two days, changing the water two to three times each day. The cod will expand as it absorbs the water. Remove the cod from the water and pat dry.

Put the potatoes in a pan with enough water to cover them; add a pinch of fine sea salt and bring to a simmer over moderate heat. Cook the potatoes for about 20 minutes, or until a paring knife inserted in several of them meets not resistance. Remove from the heat, drain, and peel the potatoes; use a ricer or potato masher to mash them until they are smooth. Season with fine sea salt to taste.

Rinse the pan and return it to high heat; bring 3 cups water to a boil. Reduce the heat to poaching temperature, then add the soaked cod. Poach the fish for 25 minutes, or until it flakes easily when pressed with a fork. Remove the cod from the heat, drain, and transfer to a medium mixing bowl. Flake the fish apart thoroughly with a fork, discarding any bones and skin. Add about ¼ cup of the mashed potato to the cod, and beat the mixture with a wooden spoon or spatula, adding the olive oil gradually, followed by the remaining potato. Beat in 1 egg. Refrigerate the mixture at least 1 hour, or up to overnight.

Beat the remaining egg in a shallow bowl. Place the almond flour in another shallow bowl. Remove the cod mixture from the refrigerator and form it into golf ball–size balls. Coat the balls in the beaten egg, then roll them in the almond flour. Refrigerate for 15 to 30 minutes before frying.

In a large, deep stockpot, heat the grapeseed oil to 355°F. Line a large plate or sheet pan with paper towels. Fry the fritters in batches until they are a deep golden brown, approximately 4 to 5 minutes per batch. Remove from the oil and drain on the paper towels; sprinkle with flaky sea salt with a spider strainer. Serve with the sorrel mayonnaise.

SORREL MAYONNAISE

Sorrel mayonnaise is rich, bright, and perfect with fish in any form. Also consider spooning it on roast potatoes, inside a steak sandwich, or next to a pile of steamed vegetables.

Makes 1 cup

4 ounces sorrel leaves, thinly sliced
2 large egg yolks, at room temperature
1 tablespoon fresh lemon juice
½ teaspoon fine sea salt
1 cup grapeseed oil

In a blender, combine the sorrel leaves, egg yolks, lemon juice, and sea salt. Blend thoroughly. With the motor running on low, slowly add several teaspoons of the grapeseed oil, drop by drop, through the small opening in the blender lid, until the mixture begins to thicken. Now that the egg proteins have sufficiently unraveled, the process can move forward at a faster rate. With the motor still running, add the remaining oil in a steady stream. Stop the motor periodically and scrape down the sides of the blender with a flexible spatula; this ensures all the bits of sorrel are incorporated and puréed.

Taste for seasoning; see if you prefer more lemon juice or salt. Transfer the mayonnaise to a small container, seal, and refrigerate until ready to use.

The mayonnaise can be refrigerated in an airtight container for up to three days.

A GLASS OF GREEN

Green. Sometimes I can hear my body demanding it. I eat a hell of a lot of vegetables, but I also tend to balance them with healthy doses of coffee, meat, and whiskey. When the scale tips in favor of the more acidic foods in my diet, I reach for a dose of chlorophyll.

When your face receives the message (ofter indicated by zits, puffy eyes, or a white tongue) that you need to alkalize your system, make this green smoothie. If you've never used sorrel, this is a great way to become familiar with its sprightly flavor: green but barely grassy, tangy, and about as bright and refreshing as it gets.

2 bunches sorrel, thinly sliced

1 bunch kale, stemmed and thinly sliced

2 Armenian cucumbers (or 1 English cucumber, peeled and seeded), chopped

1 ripe avocado, chopped

3 kiwis, peeled and chopped

¼ cup fresh lemon juice

¼ teaspoon fine sea salt

3 cups cold water

Place all the ingredients in a blender. Purée until completely smooth (this can take up to 2 minutes in a home blender). Serve immediately or refrigerate for up to four hours.

SPROUTS

Sprouts of beans, grains, and seeds are relatively digestible and teem with energy and bioavailable nutrients. One ounce of sprouts can contain more beneficial nutrients than pounds of the plant's nonsprouted version. Through the process of sprouting seeds attain extraordinarily high levels of enzymes, vitamins, protein, and B vitamins. One note of caution: children and people with weakened immune systems should not eat raw sprouts unless they are absolutely sure of the integrity of the growing environment (always purchase from a grower you trust or grow your own).

Purchase only fresh sprouts that started from organic seed; if there is any sign of a slime-like dampness or a smell of spoilage, avoid or discard them. Refrigerate sprouts in an airtight container, layered with paper towels, for three to four days. They are incredibly easy to make, and I've outlined the general process on page 238. The following are a few of the legumes and grains I regularly sprout at home.

Buckwheat (not actually a cereal grain) contains all eight essential amino acids, an abundance of calcium, vitamin E, and the many of the B-complex vitamins. I only use buckwheat sprouts in raw preparations, as they are incredibly delicate and wilt with the slightest application of heat or even oil. They take approximately six to eight hours to sprout.

Chickpeas take three to four days to grow a half-inch tail. They are an exceptional source of iron and vitamin C.

Fenugreek sprouts have a bold flavor I adore, and their wispy texture enables me to pile them on. In three to four days' time, a tablespoon of fenugreek seeds yields a quart of sprouts.

Lentil sprouts develop quickly; eight to twelve hours of soaking is all that is needed. Unlike beans, lentils contain little sulfur and are therefore easier for sensitive systems to digest. They are a good source of calcium, magnesium, iron, phosphorous, potassium, and vitamin A.

You need to let *radish* seeds sprout until their tails are one or two inches long, and this can take five to six days.

Pea shoots are not actually sprouts, but since they have similar uses and effects on health, I've included them in this chapter. They are incredibly sweet and vary in size from little microgreens to large-leafed stems that require cooking.

HOMEMADE SPROUTS

Makes approximately 2 cups bean sprouts or 4 cups sprouted seeds

Sprouting beans is one of the easiest DIY projects you can take on, and after just a few simple steps, this staple ingredient is more digestible and more versatile. I like them as is; their crunchy texture and fresh, vegetal flavor are a welcome addition to salads, bowls of cooked grains or rice, even the now ubiquitous avocado toast. Yet I also use them cooked, which softens their bite and further improves their digestion (and in half the time it typically takes).

1 cup dry organic beans or seeds

Rinse the beans or seeds, and place them in a wide-mouth container. Add filtered or spring water to cover. Cover the container with cheesecloth; secure the cloth with a jar ring (or rubber band, twine, or tape; it needs to be secure for the next step), and let the seeds soak for 24 hours at room temperature.

Drain and rinse the seeds through the cloth. Repeat this twice, or until the water runs clear.

Store the jar on its side with its bottom propped up a bit, on top of a kitchen towel (which will catch the excess water draining out the top). Keep the jar at room temperature. Rinse and drain the seeds once every 4 to 12 hours (it needn't be exact) until you have a tail (for most sprouts, you are looking for ¼ to 1 inch). See the chapter introduction on the previous page for approximate times for certain seeds. The exact timing will depend on the temperature of the environment and the age and size of the seed.

Rinse and drain the seeds once more, and allow your sprouts air dry. To store, place them in an airtight container or plastic bag with a dry paper towel; refrigerate for two to five days, replacing the paper towel periodically. Do not eat sprouts that have any brown discoloration or a slimy wetness.

SAUTÉED PEA SHOOTS, GINGER, AND WHITE SHOYU

Makes 4 servings

This dish is fast, filling, and full of strong, clean flavors. When served over steamed brown rice, it makes a complete meal.

2 tablespoons grapeseed oil

1½ pounds pea shoots

Fine sea salt

4 tablespoons unsalted butter

One 4-inch piece of ginger, finely chopped

2 to 3 serrano chiles, finely chopped

5 shallots, thinly sliced

12 green garlic stalks, white and pale-green parts only, cut into 2-inch pieces

Freshly ground black pepper

¼ cup white shoyu or tamari

A splash of brown rice vinegar

12 green onions, cut into 2-inch pieces

Heat the grapeseed oil in a large sauté pan over moderately high heat. Fry the pea shoots until wilted, about 2 minutes, stirring constantly with chopsticks or tongs. Pour the wilted shoots onto a plate. Return the pan to moderate heat and add the butter.

Add the ginger, chiles, shallots, green garlic, and a pinch of salt; cook until the vegetables are soft, about 10 minutes. Stir in black pepper to taste (I like quite a bit in this recipe), the white shoyu, and the brown rice vinegar.

Return the pea shoots to the skillet; cook, stirring constantly, until warmed through (this only takes a minute). Stir in the green onions; cook a minute or two more, or until the scallions wilt.

WATERMELON SALAD WITH BUCKWHEAT SPROUTS AND FETA

Makes 4 servings

I love the Ferry Plaza farmers' market. It can be chaotic and chilly, but for me, happiness can be found in a Saturday morning full of crowded tents where complete strangers mingle while sorting and storing an abundance of fresh produce. I'm often there—browsing, chatting, and lingering—for well over two hours. By the time I unload my basket and bags, I have a fiercely growling stomach. I always use this opportunity to prepare the most delicate and perishable items I've purchased, which more often than not are the items I'm the most excited to eat.

The pink stems of buckwheat sprouts, fading to white, led me to pair them with watermelon. Accented with pungent shallot, grassy cucumber, and salty feta, the result is as stunning as it is delicious.

½ cup Quick Pickled Shallots (see page 222)

1 teaspoon Shallot Vinegar (see page 222)

Fine sea salt

2 tablespoons extra virgin olive oil

Flesh of ½ watermelon, sliced into bite-size pieces, ¼ inch thick

3 small Persian or Armenian cucumbers, thinly sliced

2 cups buckwheat sprouts (or sunflower, purslane, mâche, watercress, or wild arugula sprouts)

2 cups lightly packed herb leaves (parsley, mint, and/or cilantro)

4 ounces feta cheese, sliced ¼ inch thick

¼ teaspoon sumac

Coarse sea salt

In a small mixing bowl, whisk together the shallots, shallot vinegar, a pinch of fine sea salt, and the olive oil. On a large serving platter, arrange one haphazard layer of sliced watermelon and cucumber; spoon half the vinaigrette on top. Scatter half of the sprouts and herbs on top, followed by half of the feta and sumac and a pinch of coarse salt. Repeat the layers once more. Serve immediately—the herbs and sprouts wilt quickly.

SALT-BAKED SWEET POTATOES, ALLIUMS, AND BEAN SPROUTS

When mixed with a variety of alliums—tangy pickled shallots, potent green onions, and green garlic—sweet potatoes make an exciting side. Salt-baking them lets you slice them especially thin; this technique can be applied to any root vegetable you like. If you have difficulty digesting legumes, I recommend that you cook the sprouted beans in salted water for 15 minutes; drain, cool, and proceed with the recipe.

4 cups kosher salt

About ½ cup water

4 Japanese sweet potatoes, scrubbed

2 cups bean sprouts (lentil, mung, or chickpea)

2 serrano chiles, finely diced

Juice of ½ lemon

Extra virgin olive oil

Fine sea salt

Coarse sea salt

½ cup Quick Pickled Shallots (see page 222)

3 green onions, thinly sliced

2 green garlic stalks, white and pale-green parts only, thinly sliced

2 cups roughly chopped dill

2 cups loosely packed parsley leaves

Lemon wedges, for serving (optional)

Preheat the oven to 425°F. In a medium bowl, toss the kosher salt (I use kosher for this, as it is more affordable and there is no real loss of flavor) with the water, tablespoon by tablespoon, until the mixture looks like shaved ice. Spoon a layer of the dampened salt onto the bottom of a large skillet or roasting pan; pat it down to make a nice bed. Set the sweet potatoes on top of the salt; pack the remaining salt on and around them. Roast for 90 minutes, or until a skewer or paring knife inserted through the salt and into the sweet potatoes meets little resistance. Remove from the oven and cool slightly, about 10 minutes. Crack the outer salt shell with a spoon and pull it away. Brush away any excess salt from the sweet potatoes with a dry pastry brush or kitchen towel. Peel the potatoes, if you'd like; then cut them crosswise in ⅛-inch slices.

In a small bowl, toss the bean sprouts with the serrano chiles, lemon juice, 2 tablespoons of the olive oil, and a pinch of fine sea salt. Place a single layer of sweet potatoes on a serving platter or in a wide, shallow bowl; season with a pinch of coarse sea salt. Top with a thin layer of the pickled shallots (I like to sprinkle a bit of the pickling vinegar on as well), green onions, green garlic, seasoned sprouts, dill, and parsley. Give the herbs a pinch of coarse sea salt and a drizzle of olive oil. Repeat these layers until you've used up all of your ingredients, ending with a final layer of herbs, coarse salt, and olive oil. Serve with a side of lemon wedges or more pickled shallots for those who (like me) prefer a more acidic bite.

BEEF BROTH WITH BEAN SPROUTS

Makes 6 servings

I keep a shelf stocked with whiskey and mezcal; I love spirits and the spirit they invoke. For the occasions when I drink a shade too much, I know I can make this soup the following day. Beef broth with bean sprouts alkalizes the body and grounds an expanded mind. For a more substantial, pho-like meal, add cooked and rinsed rice noodles right before serving.

2 pounds beef short ribs

Fine sea salt

6 cups filtered water

One 2-inch piece of kombu

2 garlic cloves

1 yellow onion, cut in half
   lengthwise

1 leek, cut in half lengthwise

3 cups soybean sprouts,
   trimmed of roots

2 green onions, thinly sliced

Extra virgin olive oil

Chile flakes (optional)

Season the ribs with sea salt. If you have the time, let the ribs sit for a few hours at room temperature (or refrigerate overnight).

Place the ribs, water, kombu, garlic, onion, leek, and ½ teaspoon salt in a large pot set over high heat; bring to a boil. Reduce the heat to poaching temperature; there should be small and sporadic bubbles. Braise the ribs for approximately 2 hours, or until the meat leaves the bone with only the slightest pressure from tongs.

Remove from the heat. Strain the broth through a fine-mesh strainer or chinois, reserve the meat, discard the vegetables, and rinse the pot. Return the broth to the pot and season to taste with salt. At this point, you can add a bit of the meat back to the soup, or reserve it for another meal (think: hash, pasta sauce, tacos, or fried rice).

Bring the broth to a simmer over moderate heat. Add the bean sprouts and green onions; cook gently for a minute or two. Serve the soup warm, with a drizzle of olive oil and, if desired, a sprinkle of chile flakes.

SPROUTED CHICKPEA CROQUETTES, YOGURT, TAHINI, AND CORIANDER

Makes 4 to 6 servings

These croquettes have a falafel-like appearance but a lighter texture, and they can be made with any bean you like. Cold the next day, you can halve them on a sandwich; break them into a chopped salad of cucumbers, tomatoes, feta, and chiles; or simmer them gently in a spicy tomato sauce.

2 cups cooked or sprouted chickpeas (see page 238 to make your own)

2 spring onions, finely chopped

Zest of ½ lemon

2 tablespoons finely chopped fresh mint

2 tablespoons finely chopped fresh cilantro

1 teaspoon ground coriander

½ teaspoon ground cumin

1 teaspoon fine sea salt, plus extra for seasoning

1 teaspoon ground toasted sesame seeds

1 cup chickpea flour

1 teaspoon whole toasted sesame seeds (white, brown, or black), plus 2 table spoons, for serving

¼ cup whole sheep's milk yogurt

¼ cup tahini, plus more for drizzling

1 garlic clove

Juice of ½ lemon

½ cup water

Rice bran oil or grapeseed oil

4 radishes, thinly sliced

1 cup mixed cilantro, mint, and/or fava leaves, picked

Place the sprouted chickpeas in a small saucepan and add water to cover. Bring to a simmer over moderate heat, and cook the beans for 10 to 12 minutes. Remove from the heat and strain. Place the sprouted chickpeas in the bowl of a food processor. Add the spring onions, lemon zest, mint, cilantro, coriander, cumin, ground sesame seeds, and the teaspoon of salt. Process until all ingredients are coarsely blended. Sprinkle in the chickpea flour and pulse to combine; add flour until the dough forms a ball that no longer sticks to your hands. Turn the dough into a bowl and refrigerate, covered, for at least 1 hour (or up to overnight).

Meanwhile, place the yogurt, tahini, garlic, lemon juice, a pinch of salt, and ½ cup water in a blender; blitz until smooth. Add more water as needed to achieve your desired consistency.

Form the chickpea mixture into balls about the size of walnuts (you can use an ice cream scoop to make it easier). Line a sheet pan with paper towels; have a spider strainer or a slotted spoon handy. Heat 3 inches of oil to 325°F in a deep pot or wok, and fry a croquette to test the temperature of the oil and the consistency of the dough. If the ball falls apart, add a little flour to the mix.

Fry 6 to 8 croquettes at a time, for a few minutes on each side, or until golden brown; drain on paper towels when they are done.

Serve with a drizzle of tahini sauce and a scattering of sliced radishes, mixed herbs, and toasted whole sesame seeds.

CHOPPED SUMMER SALAD

Makes 4 to 6 servings

My favorite summer salad is a quirky and substantial one: sprouts with strongly flavored salumi, fresh chiles, and Swiss cheese. Sprouted—as opposed to boiled—legumes add a much-needed, refreshingly vegetal flavor and subtle crunch. To make this salad vegetarian, simply omit the meat.

2 shallots, finely chopped

1 serrano chile, finely chopped (or if you really like heat, 2 serrano chiles, thinly sliced)

1 tablespoon red wine vinegar

Fine sea salt

3 tablespoons extra virgin olive oil

2 pounds little gem lettuce or baby romaine, cut into ½-inch dice

1 cup baby spinach leaves

2 cups mixed sprouted beans

1 cup sunflower sprouts, cut in half crosswise

¼ cup flat-leaf parsley leaves, roughly chopped

¼ pound sliced salumi (such as Nostrana), thinly sliced

5 ounces Gruyère or Comté cheese, shaved with a Swiss peeler or sharp knife

1 cup pitted green olives, cut in half

1 pound green zebra tomatoes, cut in quarters

Coarse sea salt

Freshly ground black pepper

In a large bowl, whisk together the shallots, chile, red wine vinegar, and 2 pinches of fine sea salt. Set aside for a minute or two while you prep the other ingredients, then whisk in the olive oil. Add the remaining ingredients along with some coarse sea salt and black pepper; toss gently to combine.

SQUASH BLOSSOMS

Squash blossoms are edible flowers, but they have their own chapter because their relatively large size, sturdy structure, and barely floral flavor make them suitable to a wider range of techniques.

Squash blossoms start showing up in late spring and are often available until early fall (depending on your local climate and a particular year's weather). I try to find perky, closed buds, but often they are slightly open and a little limp. I purchase what I can find and choose applications suited to the quality. I use the tightest, brightest blossoms for salads and tempura and keep the others for fillings and soups.

To prepare the golden flowers, cut off the stems and remove the sepals (the stamens are edible). Remove any bugs and clean gently with a brush, if needed. Squash blossoms can be eaten raw or cooked. When they hit the heat, they wilt to more than half of their raw size, so plan accordingly.

Here are a few simple techniques for using squash blossoms:

- Chop and add them—along with fresh goat cheese—to a big, puffy, egg white omelet showered in freshly cracked black pepper.
- Tear and toss them into a salad of avocado, jicama, little gem lettuce, and queso fresco or Chopped Summer Salad (see page 247).
- Keep them whole and fry them into fritters or tempura; keep the batter light, using whipped egg whites or sparkling water.
- Cut them in thin slices and right before serving stir into a brothy soup of summer vegetables that includes red torpedo onion, baby zucchini, tomatoes, hot and sweet peppers, and basil.

QUESADILLAS CON FLOR DE CALABAZA

Makes 1 to 2 servings

Quesadillas are classic Mexican street food. At home, I enjoy replicating the process I've learned from observation: preparing masa, pressing my own tortillas, and cooking them on a lightly greased *comal* (clay griddle).

Starving after surfing and in the middle of nowhere in Mexico (without a *comal*), I watched my friend Eve (a superb cook) employ this speedier technique with delicious results.

1 to 2 teaspoons lard, rice bran oil, or grapeseed oil

2 ounces queso Oaxaca (or other string cheese)

2 corn tortillas

4 squash blossoms, roughly chopped

Fine sea salt

SERVING SUGGESTIONS

Salsa cruda

Lime wedges

Pickled jalapeño pepper

Radishes, cut in quarters

Place a medium skillet over moderate heat; add enough lard to reach a depth of ¼ inch.

Pull apart about 1 ounce of the queso Oaxaca, and place on one side of a tortilla. Top the cheese with a handful of squash blossoms and a pinch of sea salt; fold the tortilla in half to enclose the filling. Fry the quesadillas in the lard for 2 to 3 minutes on one side. Use a spatula to flip from the open end, making the movement decisive and swift (a fish spatula is a handy tool here). Fry for 2 to 3 minutes on the second side, or until a deep golden brown.

SHAVED SUMMER SQUASH
AND BLOSSOM SALAD

Makes 4 servings

Thin-skinned summer squash comes in a variety of shapes and a range of greens and yellows. It's fun to seek out a few and shave them lengthwise so that their unique form remains apparent on the plate: squat and sunny pattypan, pale green scallop, pine-hued Ronde de Nice, and color-blocked Zephyr. Because this dish features raw squash and little else, I recommend using the smallest ones you can find because their flavor diminishes as their size increases. Even then, their flavor is quite neutral and must be coaxed out by a warm bath of olive oil, butter, and aromatics.

4 tablespoons extra virgin olive oil

2 tablespoons unsalted butter

2 tablespoons finely chopped garlic

1 chile de arbol, torn in half crosswise

Fine sea salt

Zest and juice of 1 small lemon

1 pound baby summer squash (multiple varieties)

3 cups baby opal basil leaves

10 squash blossoms

5 ounces Parmigiano-Reggiano

Set a small pot over low heat; add the olive oil, butter, garlic, chile de arbol, and a pinch of fine sea salt. Cook for 2 minutes, then set aside to infuse. Stir in the zest and juice of half the lemon. Discard the chile.

Thinly slice the squash with a mandoline or Swiss peeler. In a large bowl, toss the squash with the warm marinade. The marinade will steam the squash slightly, and this is what you want. Set aside for at least 5 minutes.

Lay the marinated squash on a platter. It shouldn't look too perfect; let the slices fall onto the plate—some folding, some flopping, some flat. Scatter the basil leaves and the torn squash blossoms on top. Quickly run a Swiss peeler across the Parmigiano-Reggiano to create shavings. Add more basil leaves (they are an integral ingredient). Repeat the layering once more. Spoon 1 to 2 teaspoons of the remaining marinade on top.

TOASTED QUINOA, BABY ZUCCHINI, AND SQUASH BLOSSOMS

Makes 6 servings

Rinsing, draining till dry, and toasting may seem like extraordinary measures for a humble quinoa salad. But these three steps result in a fluffy, nutty, delicious dish that pleases even the most adamant quinoa skeptics. If you really want to cut down on prep time, this dish is also delicious made with bulgur, which requires nothing more than a pot of boiling water and 20 minutes to steep.

½ cup pine nuts

3 cups water

2 cups white quinoa

Fine sea salt

2 tablespoons fresh lemon juice

½ cup extra virgin olive oil

8 baby zucchini, about 1 inch in diameter (1 pound), sliced ¹⁄₁₆ inch thick

¼ cup currants

1 chile de arbol, thinly sliced

¼ cup fresh oregano leaves

10 squash blossoms, torn

Preheat the oven to 350°F. Spread the pine nuts on a sheet pan lined with parchment paper and toast them for 5 to 7 minutes. Remove from the oven and let cool.

Rinse the quinoa: pour the grains into a fine-mesh strainer set over a large bowl and run water over them. Swish the grains around with your hand. Raise the strainer. If the water is clear and there are no bubbles, no more rinsing is needed. If the water is cloudy or sudsy, rub the grains gently against the strainer. Lift the strainer and empty the bowl. Fill with fresh water, and repeat until the water remains clear and there are no bubbles on the surface. (Red and black quinoa may bleed color, not to be mistaken with dirt or other impurities.) Allow the quinoa to dry in the strainer. This rinsing and drying step can be done 8 to 12 hours ahead.

Bring the 3 cups of water to a boil in a kettle or small pot. Reduce the heat and keep at a simmer until ready to use. Toast the dry quinoa in a medium saucepan set over moderate heat, stirring constantly with a wooden spoon, until the quinoa gives off a nutty aroma and is a few shades darker. Carefully pour the hot water over the quinoa (do this slowly or it will boil over). Add 2 pinches of sea salt. Reduce the heat and simmer for approximately 15 to 17 minutes, until the water is absorbed. Add the lemon juice and olive oil. Fluff with a fork, cover, and cool to room temperature. Toss the quinoa with the remaining ingredients and another pinch of salt. Taste and add more chile, lemon juice, olive oil, or salt to suit your palate.

SQUASH BLOSSOM FLATBREAD WITH ANCHOVY BUTTER AND ARUGULA

This anchovy butter is similar to Italian bagna cauda (hot bath). It is an ideal sauce for bitter or relatively bland foods (such as radicchio, kale, zucchini, pasta, bread, and so on), all of which benefit from the sweetness of butter, the punch of chile, and the uniquely addictive quality of pounded anchovy. It also makes an impressive spread for an odd but fabulous sandwich: baguette, ricotta, grilled green garlic (see page 116), butter lettuce, and anchovy butter. Like all yeasted breads, you'll need to start this recipe (pictured on page 248) a few hours before you plan to serve it.

1 recipe Semolina Dough
  (see page 285)

¼ cup extra virgin olive oil

¼ cup Anchovy Butter
  (recipe follows)

8 squash blossoms, stemmed

A handful of baby arugula or
  arugula sprouts

Coarse sea salt

Prepare a grill; the heat should be fairly high and the rack about 4 inches from the fire. Alternatively, place two ungreased sheet pans in the oven and preheat it to 500°F.

Once the dough has risen fully, cut it into 4 equal pieces and roll each one out until it's about 6 inches in diameter; I prefer an oval shape. Brush one side with olive oil and put as many on the grill or hot sheet pans, oiled-side down, as will comfortably fit at one time. Brush the top with oil and close the grill or oven. Cook for approximately 7 to 9 minutes, or until the flatbread is puffed and golden brown. Remove the bread from the heat and brush liberally with anchovy butter; top with the torn squash blossoms, arugula, and coarse sea salt.

ANCHOVY BUTTER

Makes approximately ½ cup

½ cup unsalted butter

2 salt-packed anchovies,
  soaked, deboned, and minced

Fine sea salt

6 garlic cloves, minced

2 chiles de arbol, cut in half

Zest of 1 lemon

2 teaspoons fresh lemon juice

Place the butter in a medium saucepan over moderate heat to melt. Add the anchovies and stir constantly with a wooden spoon until they begin to dissolve, about 3 minutes. Reduce the heat to low and add a pinch of sea salt, the garlic, and the chiles de arbol (seeds and all). Continue to cook for 1 minute more. Turn off the heat and allow the garlic to finish cooking in the residual heat. Add the lemon zest and juice; stir to combine. Refrigerate in an airtight container for up to two days; reheat gently before serving, readjusting the acidity (lemon juice) and salt as needed.

SUNCHOKES

Sunchokes are dirty, knotty kids. You can either scrub them in a bowl of water or peel them. Once peeled, the alabaster flesh of this tuber will quickly turn brown. If you want the final product to remain relatively white, you must add them to acidulated (lemon) water or vinaigrette as you work.

Sunchokes thrive in the cooler months and are most readily available September through January. They are also referred to as Jerusalem artichokes, but considering they are members of the sunflower family, this seems like a misnomer. Purchase firm tubers that show no signs of sprouting. Sunchokes are a good source of vitamins A and B, potassium, calcium, and even iron. They also provide inulin, a type of dietary fiber that is especially beneficial for regulating blood sugar.

A sweet, subtle, earthy flavor and a crisp texture with no starch make sunchokes suitable for a wide range of cooking techniques. Beyond the following recipes, there are a few more ways to prepare them:

- Shaved on a mandoline and deep-fried or baked into chips
- Cut into ½-inch dice; pan-fried with Brussels sprouts and apple (and bacon, if that's your thing); and finished with a splash of cider vinegar
- Sliced ¼-inch thick and sautéed with chicories, olive oil, and chile de arbol; finished with a squeeze of lemon; and tossed with a farro pasta and grated cheese
- Braised with beef cheeks, beef stock, and red wine and garnished with coarsely chopped parsley

SHAVED SUNCHOKE SALAD WITH SUNFLOWER SPROUTS, SUNFLOWER SEEDS, AND MANCHEGO

Makes 4 servings

Perhaps this salad leans precariously close to a gimmick with its heavy-handed motif. But I assure you, the flavors and textures all work wonderfully well together. This is one of my favorite fall dishes.

1 shallot, minced

2 teaspoons sherry vinegar

Freshly ground black pepper

Fine sea salt

¼ cup extra virgin olive oil

1 pound sunchokes

1 pint sunflower sprouts, cut in half crosswise

¼ cup toasted sunflower seeds

4 ounces manchego cheese

In a medium mixing bowl, whisk together the minced shallot, sherry vinegar, a few grinds of black pepper, and a pinch of sea salt. Whisk in the olive oil.

Using a mandoline or a sharp knife, thinly slice the sunchokes to about ⅛ inch thick; add them to the vinaigrette as you work. Add the sunflower sprouts and another pinch of salt; toss gently to combine.

Arrange the salad on a serving platter (leave excess vinaigrette behind); scatter the sunflower seeds on top, and finish with shavings of manchego cheese.

SUNCHOKE AND CHESTNUT SOUP WITH CARAMELIZED CHESTNUTS AND PUMPKIN SEED OIL

Makes 4 to 6 servings

This soup is simple, enticing, and comforting. Puréed sunchokes are a canvas on which many flavors can be painted, and caramelized chestnuts and potent pumpkin seed oil create a special hue. Try them on a number of puréed fall and winter soups, such as pumpkin, celeriac, cauliflower, or potato-leek.

5 tablespoons unsalted butter

2 leeks, thinly sliced

Fine sea salt

2 pounds sunchokes, scrubbed

8 ounces cooked and peeled chestnuts (see page 176)

6 to 8 cups water (or Kombu Stock; see page 281)

2 tablespoons olive oil

½ teaspoon whole cane sugar

Freshly ground black pepper

2 tablespoons fresh thyme leaves, roughly chopped

¼ cup crème fraîche

2 tablespoons pumpkin seed oil or brown butter

Melt 4 tablespoons of the butter in a 4-quart, heavy-bottom pot over medium heat. Add the sliced leeks and a good pinch of sea salt (the salt will help prevent browning). Sweat the leeks until they have softened and turned translucent, about 8 minutes.

Meanwhile, thinly slice or roughly chop the sunchokes. Add the sunchokes, half the chestnuts, 6 cups water, and another pinch of salt to the leeks. Simmer the soup for 30 to 35 minutes, or until the sunchokes yield to the pressure of a wooden spoon (the length of time will depend on the thickness of your cut).

While the soup simmers, cut the remaining chestnuts into a ¼-inch dice. Heat a medium sauté pan over moderate high heat, and add the olive oil and remaining tablespoon of butter. Once the bubbles from the butter have subsided, add the diced chestnuts, cane sugar, a pinch of salt, and a few grinds of black pepper. Cook the chestnuts over moderately high heat until they turn a deep, golden brown, tossing them occasionally (but not constantly) to ensure they don't burn. Remove from the heat and add the thyme leaves. Taste, and adjust the seasoning.

Remove the soup from the heat; purée using a blender or a food mill, adding a bit of water as necessary to achieve the desired consistency. Return the soup to the pot and keep warm over low heat. Stir in the crème fraîche. Taste again, and adjust the seasoning. Serve the sunchoke soup in warmed bowls, topped with a spoonful of caramelized chestnuts, and a drizzle of pumpkin seed oil.

SUNCHOKES IN DUCK FAT

Makes 4 to 6 servings

Duck fat is a superior choice for roasting winter roots and tubers, frying rice, and sautéing any plant in the cabbage family. The combination of its richness and lovable funkiness with the earthy sunchokes is dramatic and satisfying. Serve this as a side for a pan-grilled steak and a pile of lightly dressed, sharp, spicy greens.

¼ cup duck fat

1   pound sunchokes, cut into
     1-inch pieces

Fine sea salt

2   tablespoons water

4   thyme sprigs

¼ teaspoon Shallot Vinegar
     (see page 222), or red wine
     vinegar

Coarse sea salt

Freshly ground black pepper

Preheat the oven to 400°F. Heat a large, ovenproof skillet over medium heat, and add the duck fat. Add the sunchokes in one even layer along with 2 pinches of fine sea salt; leave them alone for 4 to 5 minutes. Once they are brown on the first side, use tongs to flip them. Add the water and thyme sprigs. Shake the skillet a little, then transfer it to the oven.

Roast sunchokes for 15 to 17 minutes, or until they are golden brown and tender. Finish with a drizzle of vinegar, a pinch of coarse sea salt, and a pinch of freshly ground black pepper.

SUNCHOKE PURÉE

Makes 4 to 6 servings

A food mill is perfect for this recipe; the texture this old tool provides can't be replicated. You can make a variation of this recipe by smoking the sunchokes. Place half the sunchokes in a small smoker (see page 289) with cherry wood for 35 minutes. Once cooled to room temperature, peel, slice, and place them in the milk.

3 cups whole milk

Extra virgin olive oil

Fine sea salt

Freshly ground black pepper

1 pound sunchokes

½ pound russet potatoes

Pour the milk into a medium saucepan and season with 2 tablespoons of olive oil, 4 grinds of black pepper, and 3 pinches of sea salt.

Peel the sunchokes and slice them ½ inch thick. Throw them in the milk as you work, which will prevent further discoloration. Peel the potatoes and cut them into a ½-inch dice; add them to the pot as well.

Set the pot over moderately high heat and bring to a simmer. Lower the heat as needed to achieve small, steady bubbles. Cook, uncovered, for 35 minutes, or until the sunchokes and potatoes are soft. Pass the vegetables through a food mill into a large serving bowl. Ladle ½ cup of the hot milk through a fine-mesh strainer into the purée; stir to combine. Taste for salt and pepper. Add more milk and perhaps another tablespoon of olive oil, until you achieve your desired texture. Garnish with a drizzle of olive oil and more black pepper.

TOMATILLOS

The husk of a tomatillo is like a paper lantern. Beneath its ethereal wrapping, you'll find a plump, shiny fruit with a pale green hue and a citrus-like aroma. It is a lovely thing to slow down for and pay attention to in your cooking.

Tomatillos are actually yellow when ripe, but they are most often used when they're young and green. They taste more like an unripe plum than a tomato and have a faint grassiness you might associate with a dark, leafy vegetable. They are at once sour and sweet. They boast a crisp, refreshing texture and can be eaten raw, although I prefer to roast them, enhancing their flavor and softening their skins.

Tomatillos show up in markets in mid-June and are around through October. Select specimens that have an intact husk and firm, evenly colored fruit. Store them in the refrigerator in an airtight container lined with a paper towel, and they will last for more than a week. Remove the husk and rinse the slightly sticky skin before using. Tomatillos are part of the nightshade family and should be consumed in moderation by those with sensitive constitutions or health conditions.

The absolute easiest way to use tomatillos is to blend them into a mild or spicy salsa (see page 266). This salsa can then be the base for sauces, stews, and dressings, and it is a versatile condiment all on its own:
- Spooned next to stewed black beans, fried eggs, and shaved radish
- Spread on a turkey sandwich with mayonnaise, shredded iceberg lettuce, and pickled jalapeños
- Mixed into a smashed avocado destined for toast
- Slathered on Quesadillas con Flor de Calabaza (see page 250)
- Swirled into a bowl of soup or stew, especially one with a beef, bean, or summer vegetable base

TOASTED BREAD SALAD WITH ROASTED TOMATILLOS AND TOMATILLO WATER

Makes 6 servings

Vegetable water is a fun ingredient and a crafty solution to using up less-than-ideal produce. Make it with overripe or bruised tomatoes, melons, cucumbers, or tomatillos. Try it as a light sauce for ceviche or warmed as broth.

TOMATILLO WATER

½ pound tomatillos

2 green onions, thinly sliced

2 garlic cloves, smashed

1 cup basil leaves

1 cup parsley leaves

A pinch of whole cane sugar

Freshly ground black pepper

½ teaspoon fine sea salt

¼ teaspoon red wine vinegar

SALAD

½ pound tomatillos, cut in half

1 chile de arbol, torn crosswise

Extra virgin olive oil

Fine sea salt

Whole cane sugar

Freshly ground black pepper

1 medium loaf stale sourdough
   bread

4 cups loosely packed wild
   (or baby) arugula

1 cup baby basil leaves (or
   large leaves, torn or roughly
   chopped right before use)

½ cup parsley leaves

Coarse sea salt

2 avocados, ripe but still
   slightly firm

½ lemon

Cut ½ pound tomatillos into wedges and puree them in a blender with the green onions, garlic, basil and parsley leaves, sugar, a few grinds of black pepper, and the fine sea salt. Place a piece of cheesecloth over a fine-mesh strainer and set the strainer over a bowl. Pour the tomatillo mixture into the lined strainer; let it drip overnight. Alternatively, you can speed the process by using a wooden spoon to press on the mixture to extract the juice more quickly (it won't be as clear a water, but for this recipe, that's fine). Discard the pulp and add the vinegar. The tomatillo water can be refrigerated in an airtight container for up to three days.

Preheat the oven to 400°F. On a sheet pan lined with parchment paper, toss the ½ pound of tomatillos for the salad with a chile de arbol, enough olive oil to coat, a pinch of fine sea salt, a pinch of cane sugar, and a few grinds of black pepper. Roast until caramelized, about 18 to 20 minutes.

Cut the bread into approximately 1-inch cubes (or pull it apart with your hands). Spread the cubes on a sheet pan lined with parchment paper, and toss with olive oil (enough to coat each cube) and a pinch of fine sea salt. Spread the cubes into an even layer, making sure you don't overcrowd the pan (use two pans, if needed). Bake the croutons for 17 to 20 minutes, or until they are a deep golden brown. Cool to room temperature before composing the salad.

In a large mixing bowl, combine ½ cup tomatillo water with about ¼ cup olive oil; taste and add more salt or olive oil to suit your palate. Add the croutons, roasted tomatillos, arugula, herbs, and a pinch of coarse sea salt. Pit the avocados and cut them into wedges; peel away the skin. Season the avocado wedges with a squeeze of lemon and some coarse sea salt. Plate the salad: alternate layers of the tomatillo mixture with wedges of salted avocado.

TOMATILLO JAM

Tomatillo jam is bright and sweet, and it is a wonderful alternative to barbeque sauce. It is particularly good on fried eggs, avocado toast, and grilled flank steak or chicken.

2 pounds tomatillos

1 chile de arbol

½ cup granulated sugar

½ teaspoon fine sea salt, plus more to taste

½ teaspoon red wine vinegar

Chop the tomatillos into a ½-inch dice and toss them with the chile de arbol, granulated sugar, and ½ teaspoon sea salt in a wide, shallow pot (this shape will facilitate evaporation). Let the mixture stand at room temperature for 10 minutes, so the sugar and salt can pull out some of the water from the fruit (this saves you from needing to add liquid, which would dilute the flavor).

Bring the mixture to a boil over high heat, stirring gently. Boil, stirring often, for about 20 minutes, or until reduced. It should be thick enough to coat the back of a wooden spoon. Remove from the heat, and stir in the red wine vinegar. Taste, and adjust the seasoning. Cool to room temperature before serving.

If you'd like to save this jam for future use, ladle the hot jam into a sterilized, hot pint jar; wipe the rim, seal the jar, and process in a boiling water bath for 10 minutes. Store in a cool, dark place for up to two months.

COLLARD GREEN TACOS WITH TOMATILLOS

Makes 4 to 6 servings

I grew up eating fried cornbread next to bacon-infused collard greens, often for breakfast. My grandfather would rise with the sun, don his button-up flannel and loose Wranglers, and prepare a hearty meal that would keep his stomach humming for hours while he toiled in his vegetable garden and woodshop. The combination of rich, nutty cornmeal and those sweet, slow-cooked collards is a memory worth keeping. Here I've paired those well-suited mates in a more unusual but still delicious way. I think Papa would approve.

COLLARD GREENS

1 large bunch collard greens (1½ pounds), stemmed
2 tablespoons organic virgin coconut oil (or bacon fat)
1 serrano chile
Fine sea salt
½ cup water
½ lime

SALSA

½ pound tomatillos, cut in quarters
½ serrano chile, finely chopped
1 garlic clove, minced
½ bunch cilantro, roughly chopped
Fine sea salt
Freshly ground black pepper

TO SERVE

6 to 8 corn tortillas
Seasoned and smashed avocado
Cooked beans (I use Rancho Gordo pinquitos, but any bean will do)
Sliced radishes
Sliced green onions
Crème fraîche
Chopped cilantro and/or cilantro flowers
Lime wedges

Cut the collard greens into approximately 3-inch squares. Heat the coconut oil in a large skillet or medium pot over moderately high heat. Add the serrano chile and a pinch of sea salt; cook for a minute or two (the chile will infuse the fat). Add the collard greens, 2 more pinches of salt, and the water; stir to combine. Cover the pan and cook for approximately 30 to 35 minutes, or until the greens are sweet and tender. Uncover the pan and simmer for 10 to 15 minutes more, or until all the liquid has evaporated. Discard the chile and stir in a splash of lime juice. Taste, and adjust the seasoning.

For the salsa, place all the ingredients in a blender or food processor, and pulse until you have a coarse purée. Taste, and adjust the seasoning.

Compose the tacos: Warm the tortillas in a dry skillet (or a clay *comal*, a great tool for tortilla lovers) over moderately high heat. Top each tortilla with a smear of smashed avocado, a spoonful of cooked beans, a serving of collard greens, a spoonful of tomatillo salsa, chopped cilantro, and whatever else you want to fold inside.

GREEN FISH STEW

Makes 4 to 6 servings

In this hearty soup, fried fish is finished in a thick broth of tomatillos and green aromatics. I like mine on the spicy side (leaning toward two to three chiles), but you can easily adjust the heat according to your preferences. Prior to cooking, the puréed tomatillo mixture can be prepared up to three days in advance.

STEW

1 pound tomatillos
2 cups cilantro leaves
1 cup parsley leaves
6 green onions, white and
  green parts sliced
1 or 2 serrano chiles, sliced
2 cups Kombu Stock (see
  page 281)
1 teaspoon fish sauce
¼ cup extra virgin olive oil,
  plus more for cooking
½ teaspoon fine sea salt,
  plus more to taste
1½ pounds firm white fish fillets
  (such as rock cod or halibut)
1 lemon

TO SERVE

Crème fraîche
Cilantro leaves and/or
  blossoms
Parsley leaves
Thinly sliced white onion

Bring a large pot of salted water to a boil. Blanch the tomatillos until soft but still whole, about 5 minutes. Remove from the heat and drain; place the tomatillos in a blender with the cilantro and parsley leaves, green onions, serrano chiles, kombu stock, fish sauce, olive oil, and fine sea salt. Purée until smooth. Transfer the sauce to a medium saucepan and bring to a boil over high heat. Lower the heat and simmer for 10 to 15 minutes, or until slightly reduced.

Meanwhile, pat the fish dry with paper towels and cut into 3- to 4-inch pieces; season both sides with sea salt. Place a large sauté pan over moderately high heat; add enough oil to coat the bottom of the pan. Add the fish in one layer and cook for 3 to 4 minutes, or until each piece moves easily with a slight prod. If you fuss over the fish too much, it will fall apart—resist the urge to move, peek, or flip more than once. Flip the fish (a fish spatula is handy) and cook for 2 minutes more, or until the fish is opaque throughout.

Meanwhile, taste your sauce. Adjust the seasoning as needed: lemon will add brightness, and salt will add interest. If you'd like more heat, slice another chile and serve it on the table.

Divide the fish among the serving bowls, and ladle the sauce on top. Garnish each with a spoonful of crème fraîche and a scattering herbs and sliced onions.

TOMATILLOS 269

WEEDS WE WANT

Our backyards, surrounding parks, and countrysides are full of edible plants. It is no doubt daunting for some of us to imagine gathering our own dinner, but many farmers and foragers will happily do the work and bring their wonderful treasures to market. While several wild greens (dandelion, purslane, and so on) have gained popularity and are now grown from seed, I often use other lesser-known weeds in my home kitchen; they include lamb's quarter, chickweed, and miner's lettuce. All of these greens are incredible sources of protein, minerals, and vitamins A and C.

Lamb's quarter was once highly cultivated but was then replaced by other staple crops. You'll know it by its slender, pointed leaves, which are hunter green and shadowed in a silvery cast. It tastes subtly bitter but balanced; there are also hints of salt, lemon, and sweetness. Available for harvest from April through September, lamb's quarter can be used in place of spinach in just about any recipe (crowd favorites include gnocchi, borek, and spring vegetable risotto). You can also do the two simple things you can do with any edible leaf: stir it into a pot of simmering beans, or sauté it with lard and chiles.

Chickweed is grassy, and its tiny leaves and spindly stems are thin and tender. Its mild flavor and light texture pair well with other springtime crops—morel mushrooms, baby beets, ramps, and garlic scapes, to name a few. Look for chickweed with no yellowing leaves. Refrigerate leaves in an airtight container lined with paper towels; wash them only before using. Use them within three to four days of purchase. Try chickweed in place of purslane in Purslane and Herb Salad with Potatoes and Pancetta (see page 187), or as a garnish for any dish that would profit from a clean, green flavor (swordfish with salsa verde, a steak salad with radishes and herbs, or a poached egg atop roasted potatoes).

Miner's lettuce is a delicate, wild green that is foraged in the early spring after the first rains. It is buttery and sweet and boasts beautiful bright green leaves cusped with tiny white flowers. You'll often find it mixed in with your chickweed and vice versa, as they grow alongside one another. Like chickweed, its flavor and texture make it the perfect garnish for other springtime delicacies. Purchase or pick miner's lettuce that has crisp leaves without any slimy or yellow blemishes, and use it within a day or two of purchase. I think it is best served raw as a garnish or gently incorporated into simple preparations, such as a fluke crudo with lemon and olive oil, a salad with grapefruit and avocado, or asparagus with bottarga.

CROSTINI WITH FROMAGE BLANC AND POUNDED CHICKWEED

Makes 8 servings

After making this recipe once, I took the sheet pan to my third-floor neighbors, who were new parents. Dad opened the door, his sweet baby girl crying in his right arm. The shower was running, as were several cats. Chaos was in the air, and he looked exhausted. I tabled the food while he spoke of the day's woes—it had been a very rough afternoon. Later that evening, he knocked on my door, wine in hand. He was perky and smiling. The crostini led to the popping of a cork and thus a break that was just what he and Mom needed.

CROSTINI

½ baguette or long Italian bread loaf, sliced ¼-inch thick

Extra virgin olive oil

Fine sea salt

TOPPING

1 green garlic stalk, white and pale-green parts only, thinly sliced

1 cup mint leaves, coarsely chopped

2 cups chickweed, coarsely chopped

Fine sea salt

½ cup extra virgin olive oil

Zest of ½ lemon, plus more for serving

2 teaspoons fresh lemon juice

8 ounces fromage blanc

Baby mint leaves

3 radishes, trimmed and thinly sliced

Preheat the oven to 400°F. Arrange the bread slices on two large rimmed baking sheets; brush both sides with olive oil, and season with a pinch of sea salt. Bake until golden, 15 to 18 minutes, rotating the sheets halfway through (if the undersides are not browning, turn the crostini over once during baking). Remove from the oven and cool completely.

In a food processor (or with a mortar and pestle), finely chop the green garlic, mint leaves, chickweed, and a pinch of sea salt. Add the olive oil, lemon zest, and lemon juice; mix to combine. You should have a coarse purée. Taste, and adjust the seasoning.

Smear the fromage blanc on the crostini; top each with a spoonful of the chickweed mixture, a few baby mint leaves, a scattering of sliced radish, and a grating of lemon zest.

BEETS IN RASPBERRY VINEGAR
WITH MINER'S LETTUCE

Makes 6 servings

Beets are a perfect mate for the acidic bite and sprightly fruitiness of raspberry vinegar. Though somewhat difficult to find in local stores, it can be purchased online. If you're not a fan of beets, don't let that keep you from the treat that is raspberry vinegar; it is delicious in vinaigrettes, on top of ice cream, as a marinade for summer berries, or in a glaze for duck.

1 bunch beets (about 6 medium)

Extra virgin olive oil

1 or 2 tablespoons vinegar, preferably raspberry

Fine sea salt

1½ cups crème fraîche

¼ pound miner's lettuce

Coarse sea salt

Freshly ground black pepper

Trim the greens from the beet roots, and save them for any recipe that calls for spinach or chard.

Preheat the oven to 400°F. Place the beets in an oven-proof saucepan. Drizzle with a little olive oil and a splash of water; cover. Roast the beets for approximately 1 hour (or less, if you found some small specimens), or until they are easily pierced with the tip of paring knife. Remove from the heat; while they are still warm, peel the beets by rubbing them with a cloth. Let them cool to room temperature, then cut them into wedges; toss with the vinegar and 2 pinches of fine sea salt. Refrigerate until cold. This step can be done up to three days in advance.

Spoon the crème fraîche onto a serving platter or individual serving plates. Spoon five or so beet wedges off center and mound a bit of miner's lettuce on and around them. Drizzle olive oil over the miner's lettuce, and garnish the leaves with coarse sea salt and black pepper.

LEBANESE COUSCOUS WITH LAMB'S QUARTER, PERSIAN CUCUMBER, AND OIL-CURED OLIVES

Makes 6 servings

I affectionately call this dish my "Luma salad." I envisioned my dear friend when I started tinkering with these ingredients one morning; serendipitously, she stopped by my apartment on her way somewhere else, and we enjoyed the kismet. She stayed a while, eating, chatting, and playing guitar, and she left with a container full of her new eponymous dish.

Fine sea salt

8 ounces mughrabia (Lebanese couscous; Israeli couscous is a good alternative)

1 tablespoon red wine vinegar

¼ cup extra virgin olive oil

1 tablespoon Urfa chile flakes

2 Persian cucumbers, cut into ¼-inch dice

4 green onions, thinly sliced

1 cup oil-cured olives, drained

8 ounces lamb's quarter, leaves picked and large stems thinly sliced

4 to 5 cups fresh herbs and/or herb blossoms (such as mint, parsley, cilantro blossoms, and dill fronds)

Coarse sea salt

Bring a large pot of water to a boil; add a handful of fine sea salt. Cook the mughrabia for 10 to 12 minutes, or until al dente. Drain the couscous and return it to the pot; add the vinegar and olive oil, and toss gently to combine. Allow the couscous to cool to room temperature.

Add the remaining ingredients to the pot, along with a generous pinch of coarse sea salt; toss gently to combine, adding more olive oil and/or vinegar if the salad seems too dry for your liking. Taste, and adjust the seasoning.

WILD GREENS WITH SUMMER MELON AND AVOCADO

Makes 4 to 6 servings

For my palate, a melon salad needs some slightly peppery, earthy leaf to ground it, such as these wild greens. There are hundreds of varieties of heirloom melons, and I love them all. If you are inspired, take a look at Amy Goldman's *Melons for the Passionate Grower*.

1 ripe melon

2 medium avocados (such as Haas or Reed)

4 to 6 ounces wild greens (miner's lettuce, lamb's quarter, and/or chickweed)

½ tablespoon Champagne vinegar

1 tablespoon finely chopped Preserved Lmon rind (see page 282)

1 tablespoon finely chopped shallot

Fine sea salt

2 tablespoons extra virgin olive oil

Coarse sea salt

Freshly cracked black pepper

Find the most fragrant melon you can. Peel and seed the melon; cut it into thick wedges, then slice those wedges in half on the diagonal.

Peel and pit the avocados; cut them into wedges that are of similar thickness to those of your melon.

In a medium bowl, whisk together the Champagne vinegar, preserved lemon rind, shallot, and a pinch of fine sea salt; set aside for 5 minutes or so (this mellows the shallot and dissolves the salt). Whisk in the olive oil. Arrange the melon and avocado on a large platter or in a serving bowl. Drizzle three-quarters of the vinaigrette over both, and season with a pinch of coarse sea salt and black pepper. Toss the greens with the remaining vinaigrette and a pinch of coarse sea salt; scatter them on top. Serve immediately.

KOMBU STOCK

Makes 3 quarts

Kombu imparts that unique flavor we call umami. Like all sea vegetables, it is rich in many minerals and high in protein. Whenever I am feeling a little sick or stagnant, I turn to a bowl of this warm seaweed water; it consistently heals what ails me. As for a basic stock, it can't get easier or cheaper.

1 ounce kombu

3 quarts water

½ teaspoon fine sea salt

Place the kombu, water, and sea salt in a medium saucepan and warm over moderate heat. When the first bubbles begin to appear, turn off the heat. Cover the pot and steep for 30 minutes (or up to overnight). Strain through a fine-mesh strainer. Refrigerate the stock in an airtight container for up to three days.

PRESERVED LEMONS

Extend the lemon harvest by preserving them in salt. After a few months, it will be time for you get creative with the bright, slightly funky rind. These lemons can also act as a probiotic inoculant (meaning "kick-starter") for your other fermentation projects, such as salsa verde, hot sauce, sauerkraut, and pickled roots.

12 lemons (I prefer the Lisbon
  variety.)
1 to 2 cups fine sea salt
Freshly squeezed lemon juice or
  whey, as needed (I use lemon.)

Soften the lemons by rolling them on the counter under your palm, then make four cuts in the rind lengthwise, from tip to stem end, stopping just before you cut through the stem. Leaving them whole results in a preserved rind with more texture; when I cut the lemons into slices or complete quarters, the rind practically disintegrates over time.

Open the lemons slightly and pack the center full of sea salt. Put a layer of salt in the bottom of a 2-liter jar, followed by a layer of lemons, and another layer of salt. Continue filling the jar and pressing the fruit down to eliminate air pockets and release the juice from the fruit. If there is not enough liquid to cover the final layer by at least 1 inch, add additional lemon juice or whey; leave 1 inch of air space between the liquid and the lid. Cover the jar and store at room temperature, away from direct sunlight.

For the first week of fermentation, open the jar every day and press the lemons down so the liquid rises to cover them. If white or light green mold forms on the surface, remove it with a spoon. You'll see the fruit start to change character after a week or two, and the flavor will continue to evolve for a year or more. Taste after a month or two, and decide whether you'd like the fermentation to continue. When you are ready to halt the process, refrigerate the lemons; at this point, they can be kept for several years.

HOMEMADE CRÈME FRAÎCHE

Makes approximately 2 cups

Crème fraîche can be purchased in many stores nowadays, but it is also easy to make from scratch. It is a special product boasting the richness of cream with the tang and subtle funk of yogurt. I use it as a sauce for both vegetables and meat; as the finishing touch to a bowl of porridge, polenta, or soup; and as the secret something in the most exciting batch of whipped cream (see below).

1 tablespoon buttermilk

2 cups heavy cream

In a glass jar with a screw-top lid, whisk together the buttermilk and heavy cream; cover. Let sit in a warm room or in the oven with the pilot light on for 36 hours. Stir once more. Refrigerate until ready to use. Homemade crème fraîche lasts for a week or more in the fridge.

WHIPPED CRÈME FRAÎCHE

Makes approximately 2 cups

The natural acidity of crème fraîche elevates the heavy, monotonous flavor that whipped cream alone can have, making it suitable for sweet and savory dishes alike. Crème fraîche also acts as a stabilizer; whereas whipped cream will normally deflate and leach water after a short time, this batch will last for a day in the refrigerator.

1 cup heavy whipping cream, cold

2 tablespoons sugar (optional)

½ cup crème fraîche, cold

Whip the cream using a stand mixer fitted with the whisk attachment. Add the sugar (if using), and continue to whip on high speed until soft peaks form. Gently fold in the crème fraîche using a flexible spatula. Keep chilled until ready to use.

SEMOLINA DOUGH

Makes four 6-inch flatbreads

My imagination combined two memories to make this dough: a year spent kneading Neapolitan pizza dough, and one moment eating a semolina flatbread on a hot afternoon in a crowded Moroccan medina. It's good on its own when baked in flat, circular disks, as an accompaniment to Mustard Greens with Potatoes and Whole Spices (see page 152); Twelve-Hour Lamb Shoulder with Ras el Hanout (see page 214); or a spread of puréed almond butter, honey, argan oil, and salt.

While I cannot claim to teach breadmaking here, I do want to share a few things I've learned along the way:

- Invest in two different bench scrapers (they are cheap): metal and plastic.
- More yeast does not equal a better bread. If your dough isn't rising fast enough, either the yeast is dead (no rise at all); the room is too cold (turn your oven on and crack it open, if needed); or you are watching and waiting (that whole "watched pot" adage). Opt for more patience before more yeast.
- In many cases, a relatively wet dough is preferable for baking and eating but is more difficult to work with.
- Don't skimp on kneading.
- Did I mention patience? Luckily, many doughs will actually improve with an overnight sit in the refrigerator. Bring the dough fully back to room temperature before baking.
- Get lost in the process.

1½ teaspoons active dry yeast

Pinch of granulated sugar

1¼ cups warm water

2 tablespoons extra virgin olive oil

2 to 2½ cups (10 to 12½ ounces) unbleached bread flour, plus extra for rolling

¾ cup (5¼ ounces) fine semolina

1 teaspoon baking powder

1 teaspoon fine sea salt

Whisk together the yeast, pinch of sugar, and half the warm water in a large bowl. Let the mixture sit until it begins to froth, about 5 to 8 minutes. (If you don't see a change in the water's appearance, it may mean your yeast is dead; I recommend tossing that batch and starting again.) Stir in the remaining water and olive oil.

Meanwhile, in a medium bowl, whisk together 2 cups of the flour and the semolina, baking powder, and sea salt. Add the dry ingredients to the wet ingredients; mix with a wooden spoon until well combined. Turn the dough out onto a table or board and knead for 15 minutes, or until smooth and elastic (a stand mixer with a dough hook makes this an easy job). Place the dough in an oiled bowl, cover with oiled plastic wrap, and let it rise somewhere warm for 3 to 4 hours (but no longer than 8), or until it has more than doubled in size. Proceed according to the recipe instructions, or refrigerate overnight and bring fully back to room temperature before using.

PERFECT STEAMED RICE

Makes approximately 5 cups

This is rice the way an Azerbaijani grandmother would make it, and you should trust that it will come out perfectly dry and fluffy every damn time. It may seem daunting at first, but if you practice enough, preparing superb steamed rice will soon come effortlessly.

2 cups basmati rice

Fine sea salt

¼ cup hot water

3 tablespoons unsalted butter (optional)

Place the rice in a medium saucepan; cover with water to 4 inches or so, and use your hand to swirl it around (this releases the starch). Let the rice settle to the bottom, then pour off the starchy water. Repeat this process of filling, swirling, setting, and pouring three more times, or until the water runs clear. Cover the rice with water once more and soak for at least 30 minutes, or up to overnight. Strain the rice and set aside.

Fill the same saucepan with water; add 3 pinches of sea salt. Bring to a boil over high heat. Add the rice and parboil for 5 minutes. Strain the rice again.

Return the saucepan to moderately high heat and add ¼ cup hot water. Using a fork, mound the parboiled rice in a pyramid in the pan, adding a pinch or two of salt as you go. Poke holes in the pyramid with the handle of a wooden spoon. Scatter pats of butter on top, if using. Cover the pan and cook on very low heat for 35 minutes.

Remove the pan from the heat. Take off the lid, place a clean tea towel over the pan, and cover it once more. Rest the rice for 15 minutes before serving (the towel will absorb extra moisture). Gently fluff the rice with a fork.

BROWN BUTTER

The toasted, sweet aroma of brown butter reminds me of hazelnuts. It can be used for regular butter in many baking recipes and is a wonderful topping for winter soups, roasted vegetables, and sautéed fish.

1 cup unsalted butter

½ teaspoon fine sea salt

In a small saucepan over medium heat, cook the butter until it turns deep golden brown (make sure you are using a stainless steel pan, so you can see the color change); this process can take 3 to 6 minutes. Keep an eye on the butter to make sure it doesn't burn. Remove from the heat, and add the salt.

Brown butter can be refrigerated in an airtight container for up to one month.

HOW TO BUILD A SMALL SMOKER

If you want to smoke whole racks of ribs or a wild-caught salmon, many great books dive into the subject with intelligence and depth. The instructions here are for smaller smoking projects that can easily take place in your home kitchen.

Smoked ingredients can provide a complexity to your cooking. I encourage you to experiment with the technique on your own, joyously smoking an egg, sunchokes, a bowl of almonds, and whatever else you may find.

I prefer hickory wood chips, since they smolder well and I like their scent. Apple, cherry, maple, and oak are also nice. I only use mesquite when smoking garlic or shallots—it is too strong for anything else. For smoking relatively small ingredients for a relatively short amount of time (for example, garlic cloves versus a goat leg), tiny wood chips work well, and no coal is necessary.

If you're smoking a large amount of food, build a smoker in a large roasting pan; if you are only smoking a few small ingredients use a 7-quart, heavy-bottom pot or Dutch oven.

Aluminum foil

1 or 2 ounces wood chips

A roasting pan or round Dutch oven (at least 3 inches deep)

A square or circular cooling rack (that inserts easily into the roasting pan or Dutch oven)

Using the foil, make a loose, little package (or two, as needed) containing about an ounce of wood chips; poke a few holes in the package and place it in the bottom of your pan. Place the rack on top of the foil. Place the foods to be smoked directly on the rack; use foil to cradle any wet foods (such as boiled beets or tomato slices), and use plates or shallow bowls to hold any foods that can't sit securely on the rack.

Set the smoker over one or two burners—depending on the size of the pan—set to high heat, and wait for the heat to ignite the chips (I sometimes use a propane torch directly on the foil, if a gas stove isn't available). Once you see smoke, wait about 5 minutes more. Cover the smoker with a tight-fitting lid or two layers of foil; wait 5 to 7 minutes more, or until you see smoke seeping out the sides. Turn the burner(s) off, and refer to your recipe for smoking time (or use your best judgment).

Once the foods have been removed, allow the wood chips to cool to room temperature, then submerge them in water to be sure they are extinguished.

IN MY LARDER

I used to have a pantry full of international bottles and jars and odd things. Now I find
happiness in simplicity. My larder has been pared down, and this chapter presents what I
consider the essentials.

Choose your favorite items from this list and add others. Personalize your pantry. Once
it is well stocked to your preferences, you may find it easier to shop without a list or menu
in mind, and the dishes that emerge from that freedom will be very much your own. With
a foundation in place, you can purchase whatever produce catches your eye and trust that
you'll be able to get home and figure things out later. Oh, and *always* buy lemons.

SALT: FINE AND COARSE SEA SALT

Sea salt is concentrated ocean, crystallized minerals and beneficial trace elements (including
iodine), and the animator of all food. I use La Baliene fine sea salt because the first restaurant that trained me to taste used it, although I've been attempting to use fine gray sea
salt instead. I use Diamond Crystal kosher salt for large brining projects, pasta water, and
salt-baking. I garnish with coarse sea salts like Maldon, Jacobsen, or fleur de sel.

EXTRA VIRGIN OLIVE OIL

Oils labeled "extra virgin" are composed of 100 percent olive oil, which is pressed fruit
juice without additives. The factors influencing its quality and taste include the variety and
quality of the olives used, the *terroir* (environmental aspects of the growing region), and the
countless decisions and production practices of the producer.

While price is not always an indicator of quality, the best oils are often expensive because
they are more complex and costly (slow) to make. I recommend having two extra virgin
olive oils in your kitchen: one that is mild and less expensive for cooking, and one that
is individuated and complex for finishing. When considering the latter, you have many
options. Some oils are aromatic, floral, and buttery; some are full and fruity; and many are
herbaceous, grassy, and peppery. Find a store or stand that will let you taste before you buy.

I typically use Frantoia Sicilian for both cooking and finishing. I know it well and am
fond of its versatile flavor: ripe fruit, green almonds, mild herbaceousness.

I have favored Tenuta di Capezzana (sweet grass, almonds, gentle flavor) and Olio Verde
as finishing oils for years, yet there are very good olive oils coming out of California, and
I rotate through local bottles regularly. I'm sure I'll soon land on a favorite or two, and I
recommend that you test a few yourself.

Olive oils should be stored in a cool, dark place. When an unopened bottle is prop-
erly stored, a good extra virgin olive oil can last two to three years. But flavors will slowly

diminish over time, so make sure to pay attention to the mill date or bottle date. Once the bottle is opened, make sure it is tightly sealed after use because oxygen is the biggest contributor to degradation. As a general rule, once you open a bottle, try to use it up within four months.

VIRGIN COCONUT OIL

Unrefined coconut oil is an impressive food. Its nutty flavor and tropical aroma easily lend complexity to dishes; its relatively high smoke point means it is good for frying foods without denaturing (see Burdock Fritters, page 31). Most strikingly, coconut oil is one of the few significant plant sources of lauric acid, also found in human breast milk, which enhances brain function and boosts the immune system. It is a proven antiviral, antibacterial, and antifungal agent; I take teaspoons of it as medicine with the first signs of a sinus infection and massage the sweet smelling balm into cuts, scrapes, burns, and blemishes.

UNSALTED CULTURED BUTTER

In addition to invaluable fatty acids, butter contains lecithin and trace minerals. Like coconut oil, it has antimicrobial and antifungal properties. I favor cultured butter as it is easier to digest; can be cooked at slightly higher temperatures; and has a slightly tangy, fuller flavor. For cooking, I use unsalted butter so I can better control the salinity of a dish.

GHEE

This ayurvedic ingredient is butter with everything removed but the fat. Ghee has a longer shelf life than butter and a higher smoke point; it is also gentler on the digestive system. Commercial ghee is available, but homemade ghee is much more delicious (see page 61).

ANIMAL FATS: PORK, CHICKEN (SCHMALTZ), DUCK, LAMB

Our bodies need the saturated dietary fats available in high-quality butter, ghee, coconut oil, palm oil, and animal fats. It is the ratio of saturated fat to unsaturated fat that really matters, and for our bodies to function optimally, we need varied sources of both. I regularly use animal fats for cooking; they impart wild amounts of flavor and are grounding to the body. Pork, chicken, duck, and lamb fat can be purchased from local farmers and specialty grocers, but you can also render your own. *Rendering* can be as simple as skimming the fat off the Twelve-Hour Lamb Shoulder with Ras el Hanout (see page 214) or saving the fat from the pan after cooking bacon. Storing these fats is a very old, healthy, and thrifty tradition that many of us could benefit from adopting (I freeze mine for up to three months).

NUT AND SEED OILS

Nut oils are my splurge. They are a luxury—absolutely unnecessary yet so very pleasing. Just a teaspoon transforms a finished dish by adding, elevating, and complicating. I store quite a few oils in my fridge: pistachio, almond, hazelnut, walnut, and pecan.

GRAPESEED AND RICE BRAN OILS

I use grapeseed or rice bran oil on the few occasions when I need a flavorless oil, sometimes with a high smoke point. This is useful when I am making mayonnaise, Crispy Shallots and Shallot Oil (see page 225), or popcorn.

RED WINE VINEGAR

I use an aged Banyuls exclusively. Many red wine vinegars are too acidic for my palate and lack depth of flavor. Banyuls is made from a fortified wine and is produced slowly, allowing the flavors of the fruit to remain and evolve. In general, choose a vinegar that does not exceed 6 to 6.5 percent acidity (check the label).

SHERRY VINEGAR

I use aged sherry vinegars made from Pedro Ximénez grapes, because they tend to have nuanced flavors of raisins, licorice, and beeswax, making them perfect for winter salads, pork preparations, and grains.

RAW, UNFILTERED APPLE CIDER VINEGAR

Good cider vinegar carries notes of apple blossoms and warm spices and contributes a bracing brightness to a dish. It is also a health tonic that alkalizes the blood: combine 1 tablespoon vinegar, 1 teaspoon raw honey, and 1 cup of hot water; stir; and drink.

VERJUS

Made from unripened grapes, this acidic juice (also spelled "verjuice") has been used for centuries in European and Middle Eastern cooking as an alternative to wine, vinegars, or lemon juice.

KOMBU

Kombu imparts that unique flavor we call umami. Like all sea vegetables, it is uniquely rich in a broad range of minerals and is high in protein. It is also a carminative, a substance that helps ease the digestion of fibrous beans and grains. I use it like bay leaf in just about every savory simmering pot.

SALT-PACKED CAPERS

These buds of a Mediterranean flowering bush lend their briny, slightly floral flavor to many dishes in this book. Salt-packed capers retain more flavor and integrity of texture than their brine-packed brethren. Soak them in water for 20 minutes and rinse before using. Fried capers are crisp, salty morsels that practically shatter in your mouth—addictive and fun. However, this step is not necessary to enjoy capers; feel free to leave them raw.

SALT-PACKED ANCHOVIES

Packed in salt, whole anchovies will keep indefinitely (refrigerate in a closed container and add more salt to cover with each use). They require a 15- to 20-minute soak in water or milk, and you must remove the backbone and tail before use. Agostino Recca is the brand most readily available in my area.

FISH SAUCE

Intoxicating and unique, fish sauce is salty and pungent, with the quality of umami. No other product can offer such a distilled flavor of the sea. It is also more versatile than you might think.

I stock several brands—some made with anchovies, some with dried shrimp—of all different ages and from disparate regions of the world. If you're only buying one, I recommend Red Boat, which is pure and aged for at least one year.

PRESERVED LEMONS

Preserved lemons are one of the easiest home fermentation projects, and the result is a marvel of melded acidity, umami, bitterness, and sweetness. The Preserved Lemons recipe in this book (see page 282) gives instructions on how to make your own.

RAW NUTS: ALMONDS, WALNUTS, HAZELNUTS, PINE NUTS

I purchase small quantities of nuts and keep them in the refrigerator; I keep pine nuts in the freezer. If your nuts smell acrid and appear rubbery, throw them out—they are rancid.

LEGUMES

Dried legumes have a long shelf life, but due to space and my desire for an uncluttered work space, I stock only five or six kinds at time. You may want to start with two varieties of lentils, one fun heirloom bean, chickpeas, and your favorite white bean. I try to keep a quart or two of frozen, precooked beans on hand. All cooked beans freeze remarkably well (and up to four months or so) if cooled and packed in their cooking water.

See the "Sources" section at the back of this book for online stores that sell high-quality legumes.

WHITE BASMATI AND SHORT-GRAIN BROWN RICE

These are staples. I am never without them. If you have rice, a bag of greens, and a pot of beans, you have yourself a nutritious, fast, and affordable dinner.

RAW, UNFILTERED HONEY

Raw honey has wonderful medicinal properties, while pasteurized honey fosters damp (mucus-forming) conditions. Local honey can also decrease pollen allergies. I use honey often: as a starter for fermenting fruits (see pages 24 and 217; as an emulsifier for vinaigrettes; in baking; and in a bowl of porridge, along with tahini and coarse salt.

UMEBOSHI PLUMS

In Japan, the *ume* plum tree is prized for its *wabi sabi* flowers, which mark the beginning of spring. The precious fruit is transformed into naturally fermented pickles that are incredibly healing and flavorful. When I am feeling lethargic or hung over, or when my skin is showing signs of dullness, I eat one plum a day for a few days.

MISCELLANEOUS STAPLES

The essential spices in my cabinet are chile de arbol, whole cumin seeds, whole coriander seeds, Urfa chile, and black peppercorns.

I always have one or two short dry pastas—such as orecchiette, penne, or couscous—on hand, as well as one or two whole grains such as farro, rye berries, or quinoa.

If you are a baker, you will want to stock kamut flour, all-purpose flour, white granulated sugar, whole cane sugar and/or muscovado sugar, baking soda, and baking powder.

SOURCES

While I have certainly seen kumquats and dandelion greens at large supermarkets, I encourage you to shop at all the farmers' markets, small co-ops, *tiendas*, Asian grocers, and roadside stands in your area. In this way, you'll support your community and be more likely to find all of the wonderful ingredients in this book. The following are a few reliable online resources to aid in your search:

ANSON MILLS—This is a remarkable company that grows organic heirloom grains and mills them to order. I learn as much from perusing its website as I do from reading a cookbook. While my wish list includes just about all of Anson Mills' products, my freezer is regularly packed with its farro (piccolo and grande), Carolina Gold rice, oats, fine cornmeal, and polenta. Visit the company's website at http://ansonmills.com.

BOB'S RED MILL—Despite the company's large size, it still mills grains and seeds with stone. Its products are on offer at www.bobsredmill.com.

COOP DIRECTORY SERVICE—Co-op markets are employee-owned grocery stores that often stock incredible foods in bulk. To find a co-op market near you, check with http://coopdirectory.org.

GOLD MINE NATURAL FOOD COMPANY—This online store stocks organic and heirloom grains, beans, Japanese fermented products, good-quality salts, and homewares at http://shop.goldminenaturalfoods.com.

GOOD EGGS—Good Eggs is an online store with local delivery; they supply many local and farm-direct products across almost all grocery categories. Currently in four cities, the company is set to expand soon. You can find it at www.goodeggs.com.

KALUSTYAN'S—I used to live a few blocks from this icon on Curry Hill in New York City. It is a fantastically fragrant little shop full of so many exciting and exotic ingredients, such as dried pomegranate seeds, mango powder, and assorted herbal tonics from India. You can visit the online store at http://kalustyans.com.

LOCAL HARVEST—Farmers' markets are some of the best sources of good food and good conversation. To find a farmers' market near you, visit www.localharvest.org.

MARKET HALL FOODS—An Easy Bay institution, Rockridge Market Hall has a wonderful online shop for those interested in Marash chiles, aged Banyuls and Pedro Ximénez vinegars, Tenuta di Cappezzana olive oil, Katz lemon olive oil, Pommery mustard, crystallized whole roses, and some of the best dried pasta imported to the United States. See the selection at http://markethallfoods.com.

MIKUNI WILD HARVEST—For a reputable, albeit expensive, source for verjus and high-quality French nut oils, try www.mikuniwildharvest.com.

MOUNTAIN FEED AND FARM SUPPLY—My colleagues and I make regular field trips to this incredible store. It pretty much has everything a cook, gardener, or foodsmith could need. You can visit the online version at www.mountainfeed.com.

NORTHWEST WILD FOODS—An online source for frozen green gooseberries and wild huckleberries is https://nwwildfoods.com.

OMEGA NUTRITION—This company is known for organic coconut oil mechanically pressed at a low temperature. You can find it at www.omeganutrition.com.

PICK YOUR OWN—There is nothing quite like picking apples on a cool, crisp day or eating strawberries in a windblown field by the sea. If you want a wonderful directory that will help you seek out such experiences, try www.pickyourown.org.

RANCHO GORDO—Steve Sando is an inspiring proprietor, and his company is one of the best sources for heirloom beans. Look it up at www.ranchogordo.com.

STRONG ARM FARMS/SONOMA COAST SEAWEED—This is the place for sustainably harvested seaweed and my first choice for kombu; visit www.strongarmfarm.com/seaweed.

ACKNOWLEDGMENTS

Danielle Svetcov, a very special literary agent—you wield honesty with compassion and warmth and humor. I wouldn't have written a book without you.

Rick Poon, photographer, food stylist, cheerleader, and eater—thank you for being calm, creative, warm, and supportive. You captured my creations gracefully and skillfully, and I am sincerely grateful.

Rochelle Bourgault, my editor, and the entire team at Roost Books—thank you for this opportunity and for offering me your trust, talent, and support.

My family and friends—I love you. You all inspired and informed my cooking, reminded me continuously of my capabilities, and allowed me to nurture you with so many plates of plants.

My colleagues in food and food education: Sarah Nelson and Emily Geis—I could not ask for better comrades; by offering me your time and energy (and humor), you both made balancing a book with a big job a possible feat. Rosie Branson Gill—this book unfolded beneath your encouraging gaze, and every mention of preserved lemon is dedicated to you. Amie Pfeiffer—thank you for your scrupulous recipe testing; your insight and input steered so many edits in this book. Kristin Cole—you picked up slack (especially in the pantry) and made me sit still when you saw my tired eyes. Sam Mogannam—you are the brave and passionate man who created a most intimate grocery store selling farm-direct produce; thank you for supplying me with the food I adore and for bestowing upon my craziness a positive connotation.

The farmers who grow my food—I am in awe. I am grateful.

Leslie C., Angela W., and Nicole H.—the women who taught me to attune to my body and to respond compassionately and creatively.

My students—thank you for giving as much as you receive. You are my teachers.

INDEX

Roost Books
An imprint of Shambhala Publications, Inc.
4720 Walnut Street
Boulder, Colorado 80301
roostbooks.com

First Edition
Printed in United States of America

♾ This edition is printed on acid-free paper that meets the
American National Standards Institute Z39.48 Standard.
♻ Shambhala Publications makes every effort to print on recycled paper.
For more information please visit www.shambhala.com.

Distributed in the United States by Penguin Random House LLC and
in Canada by Random House of Canada Ltd

Designed by Allison Meierding

Library of Congress Cataloging-in-Publication Data
McKenzie, Michelle, author.
Dandelion and quince: exploring the wide world of unusual vegetables,
fruits, and herbs / Michelle McKenzie.—First edition.
pages cm
Includes index.
ISBN 978-1-61180-287-0 (hard cover: alk. paper)
1. Cooking (Wild foods) 2. Wild plants, Edible. I. Title.
TX823.M365 2016
641.3'03—dc23
2015024808